The Seven Deadly Sins

nakaba suzuki presents

38

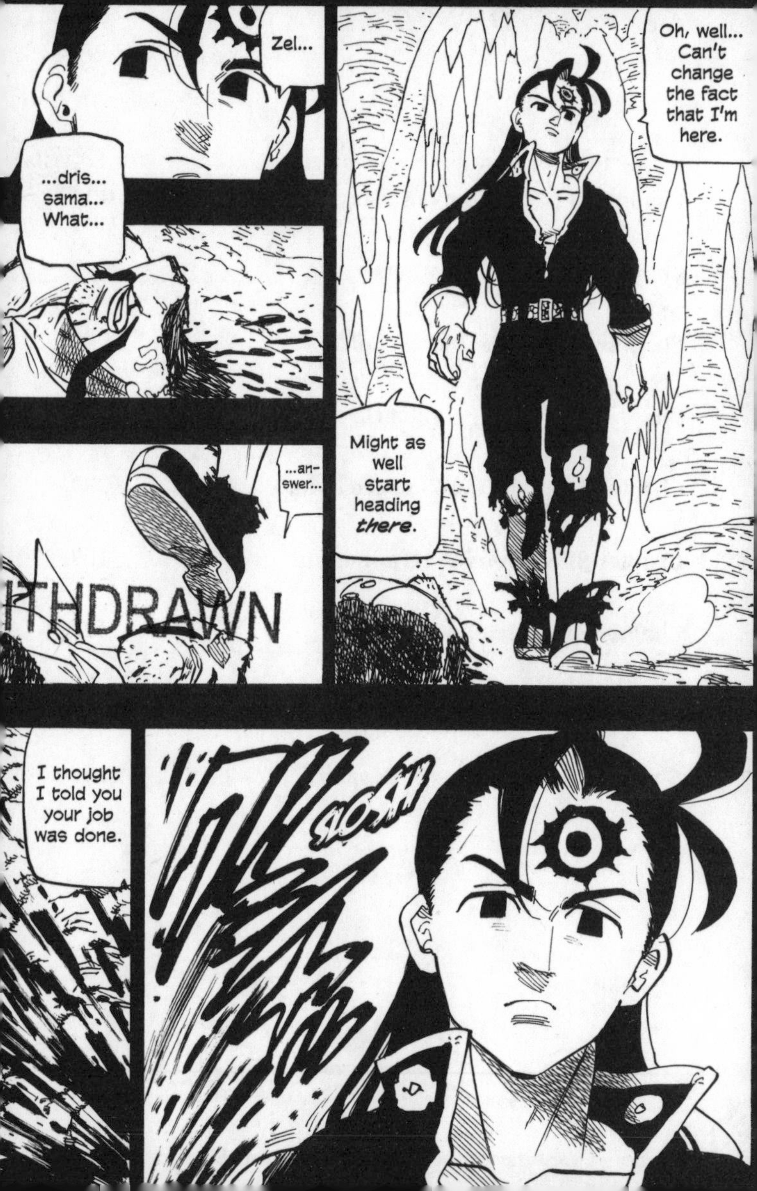
Oh, well... Can't change the fact that I'm here.
Might as well start heading *there*.
Zel...
...dris... sama... What...
...an- swer...
SLOSH
I thought I told you your job was done.

CONTENTS

BOAR HAT
The Seven Deadly Sins

Is the final volume of The Seven Deadly Sins near? A Special Essay.

75% Fiction

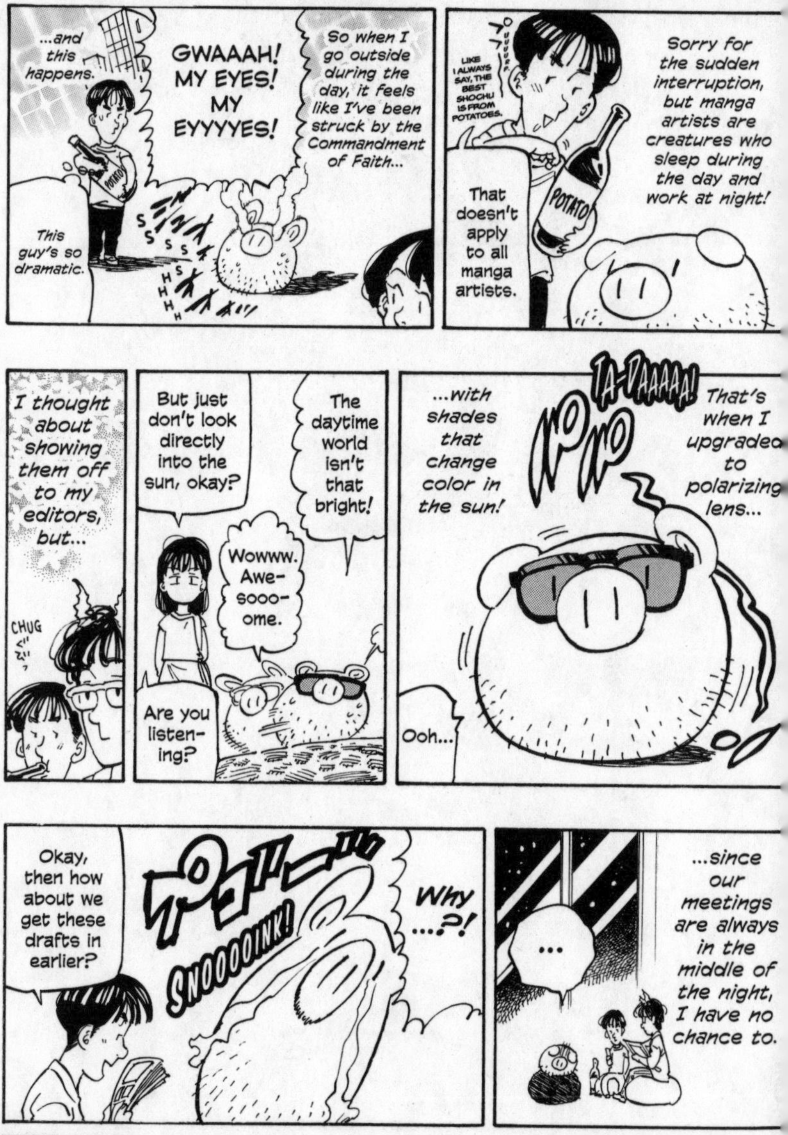
Sorry for the sudden interruption, but manga artists are creatures who sleep during the day and work at night!
LIKE I ALWAYS SAY, THE BEST SHOCHU IS FROM POTATOES.
POTATO
That doesn't apply to all manga artists.
So when I go outside during the day, it feels like I've been struck by the Commandment of Faith...
GWAAAH! MY EYES! MY EYYYYES!
...and this happens.
POTATO
This guy's so dramatic.
TA-DAAAAA!
That's when I upgraded to polarizing lens...
...with shades that change color in the sun!
Ooh...
The daytime world isn't that bright!
But just don't look directly into the sun, okay?
Wowww. Awe-sooo-ome.
Are you listen-ing?
I thought about showing them off to my editors, but...
CHUG
...since our meetings are always in the middle of the night, I have no chance to.
...
Why ...?!
SNOOOOINK!
Okay, then how about we get these drafts in earlier?

THE END

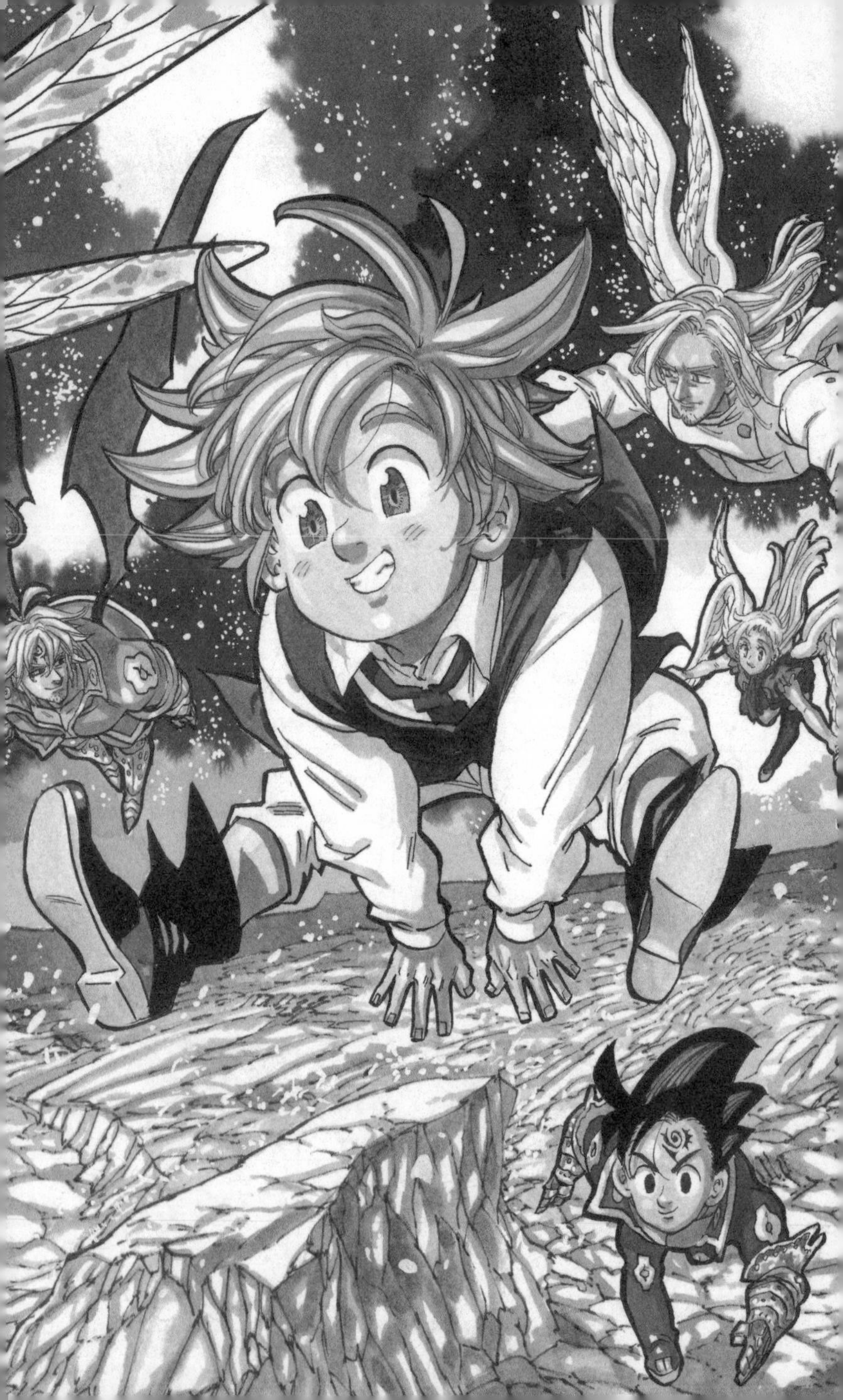

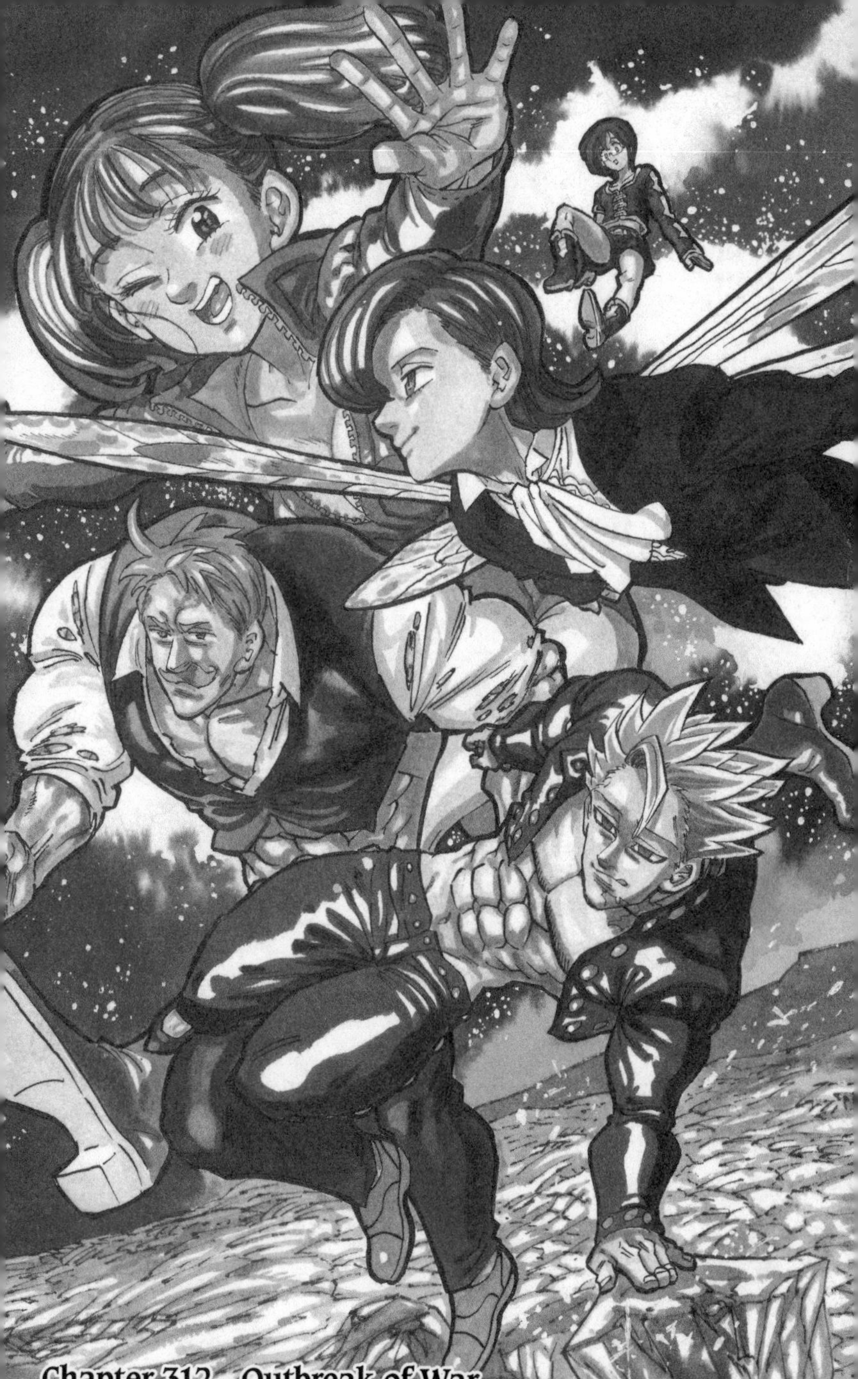

Chapter 312 - Outbreak of War

Is the final volume of The Seven Deadly Sins near? A Special Essay.

90% Fiction

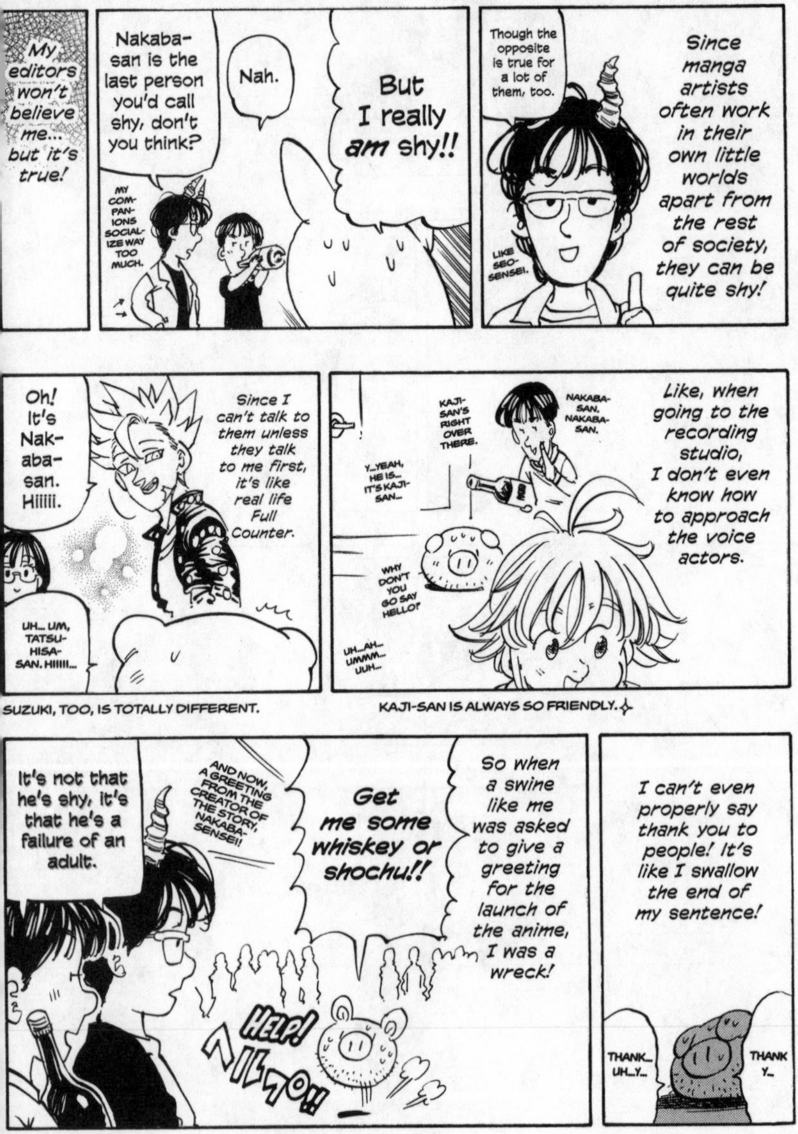

Since manga artists often work in their own little worlds apart from the rest of society, they can be quite shy!
Though the opposite is true for a lot of them, too.
LIKE SEO-SENSEI.
But I really *am* shy!!
Nakaba-san is the last person you'd call shy, don't you think?
Nah.
MY COMPANIONS SOCIALIZE WAY TOO MUCH.
My editors won't believe me... but it's true!
Like, when going to the recording studio, I don't even know how to approach the voice actors.
NAKABA-SAN. NAKABA-SAN.
KAJI-SAN'S RIGHT OVER THERE.
Y...YEAH, HE IS... IT'S KAJI-SAN...
WHY DON'T YOU GO SAY HELLO?
UH...AH... UMMM... UUH...
KAJI-SAN IS ALWAYS SO FRIENDLY.
Since I can't talk to them unless they talk to me first, it's like real life Full Counter.
Oh! It's Nakaba-san. Hiiiii.
UH... UM, TATSUHISA-SAN. HIIIII...
SUZUKI, TOO, IS TOTALLY DIFFERENT.
I can't even properly say thank you to people! It's like I swallow the end of my sentence!
THANK Y...
THANK... UH...Y...
So when a swine like me was asked to give a greeting for the launch of the anime, I was a wreck!
Get me some whiskey or shochu!!
AND NOW, A GREETING FROM THE CREATOR OF THE STORY, NAKABA-SENSEI!
It's not that he's shy, it's that he's a failure of an adult.
HELP!
ヘルプ!!

THE END

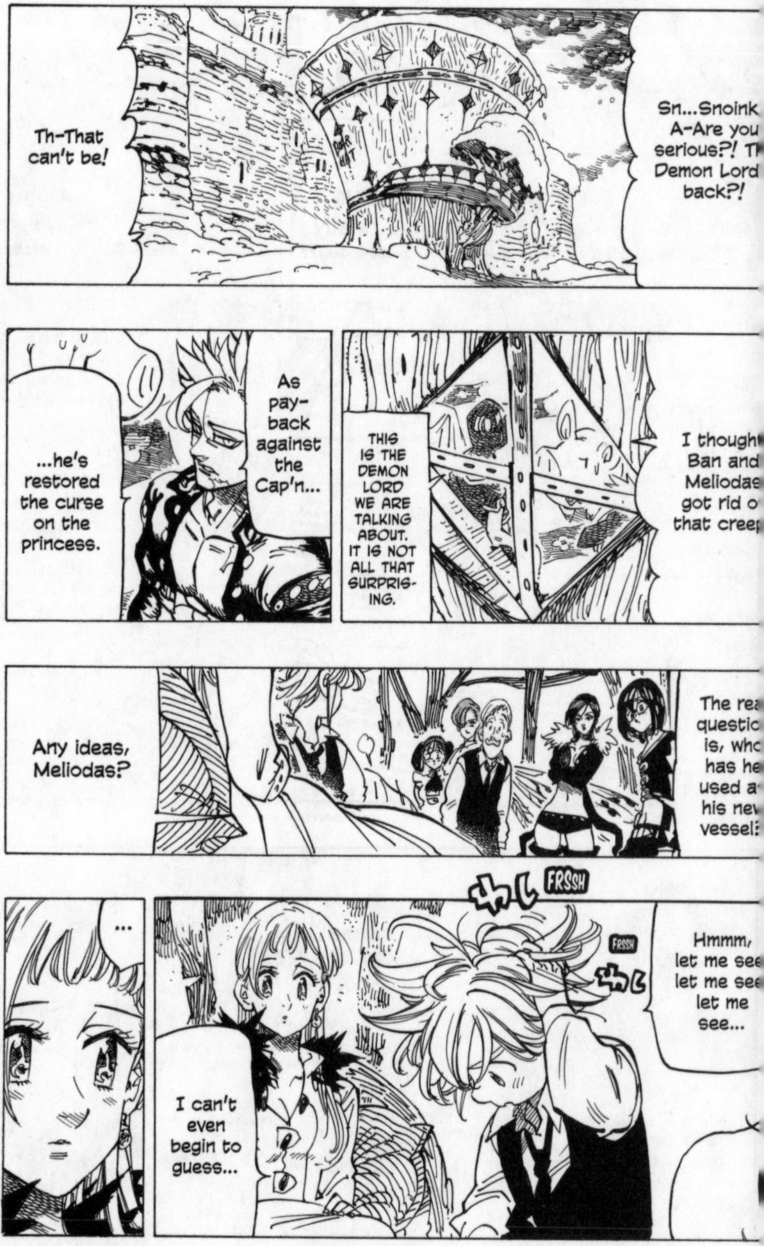

Sn...Snoink A-Are you serious?! T Demon Lord back?!
Th-That can't be!
I though Ban and Meliodas got rid o that creep
THIS IS THE DEMON LORD WE ARE TALKING ABOUT. IT IS NOT ALL THAT SURPRISING.
As pay-back against the Cap'n...
...he's restored the curse on the princess.
The re questic is, whc has he used a his nev vessel
Any ideas, Meliodas?
FRSSH
FRSSH
Hmmm, let me se let me se let me see...
I can't even begin to guess...
...

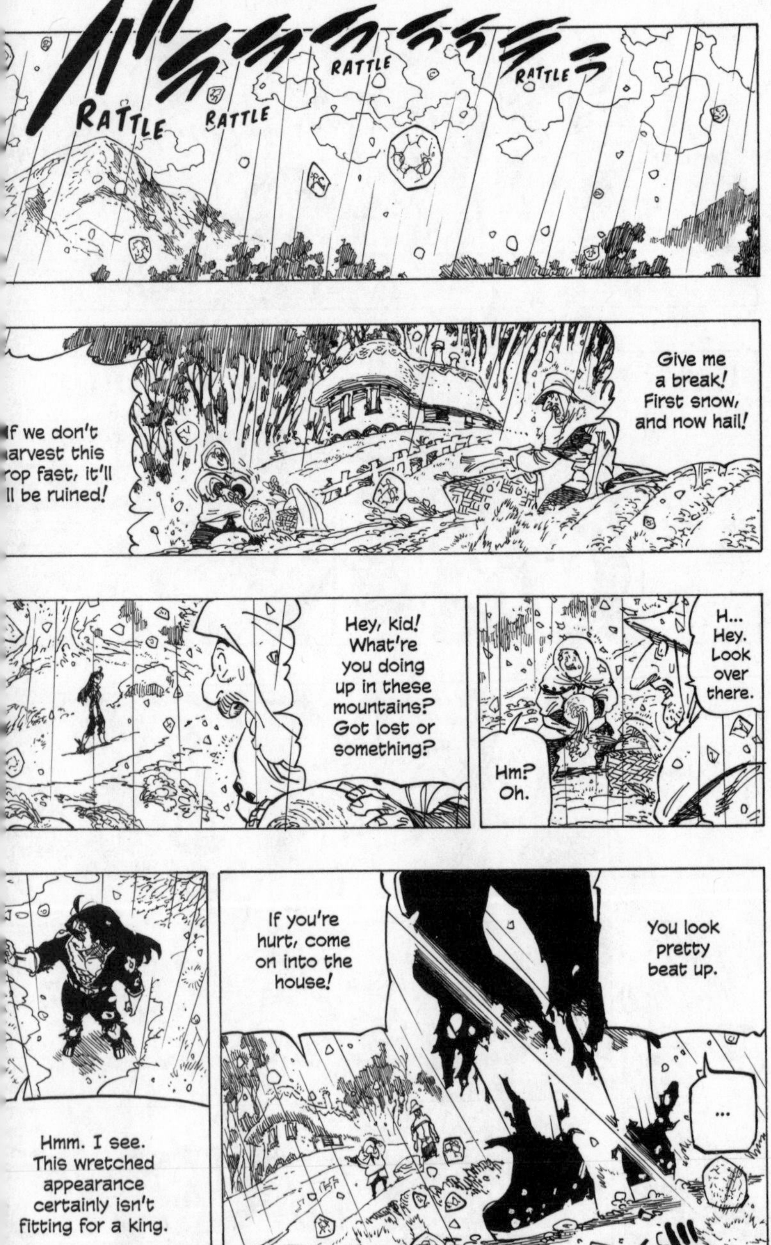
RATTLE
RATTLE
RATTLE
RATTLE
Give me a break! First snow, and now hail!
If we don't arvest this rop fast, it'll ll be ruined!
H... Hey. Look over there.
Hm? Oh.
Hey, kid! What're you doing up in these mountains? Got lost or something?
You look pretty beat up.
If you're hurt, come on into the house!
...
THUD
Hmm. I see. This wretched appearance certainly isn't fitting for a king.

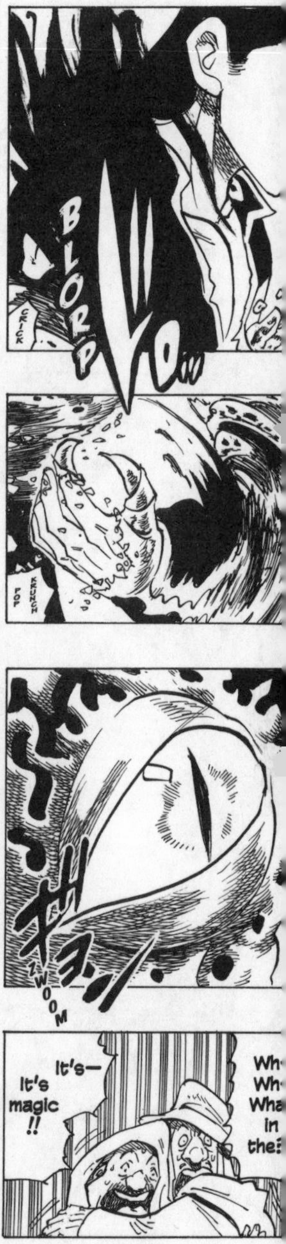
BLORP
CRICK
POP
KRUNCH
ZWOOM
Wh
Wh
Wha
in
the?
It's—
It's magic!!

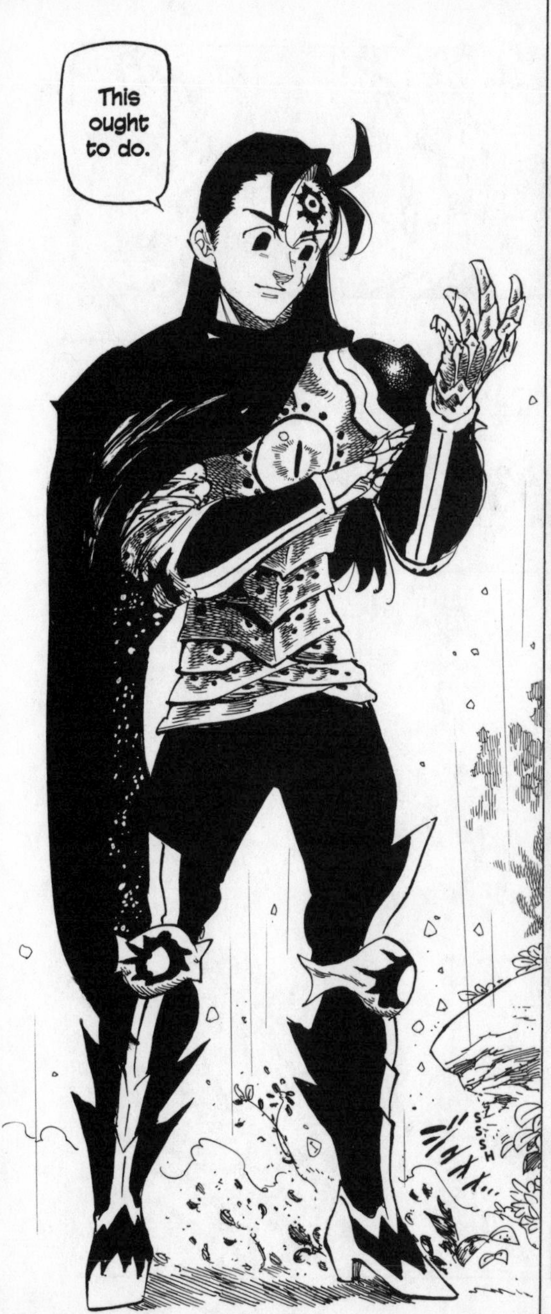
This ought to do.
SZSSSH

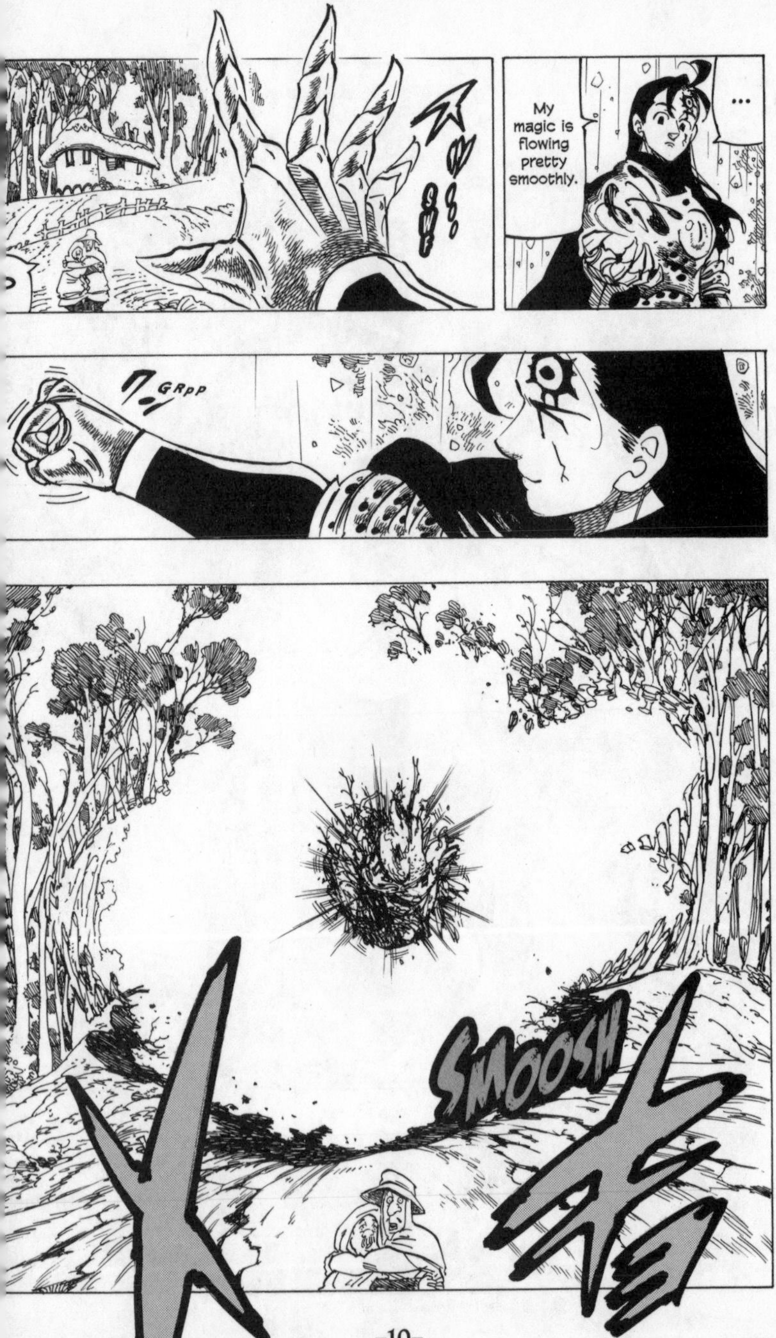
...
My magic is flowing pretty smoothly.
SWF
GRPP
SMOOSH

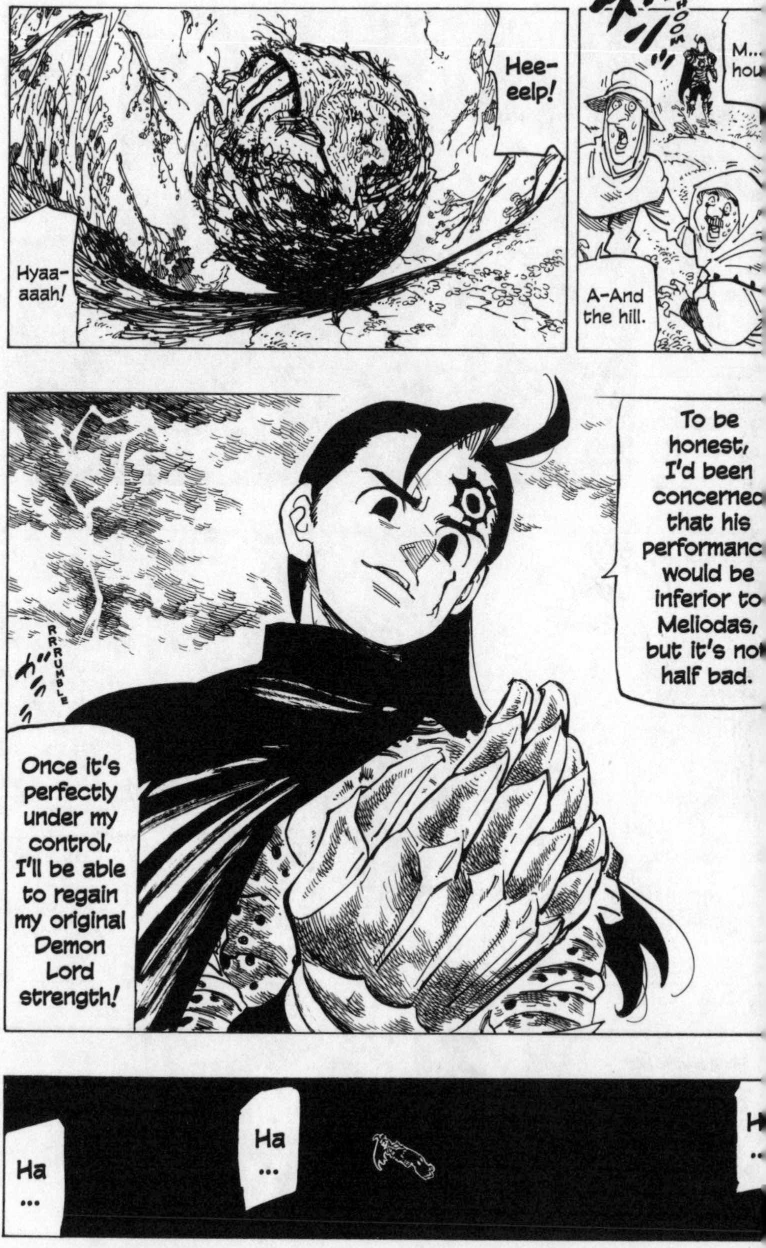
THOOM
M...
hou
A-And the hill.
Hee-eelp!
Hyaa-aaah!
To be honest, I'd been concerne that his performanc would be inferior to Meliodas, but it's no half bad.
RRRUMBLE
Once it's perfectly under my control, I'll be able to regain my original Demon Lord strength!
Ha ...
Ha ...

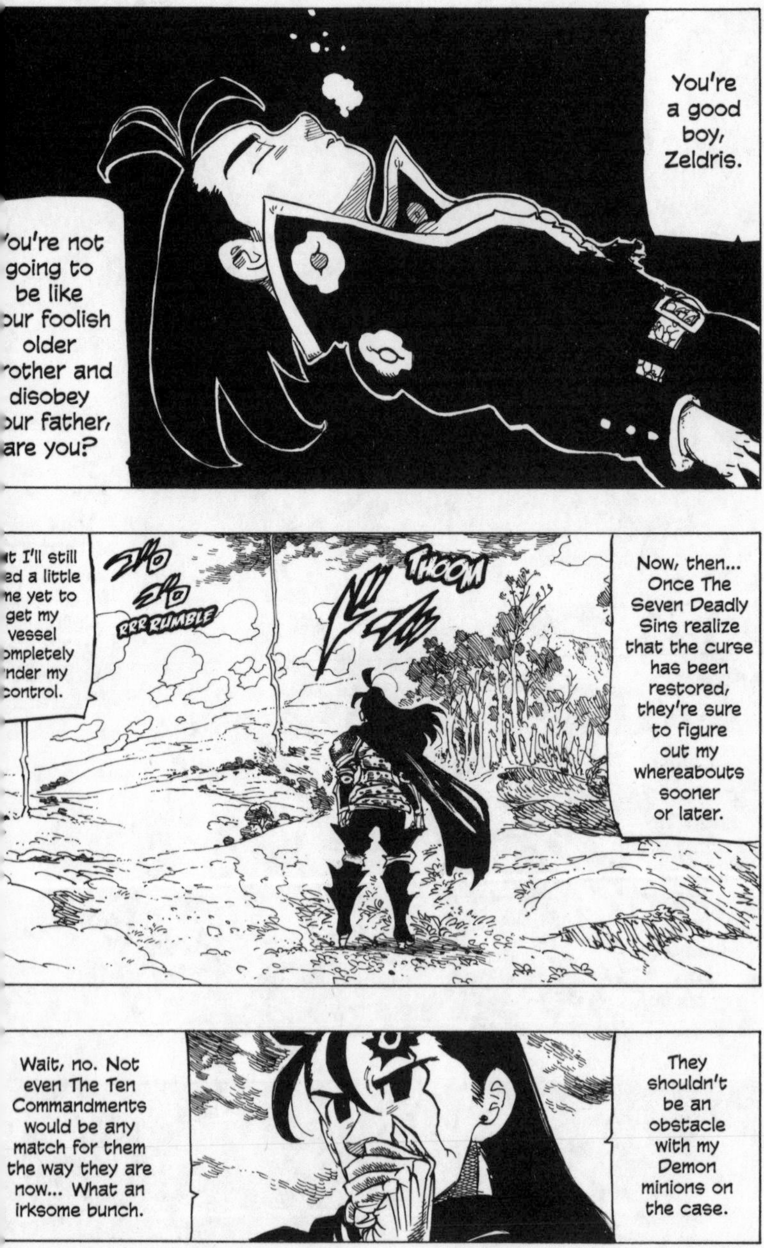
You're a good boy, Zeldris.
'ou're not going to be like our foolish older rother and disobey our father, are you?
Now, then... Once The Seven Deadly Sins realize that the curse has been restored, they're sure to figure out my whereabouts sooner or later.
THOOM
RRR RUMBLE
t I'll still ed a little ne yet to get my vessel ompletely nder my control.
They shouldn't be an obstacle with my Demon minions on the case.
Wait, no. Not even The Ten Commandments would be any match for them the way they are now... What an irksome bunch.

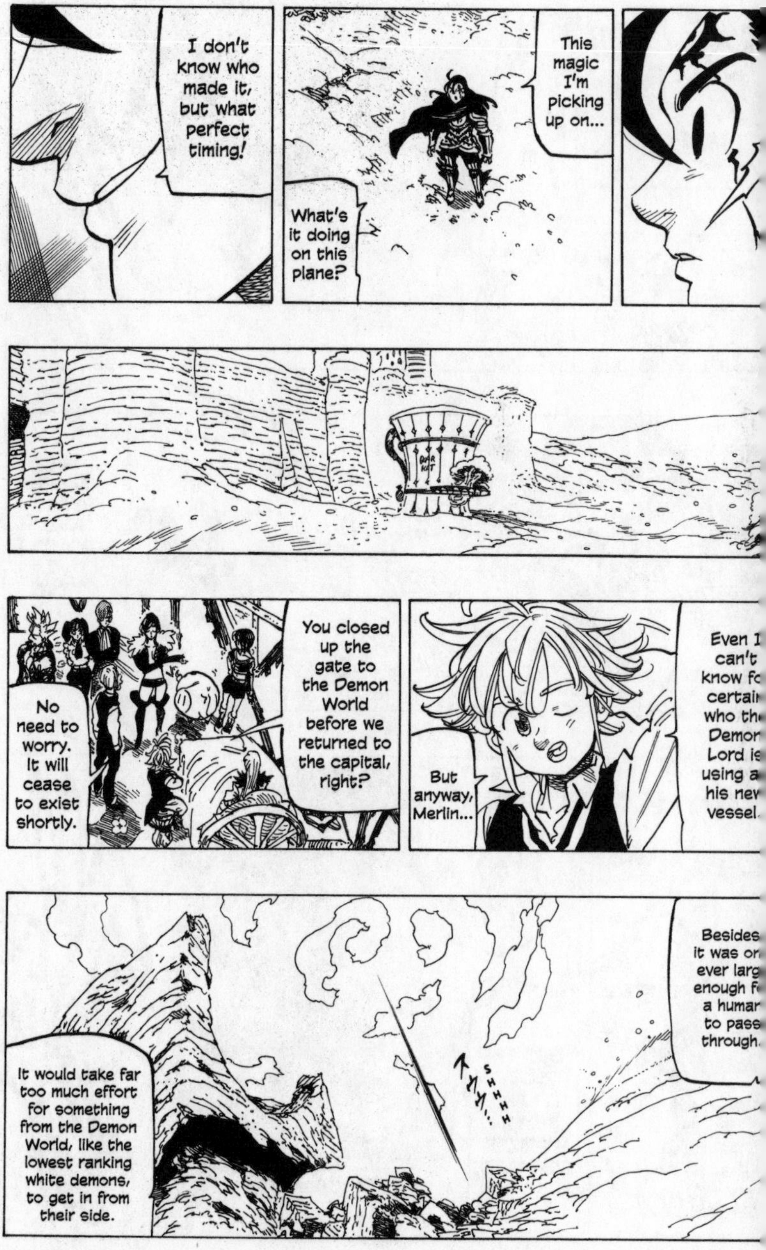
This magic I'm picking up on...
What's it doing on this plane?
I don't know who made it, but what perfect timing!
Even I can't know fo certai who th Demor Lord is using a his new vessel.
But anyway, Merlin...
You closed up the gate to the Demon World before we returned to the capital, right?
No need to worry. It will cease to exist shortly.
Besides, it was or ever larg enough f a humar to pass through.
SHHHH...
It would take far too much effort for something from the Demon World, like the lowest ranking white demons, to get in from their side.

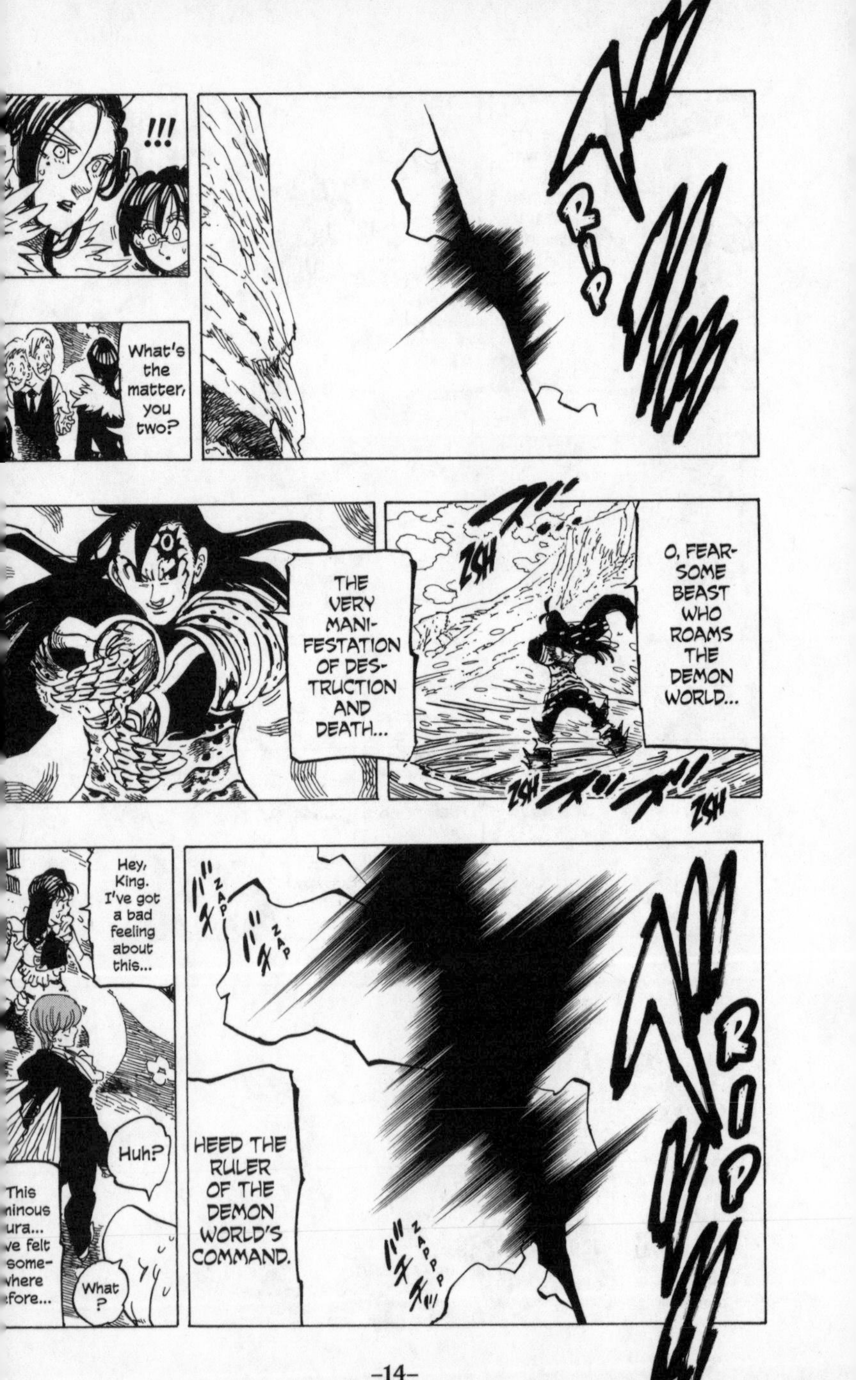
RIP
!!!
What's the matter, you two?
ZSH
O, FEAR-SOME BEAST WHO ROAMS THE DEMON WORLD...
ZSH
ZSH
THE VERY MANI-FESTATION OF DES-TRUCTION AND DEATH...
ZAP
ZAP
HEED THE RULER OF THE DEMON WORLD'S COMMAND.
ZAPPP
RIP
Hey, King. I've got a bad feeling about this...
Huh?
This minous ura... ve felt some-where efore...
What?

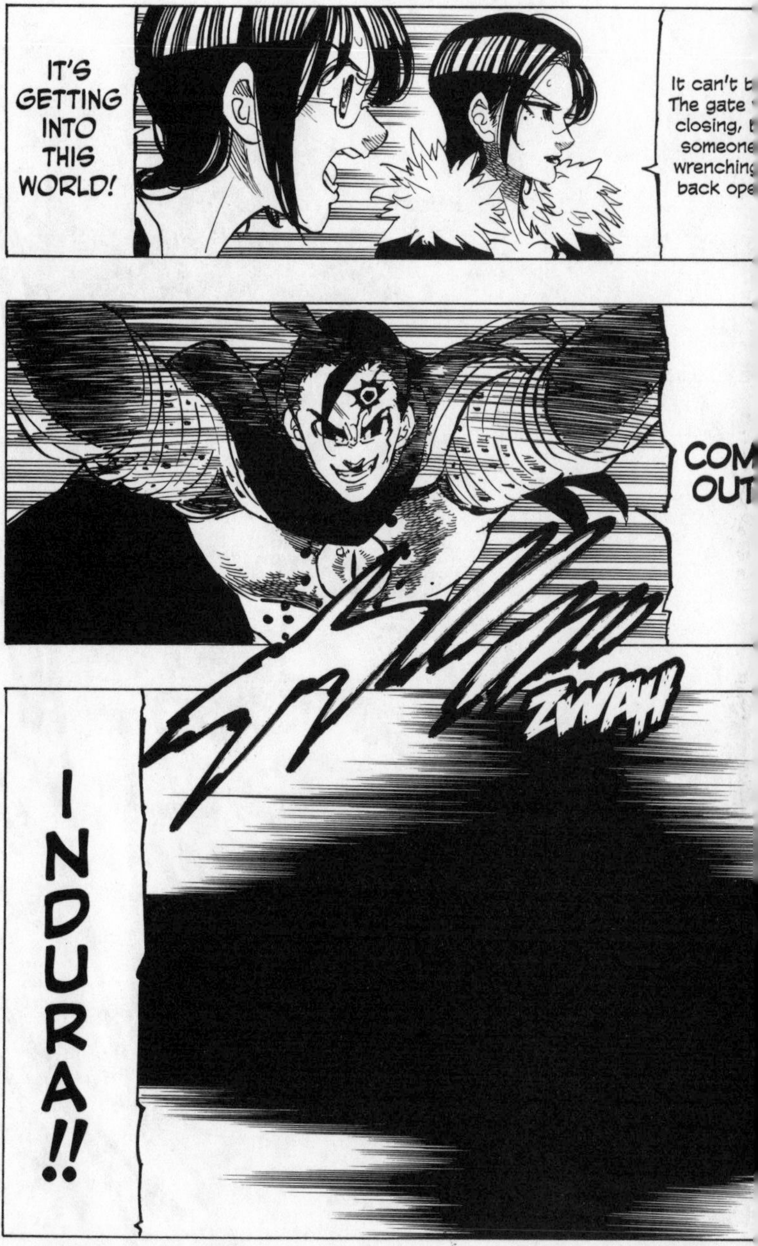
It can't b The gate closing, someone wrenching back ope
IT'S GETTING INTO THIS WORLD!
COM OUT
ZWAH
INDURA!!

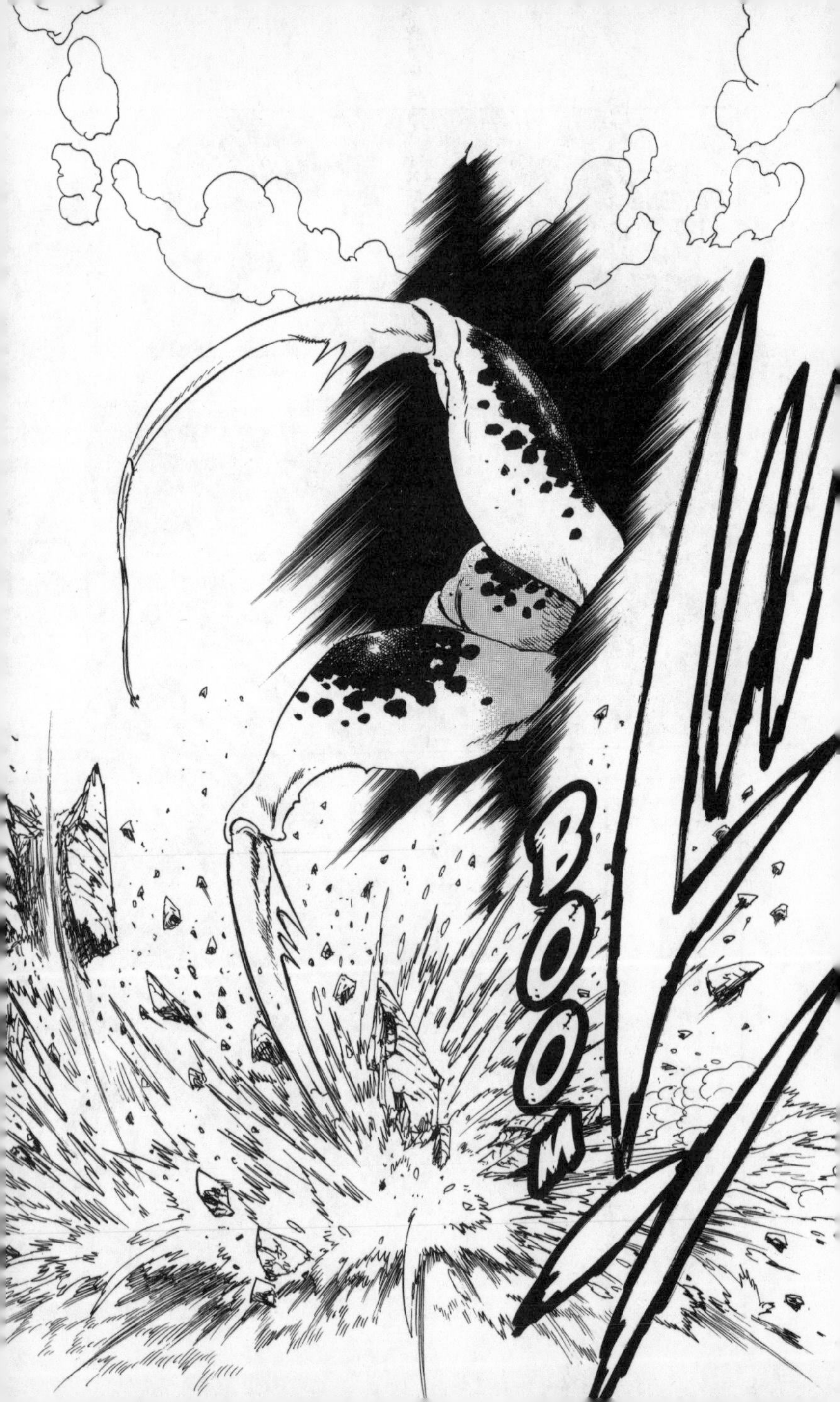
BOOOM

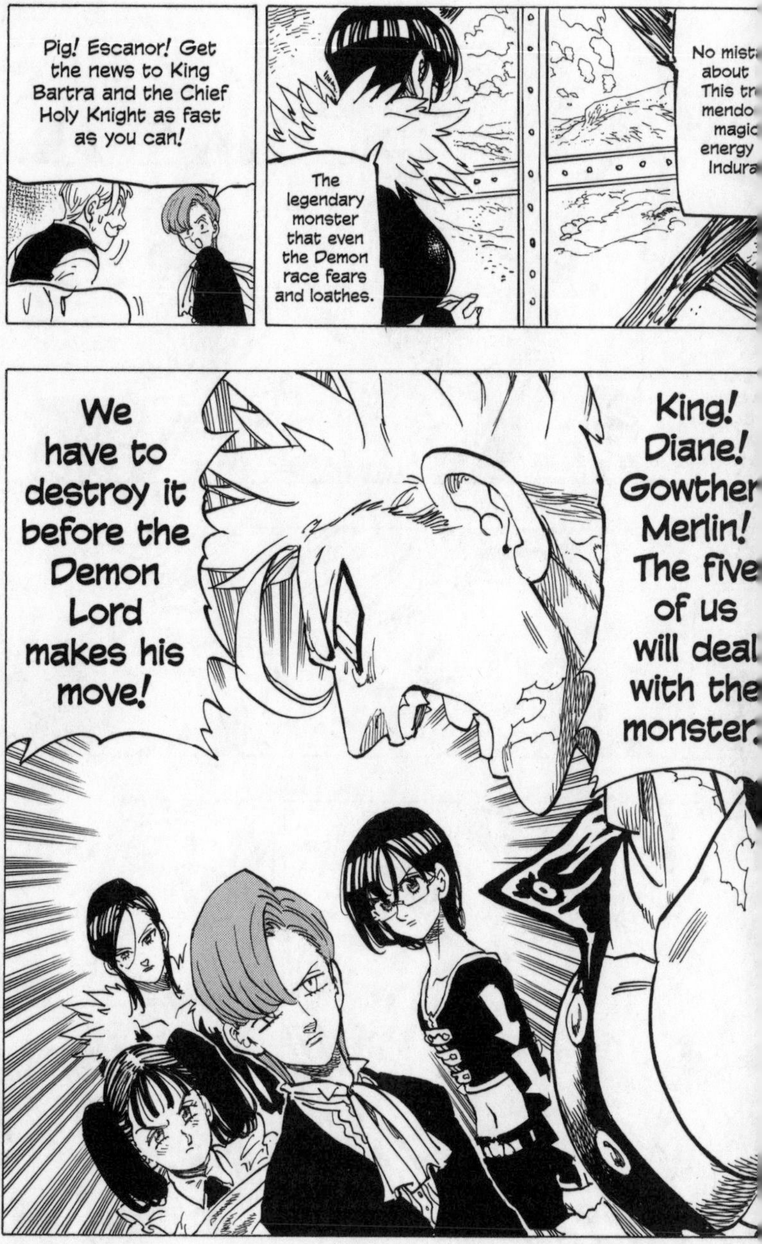
No mist
about
This tr
mendo
magic
energy
Indura
The legendary monster that even the Demon race fears and loathes.
Pig! Escanor! Get the news to King Bartra and the Chief Holy Knight as fast as you can!
King! Diane! Gowther Merlin! The five of us will deal with the monster.
We have to destroy it before the Demon Lord makes his move!

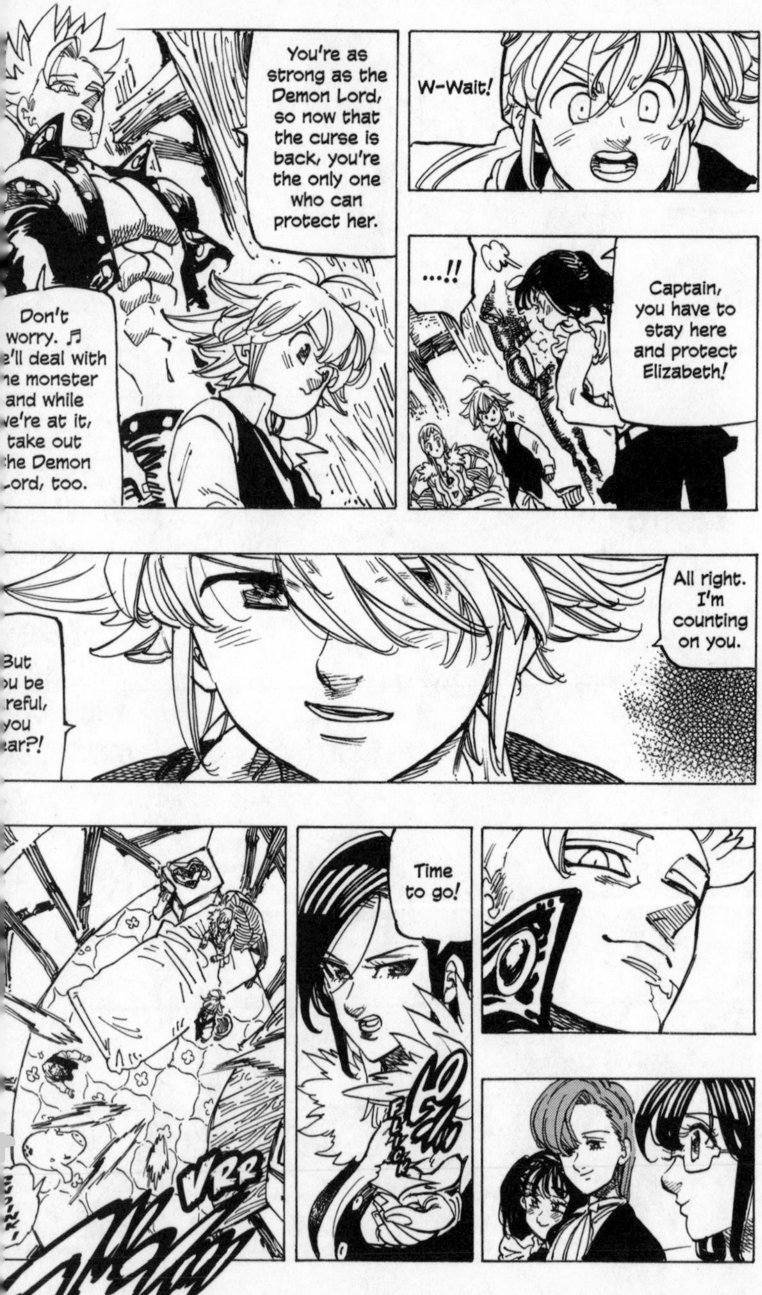

W-Wait!
...!!
Captain, you have to stay here and protect Elizabeth!
You're as strong as the Demon Lord, so now that the curse is back, you're the only one who can protect her.
Don't worry. ♫ e'll deal with e monster and while ve're at it, take out he Demon ord, too.
All right. I'm counting on you.
But u be reful, you ar?!
Time to go!
VRR

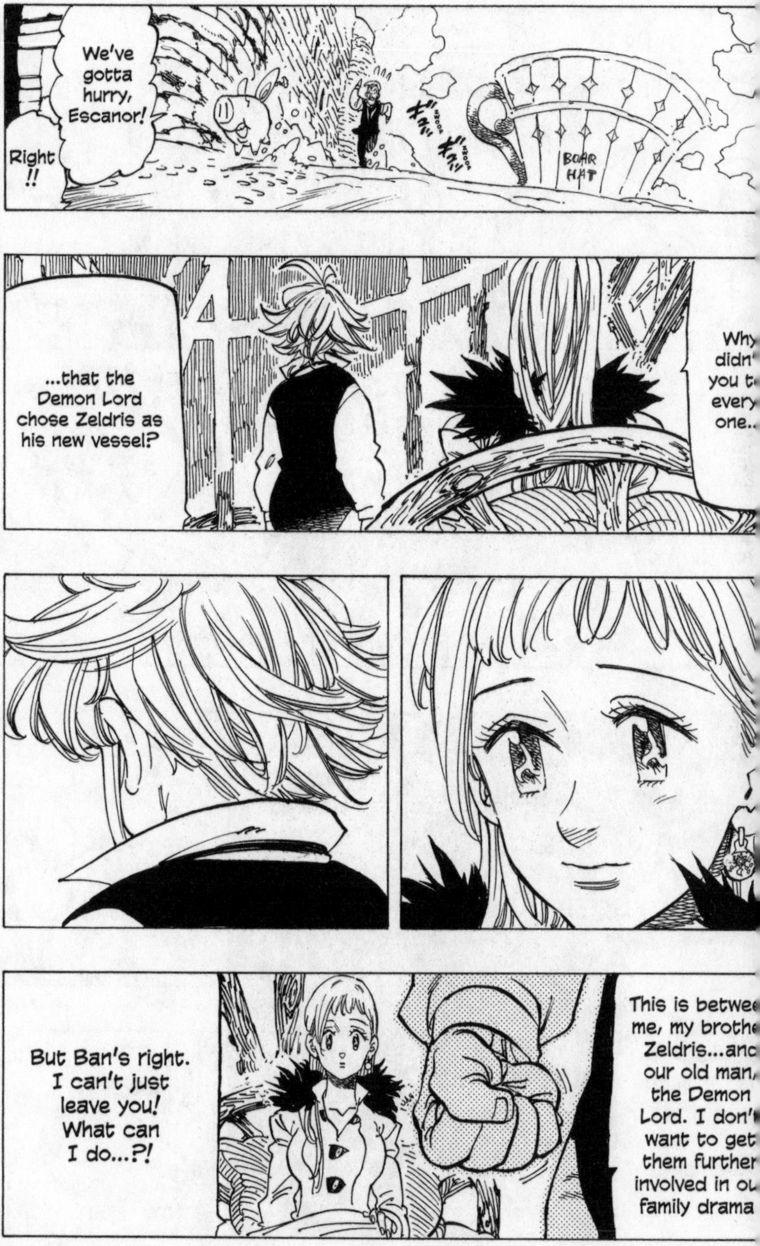
We've gotta hurry, Escanor!
Right!!
BOAR HAT
Why didn' you t every one..
...that the Demon Lord chose Zeldris as his new vessel?
This is betwe me, my brothe Zeldris...and our old man, the Demon Lord. I don' want to get them further involved in ou family drama
But Ban's right. I can't just leave you! What can I do...?!

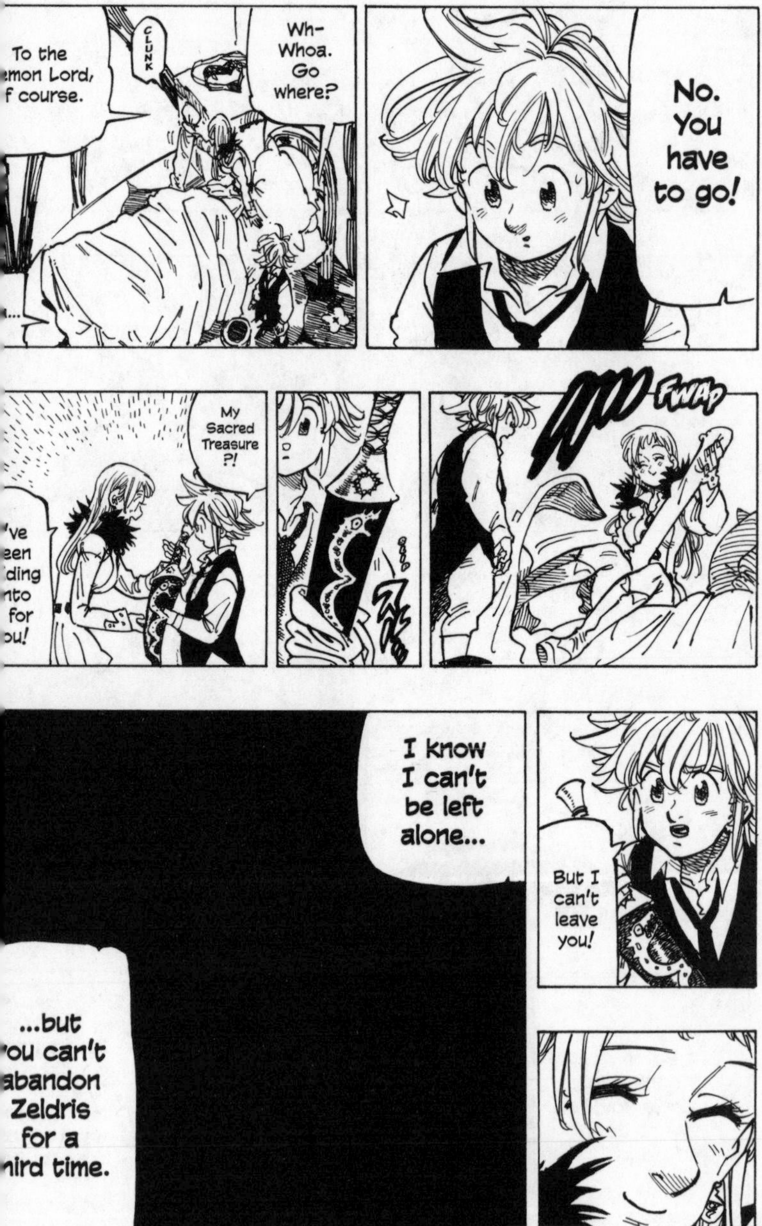

No. You have to go!
Wh- Whoa. Go where?
CLUNK
To the
emon Lord,
f course.
...
FWAp
My Sacred Treasure?!
've
een
ding
nto
for
ou!
But I can't leave you!
I know I can't be left alone...
...but
ou can't
abandon
Zeldris
for a
hird time.

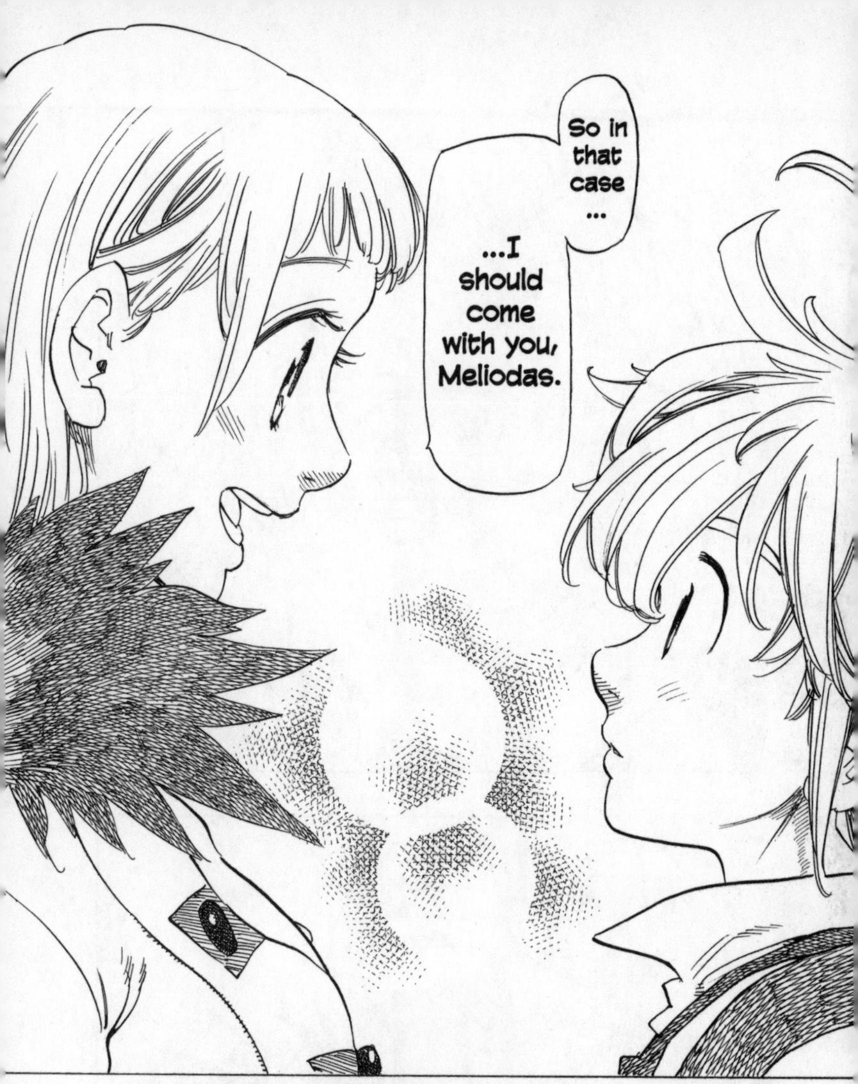
So in that case ...
...I should come with you, Meliodas.

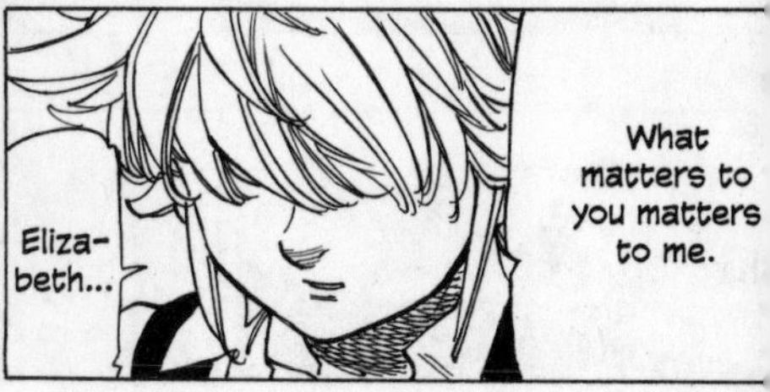
What matters to you matters to me.
Eliza-beth...

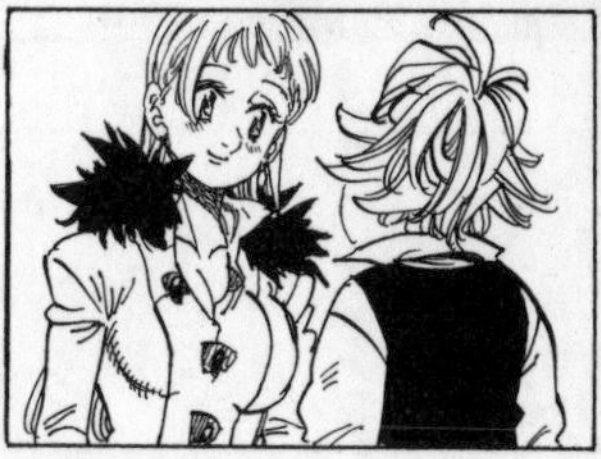

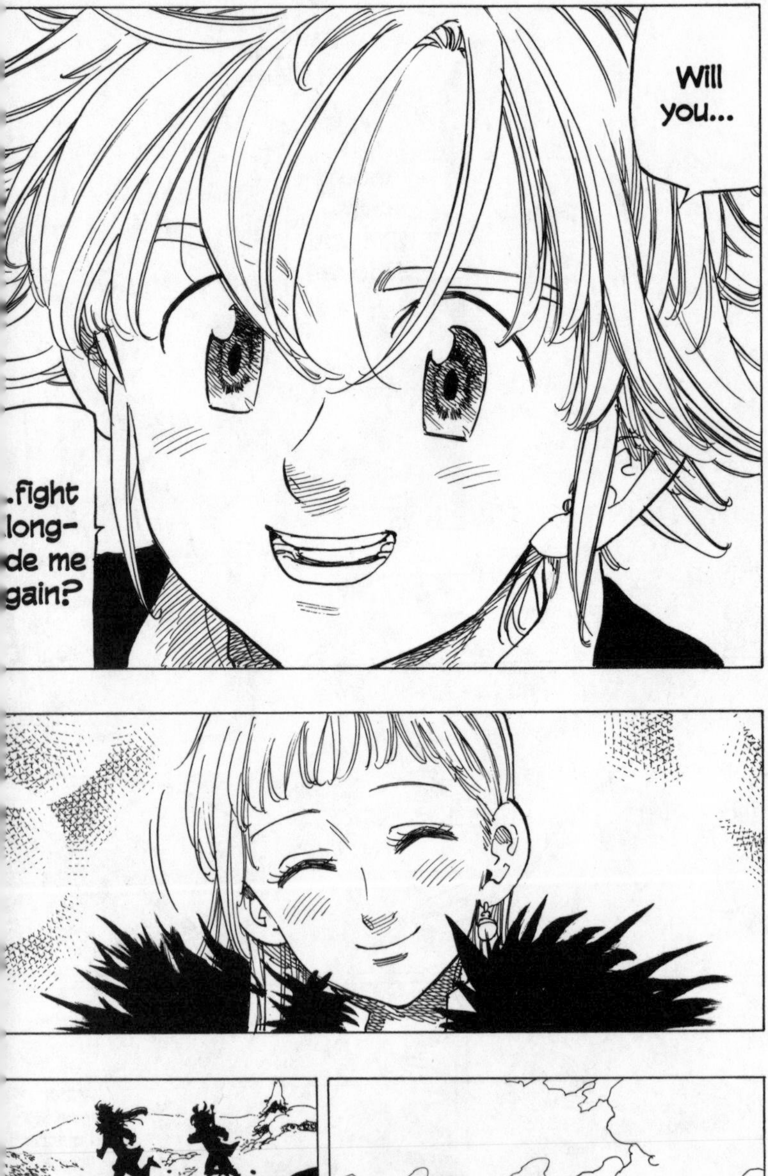
Will you...
.fight long- de me gain?

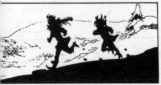

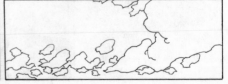

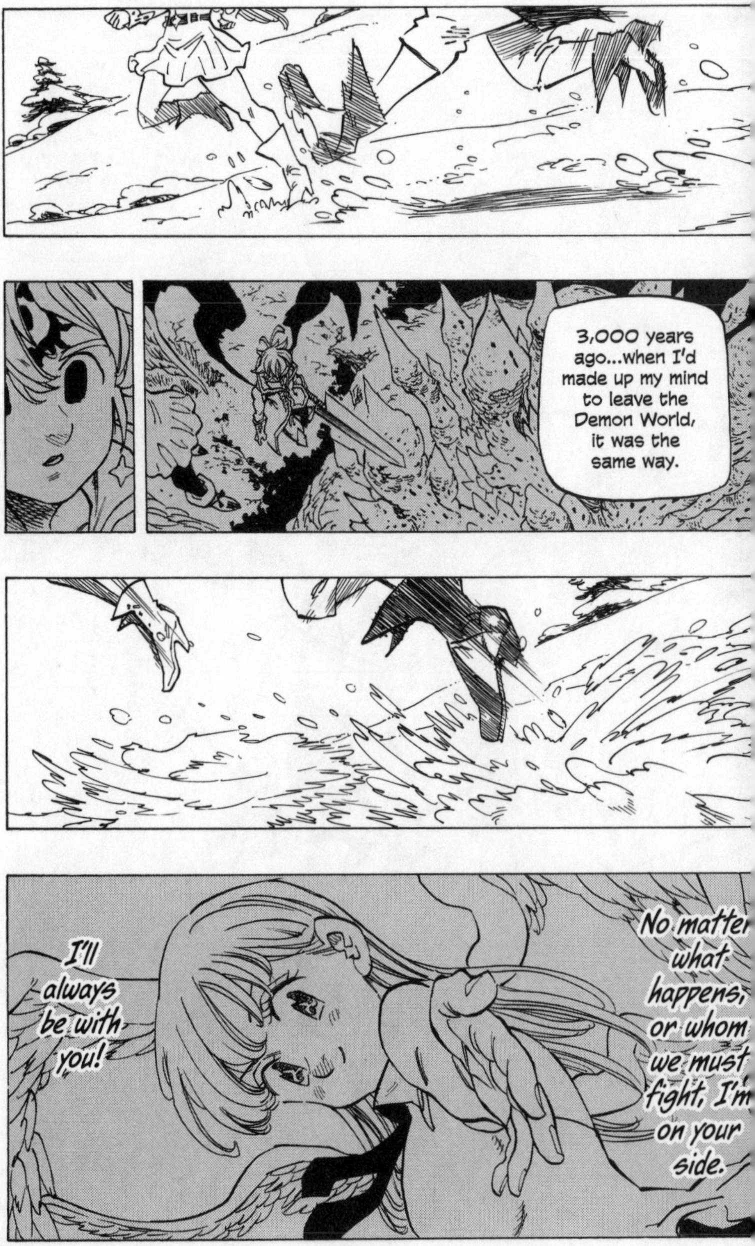
3,000 years ago...when I'd made up my mind to leave the Demon World, it was the same way.
No matter what happens, or whom we must fight, I'm on your side.
I'll always be with you!

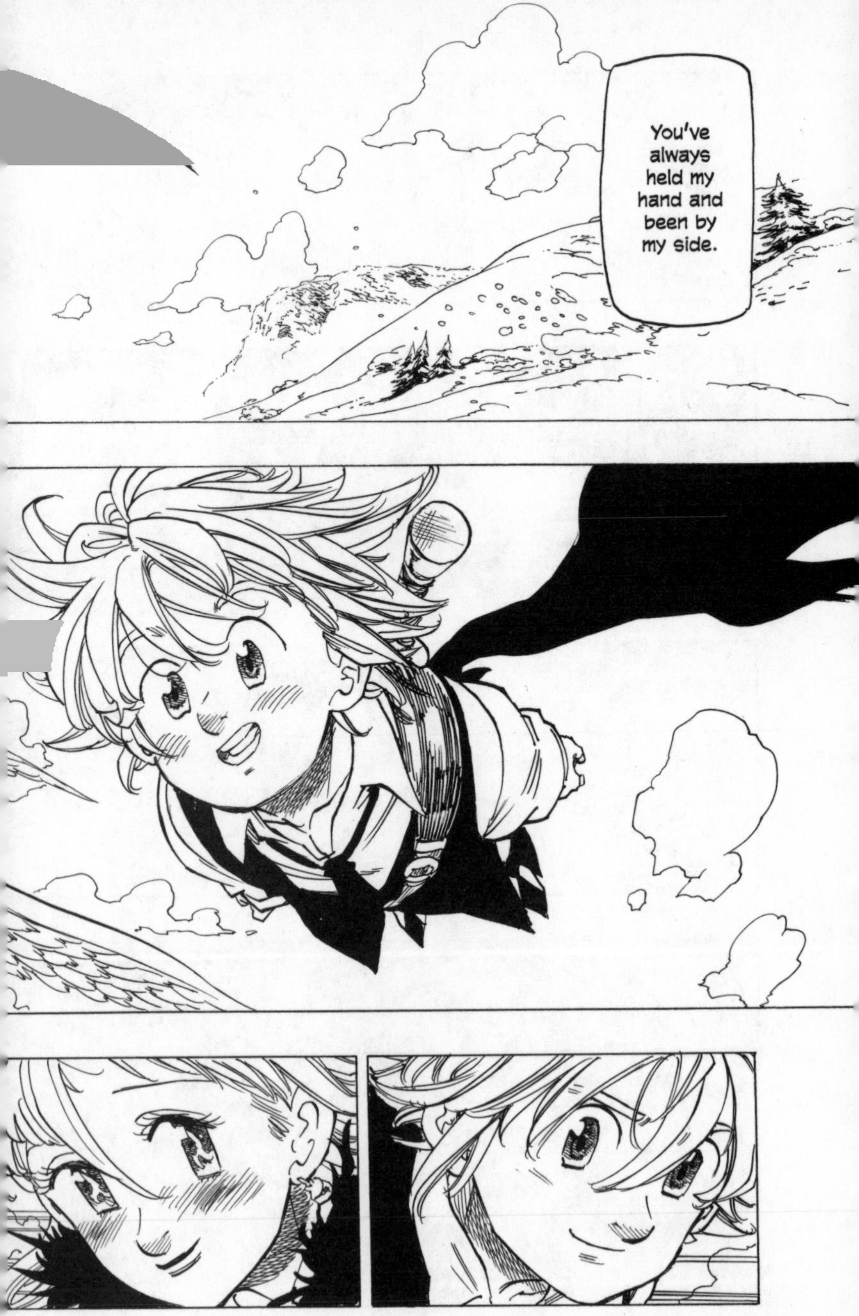
You've always held my hand and been by my side.

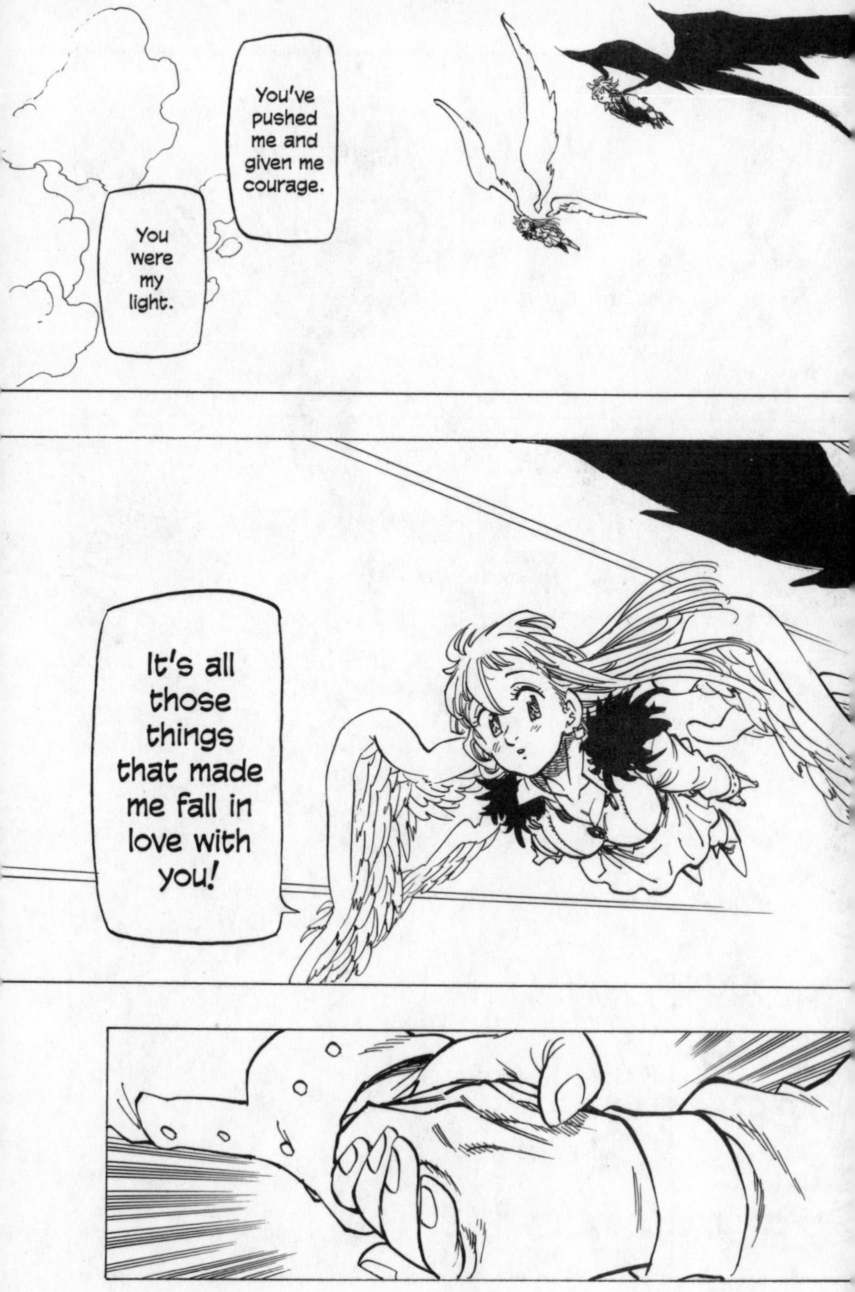
You've pushed me and given me courage.
You were my light.
It's all those things that made me fall in love with you!

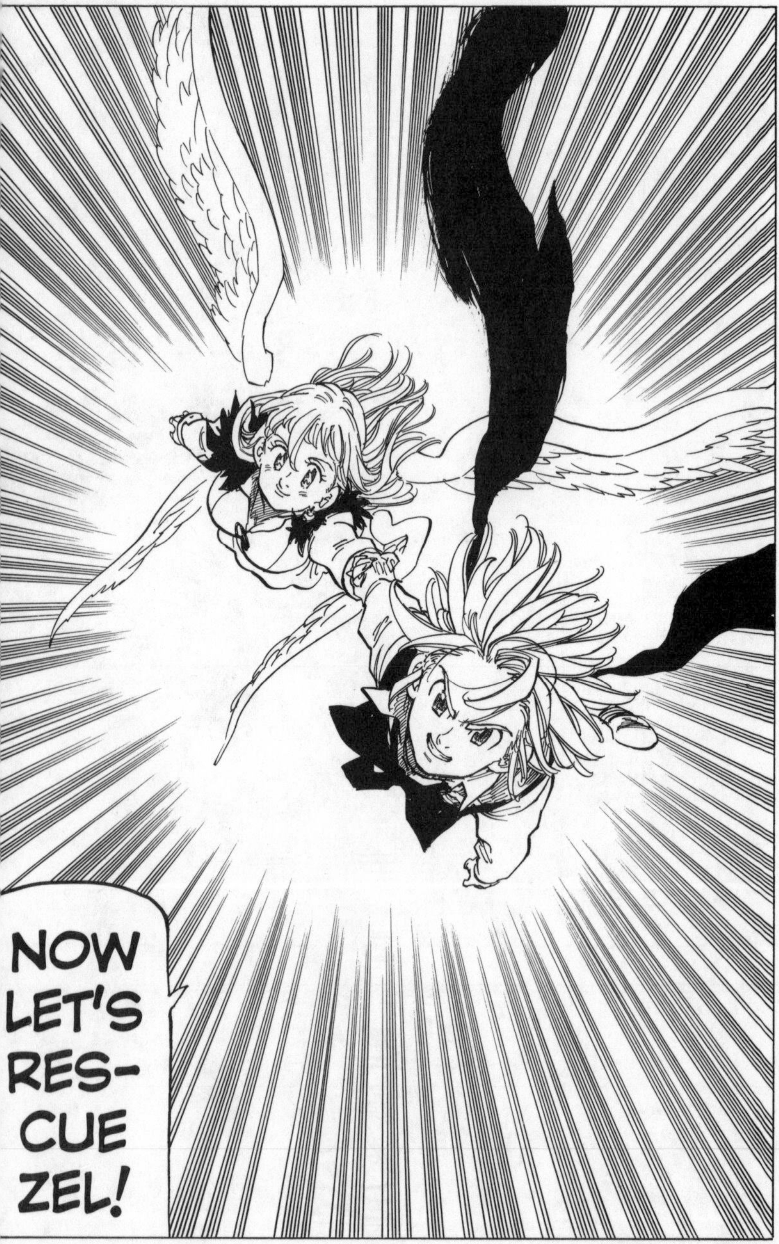
NOW LET'S RES-CUE ZEL!

THE SEVEN DEADLY SINS

Chapter 313 - Fated Brothers

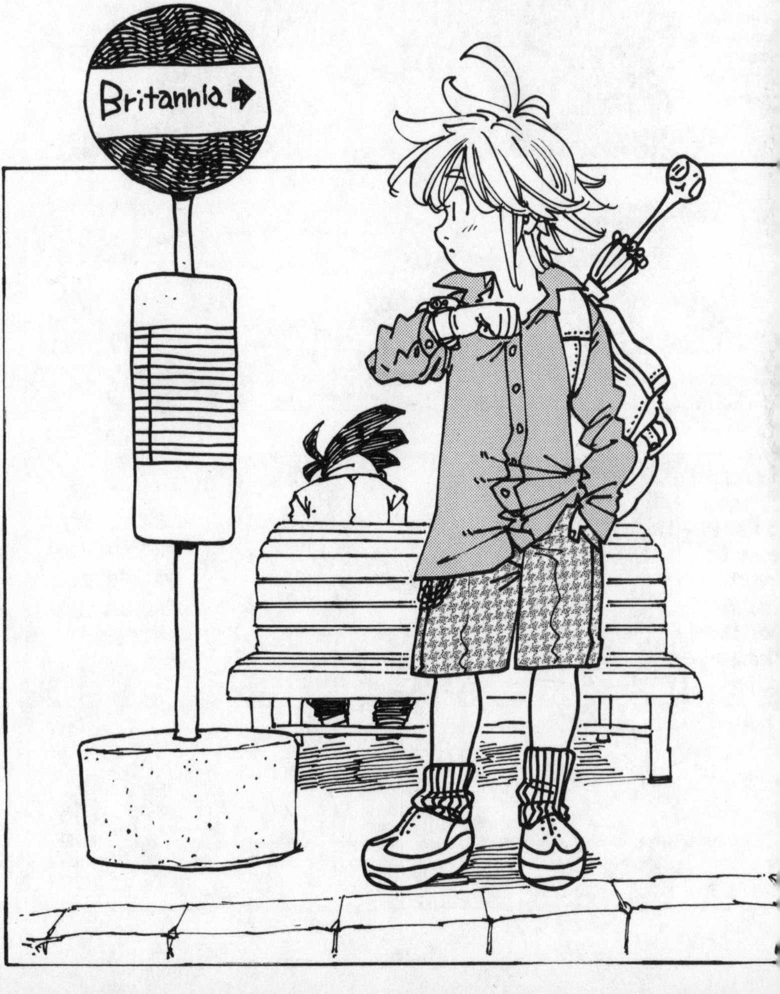
Britannia

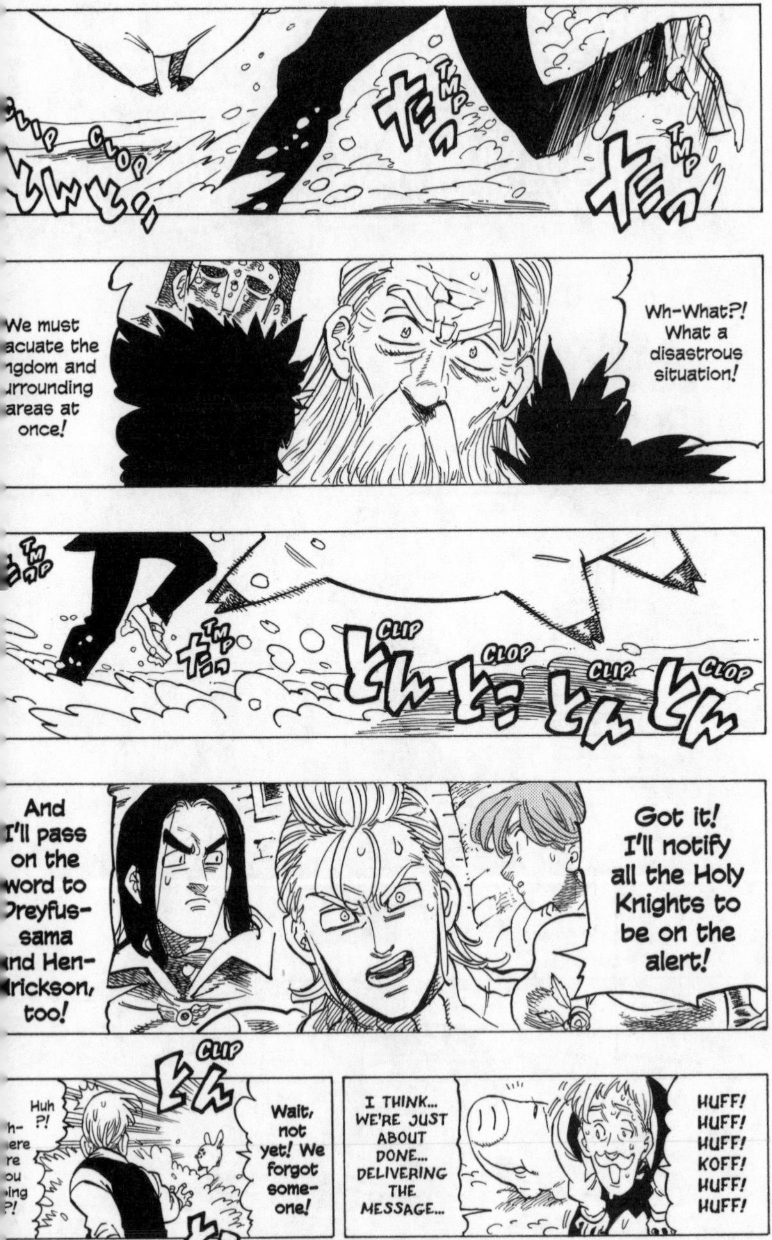
TMP
TMP
CLIP
CLOP
Wh-What?! What a disastrous situation!
We must acuate the ngdom and urrounding areas at once!
TMP
TMP
CLIP
CLOP
CLIP
CLOP
Got it! I'll notify all the Holy Knights to be on the alert!
And I'll pass on the word to reyfus-sama and Hen-rickson, too!
HUFF! HUFF! HUFF! KOFF! HUFF! HUFF!
I THINK... WE'RE JUST ABOUT DONE... DELIVERING THE MESSAGE...
CLIP
Wait, not yet! We forgot some-one!
Huh?!
CLOP

HAAH— HAAH—

KOFF! KOFF! KOFF!

H- go m ene

Haah!

The world's going to be in hot water again...

Mael- san.... If you can hea me...

...please... lend me... your power once more.

Before it's too late!

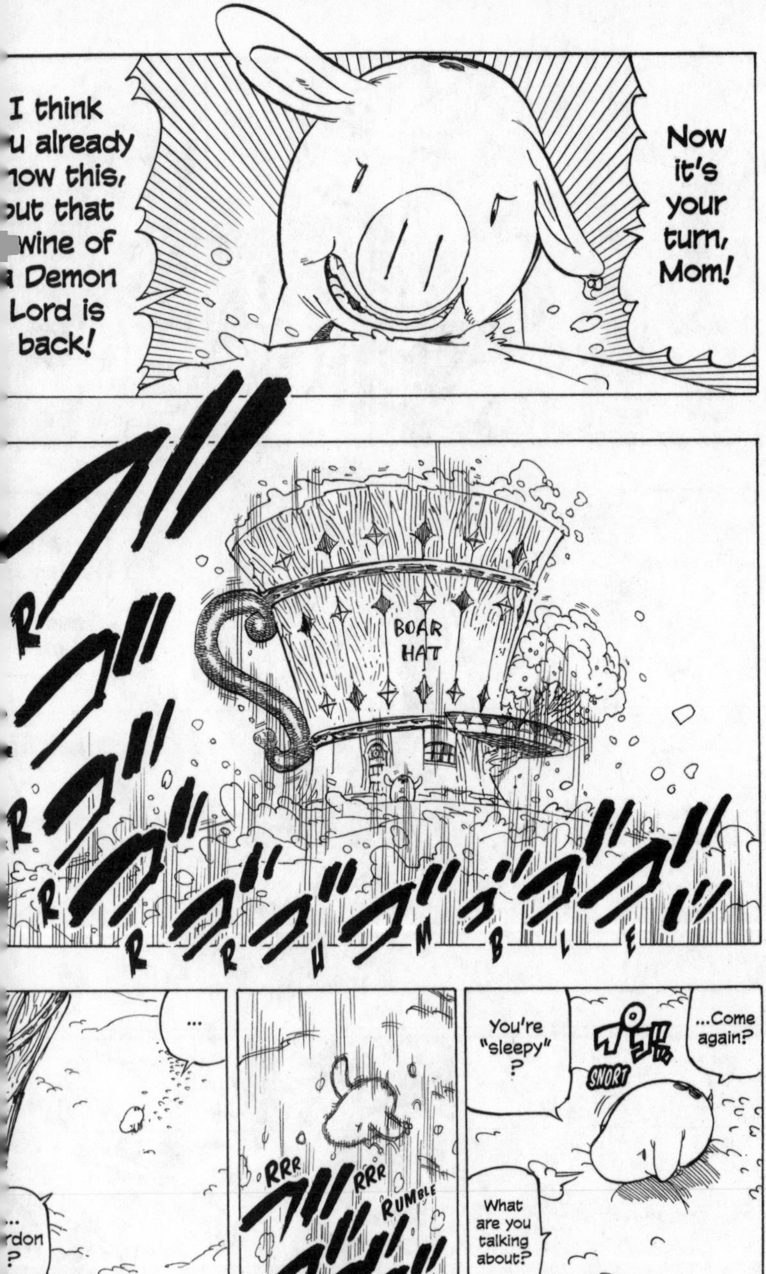

Now it's your turn, Mom!
I think u already now this, ut that wine of a Demon Lord is back!
BOAR HAT
RRRRRUMBLE
...Come again?
SNORT
You're "sleepy"?
What are you talking about?
RRR RRR RUMBLE
...
...rdon?

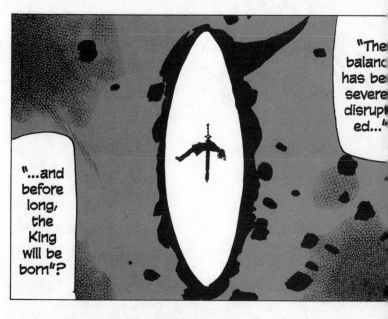

"The
balanc
has be
severe
disrup
ed..."
"...and before long, the King will be born"?
Snooooink! What did I just tell you?! He's already back! Quit talking in your sleep, Mom!
It's come down to this. I have to do something!
SPIN SPIN SPIN SPIN SPIN SPIN
Think... Think...!
Wait, no! Don't think. Feel!
ROLL ROLL ROLL ROLL ROLL ROLL
SLAM
Ow!!

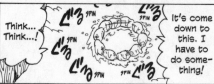

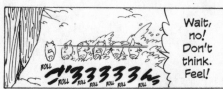

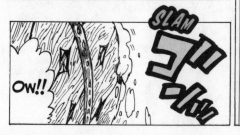

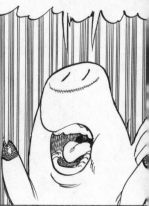

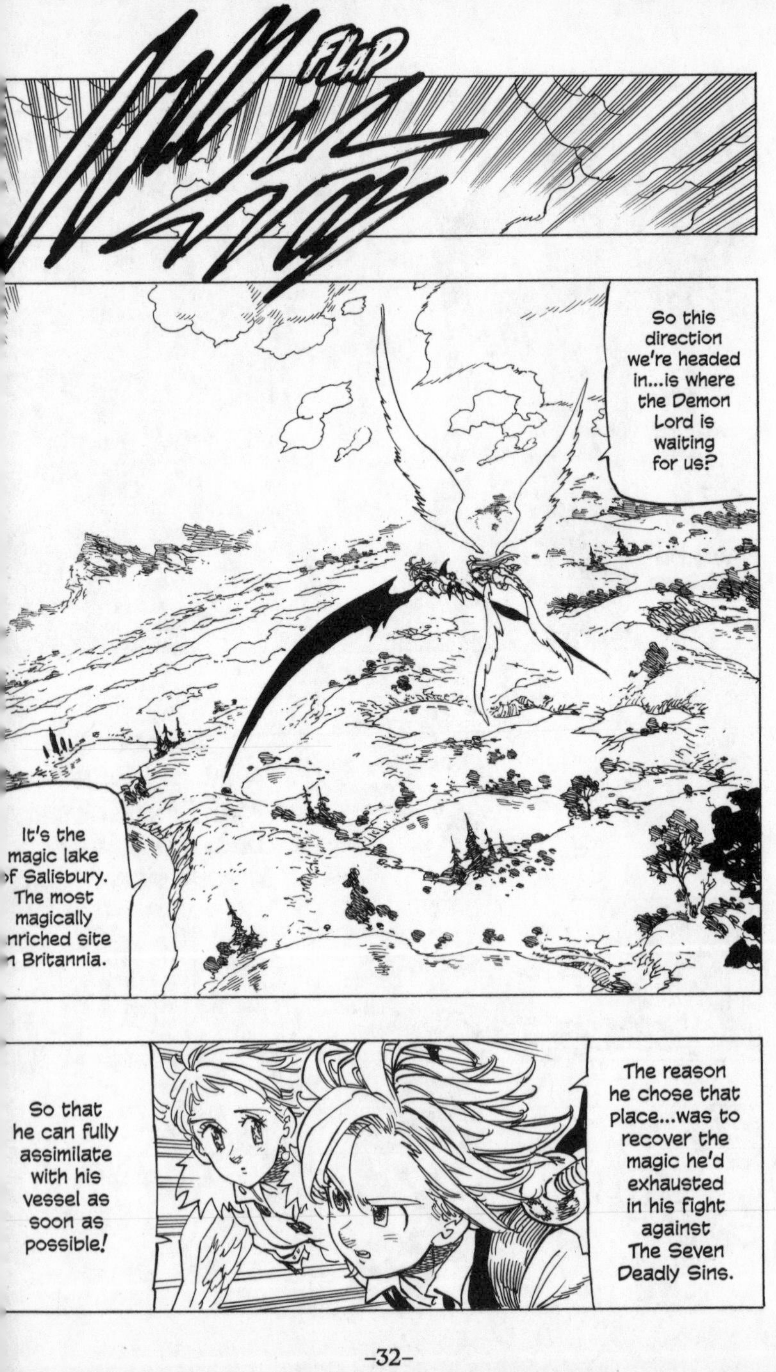
FLAP
So this direction we're headed in...is where the Demon Lord is waiting for us?
It's the magic lake f Salisbury. The most magically nriched site n Britannia.
The reason he chose that place...was to recover the magic he'd exhausted in his fight against The Seven Deadly Sins.
So that he can fully assimilate with his vessel as soon as possible!

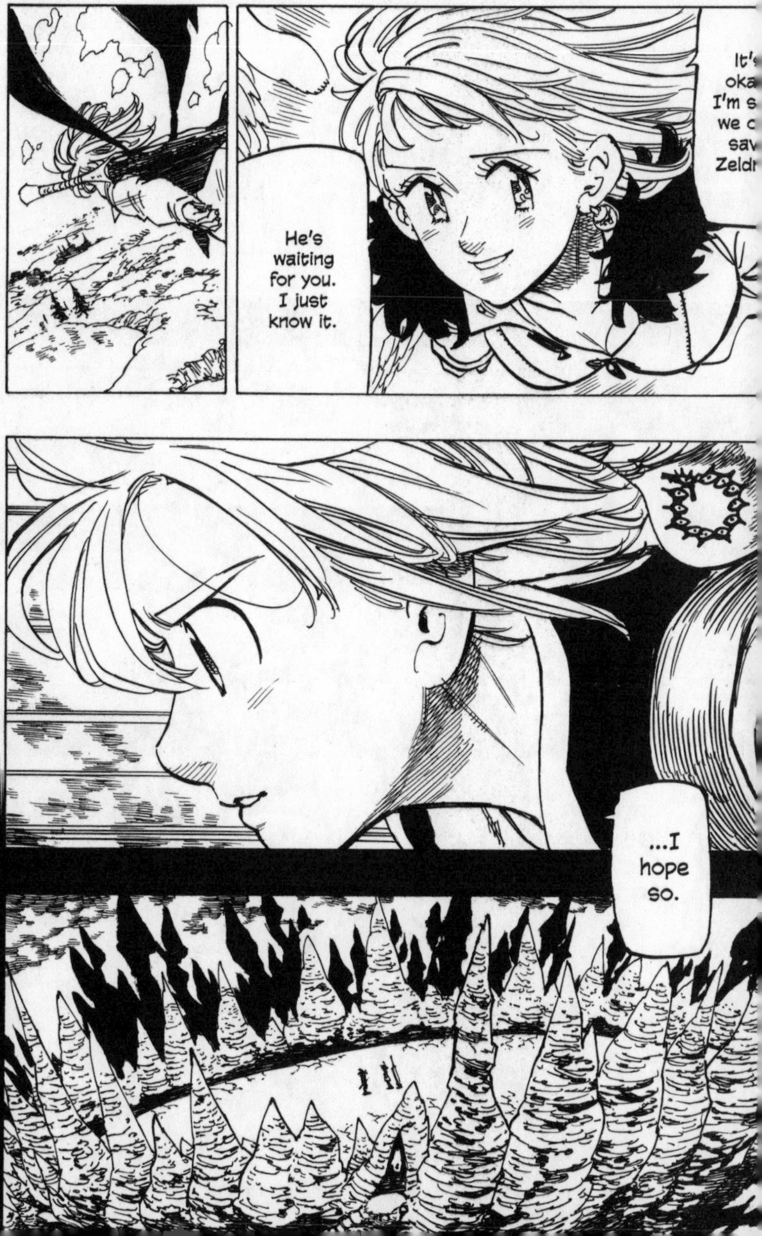
It's oka I'm s we c sav Zeldr
He's waiting for you. I just know it.
...I hope so.

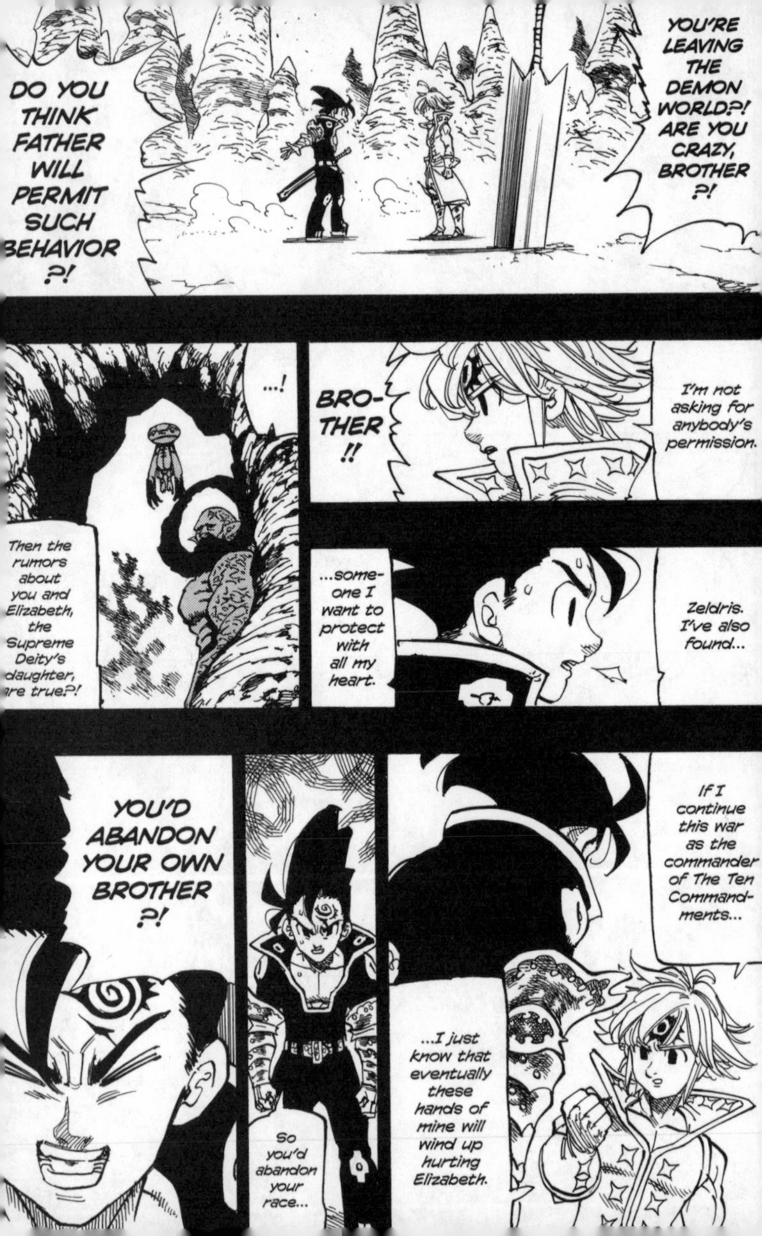
YOU'RE LEAVING THE DEMON WORLD?! ARE YOU CRAZY, BROTHER?!
DO YOU THINK FATHER WILL PERMIT SUCH BEHAVIOR?!
I'm not asking for anybody's permission.
BROTHER!!
Zeldris. I've also found...
...someone I want to protect with all my heart.
...!
Then the rumors about you and Elizabeth, the Supreme Deity's daughter, are true?!
If I continue this war as the commander of The Ten Commandments...
...I just know that eventually these hands of mine will wind up hurting Elizabeth.
So you'd abandon your race...
YOU'D ABANDON YOUR OWN BROTHER?!

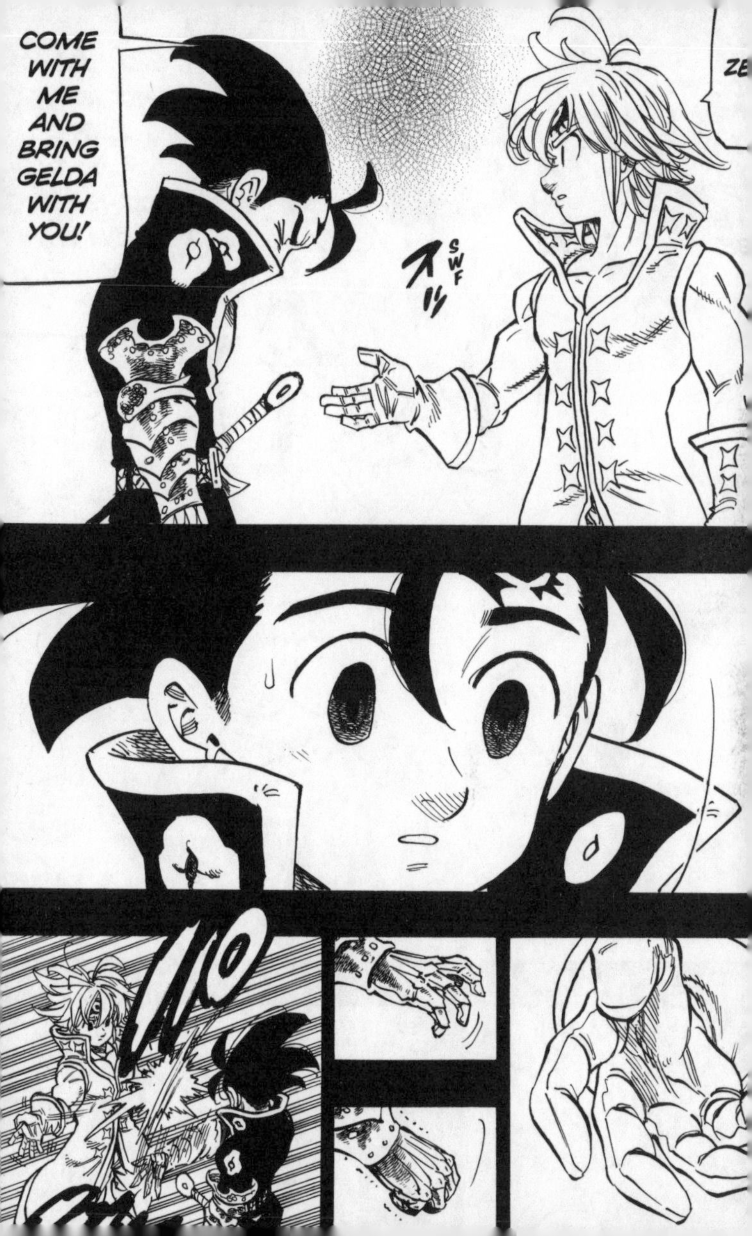
ZE
COME WITH ME AND BRING GELDA WITH YOU!
SWF

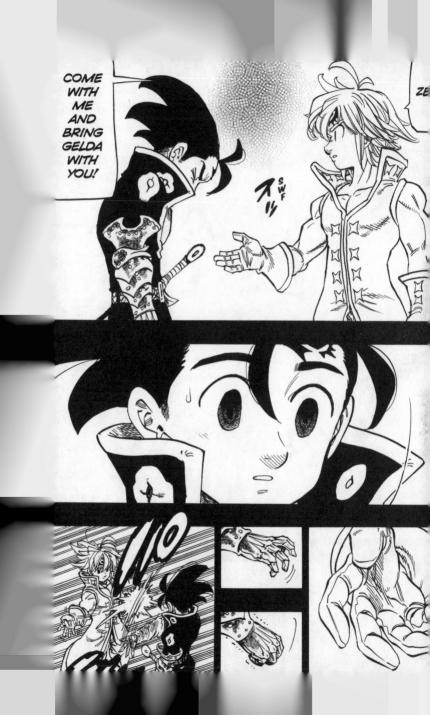

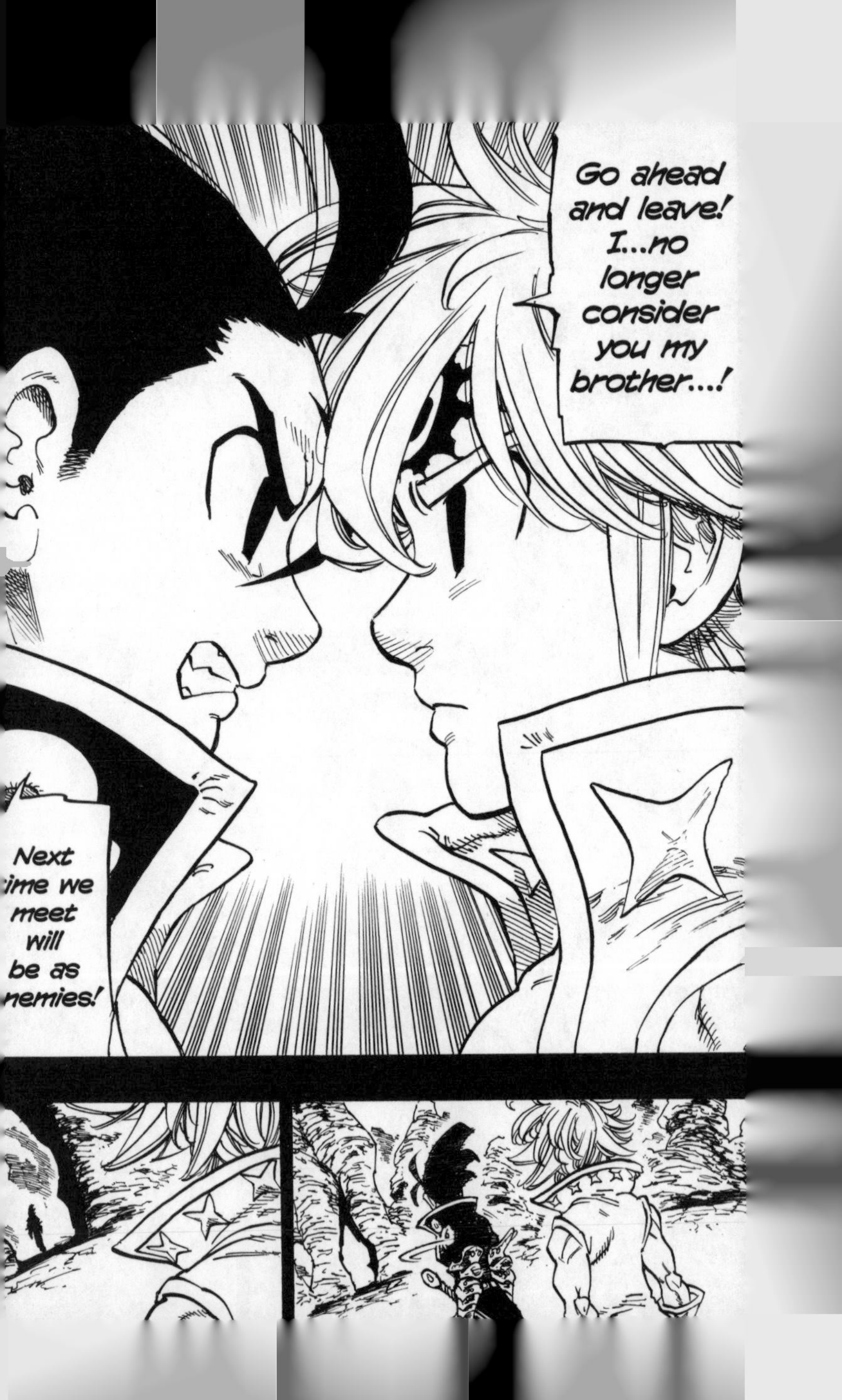
Go ahead and leave! I...no longer consider you my brother...!
Next ime we meet will be as nemies!

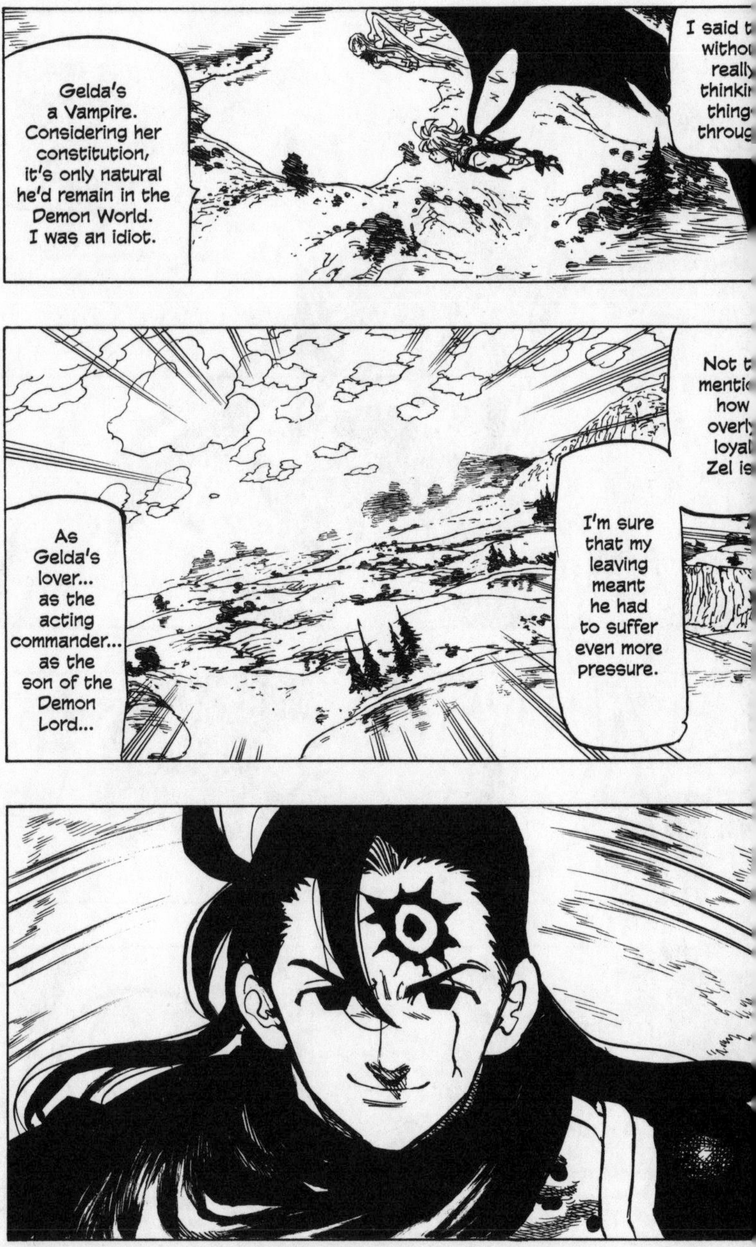
I said t withou really thinki thing throug
Gelda's a Vampire. Considering her constitution, it's only natural he'd remain in the Demon World. I was an idiot.
Not t menti how overl loyal Zel is
I'm sure that my leaving meant he had to suffer even more pressure.
As Gelda's lover... as the acting commander... as the son of the Demon Lord...

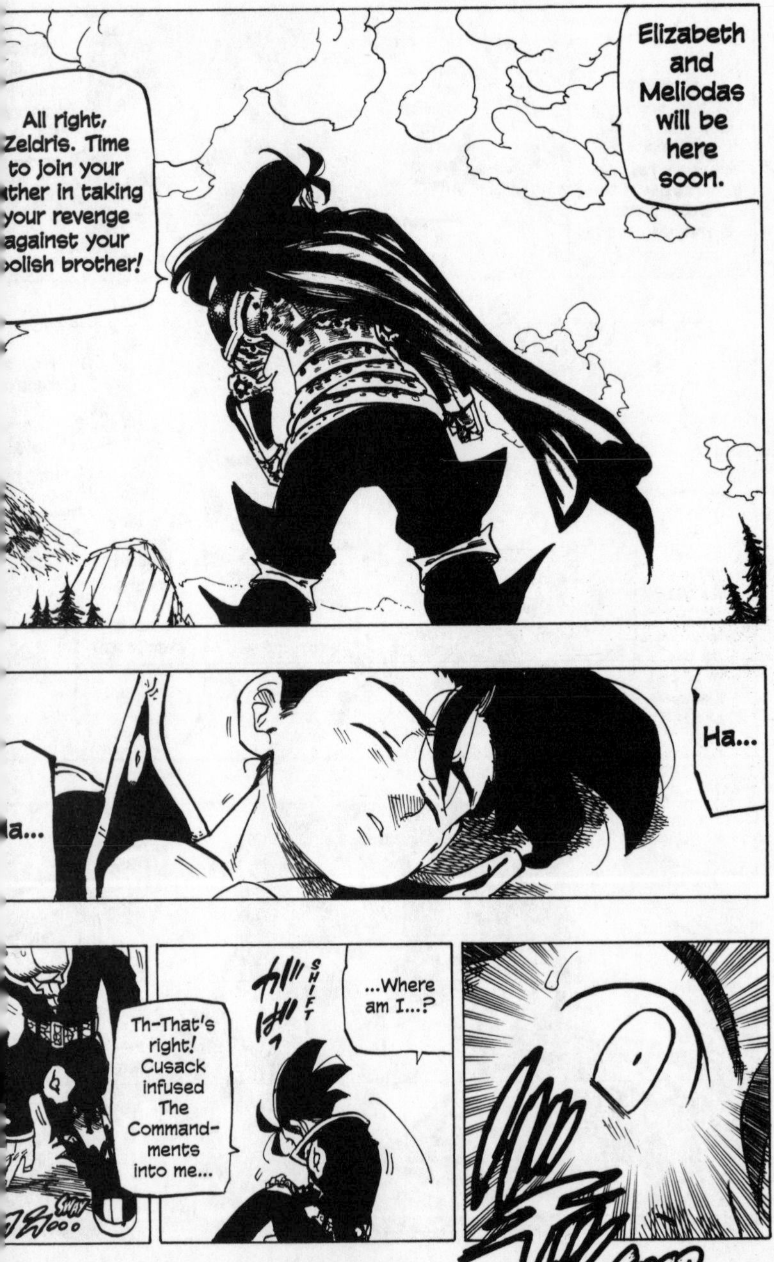
Elizabeth and Meliodas will be here soon.
All right, Zeldris. Time to join your ather in taking your revenge against your oolish brother!
Ha...
a...
SNAP
SHIFT
...Where am I...?
Th-That's right! Cusack infused The Command-ments into me...
SWAY

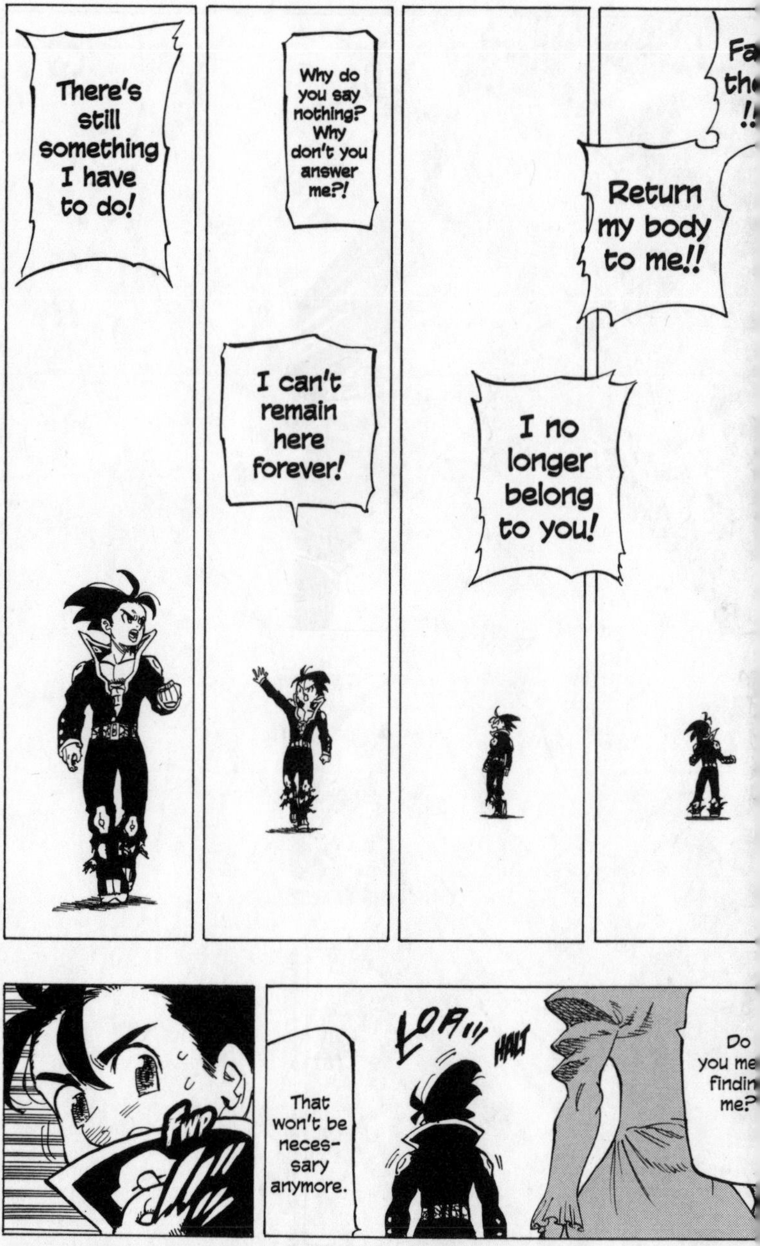

Fa th !!
Return my body to me!!
I no longer belong to you!
Why do you say nothing? Why don't you answer me?!
I can't remain here forever!
There's still something I have to do!
Do you me findin me?
HALT
That won't be neces-sary anymore.
FWP

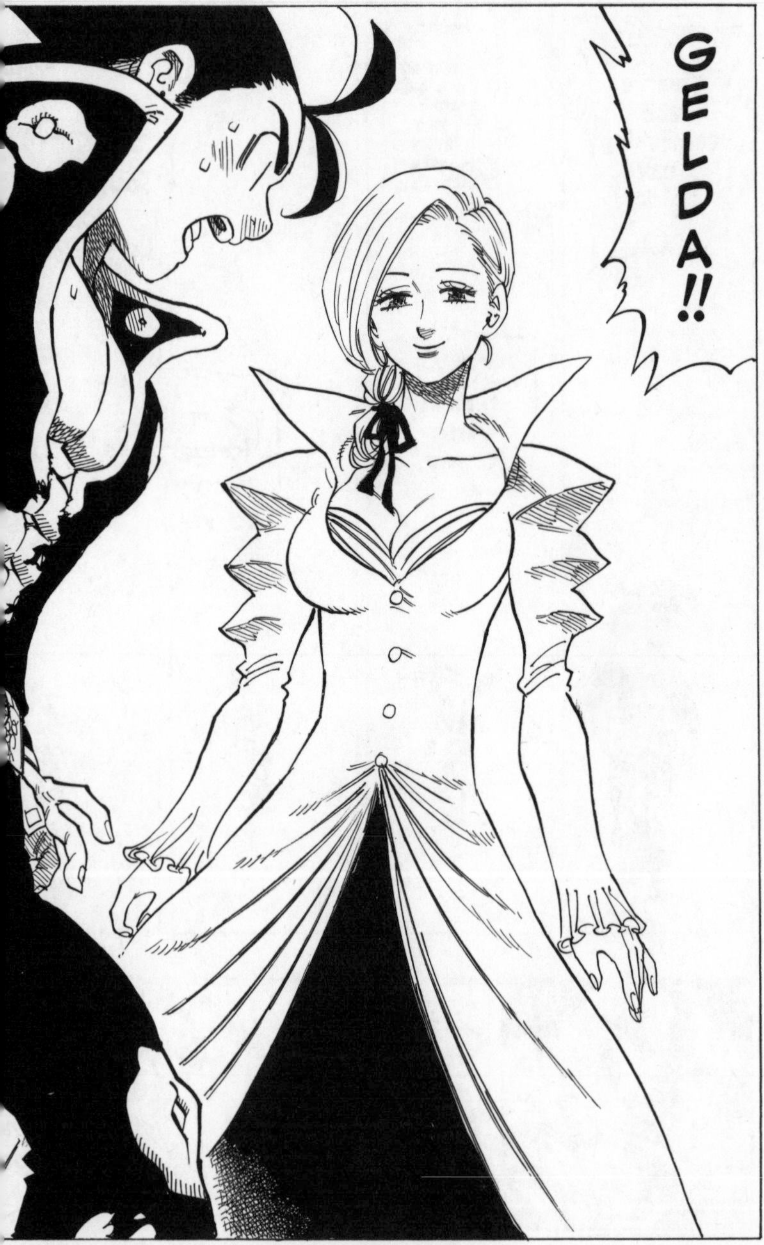
GELDA!!

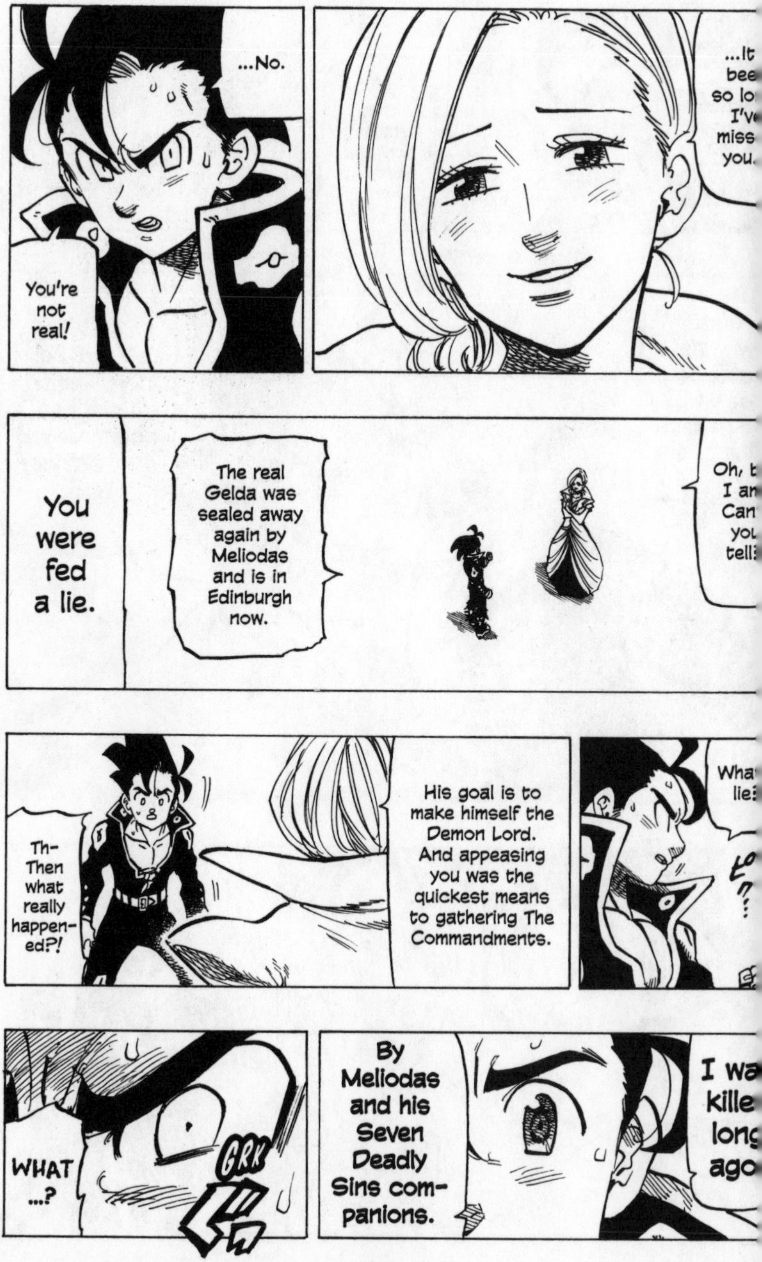

...It bee so lo I'v miss you.
...No.
You're not real!
Oh, t I an Can you telli
The real Gelda was sealed away again by Meliodas and is in Edinburgh now.
You were fed a lie.
Wha lie?
His goal is to make himself the Demon Lord. And appeasing you was the quickest means to gathering The Commandments.
Th- Then what really happen-ed?!
I wa kille long ago
By Meliodas and his Seven Deadly Sins com-panions.
WHAT ...?
GRK

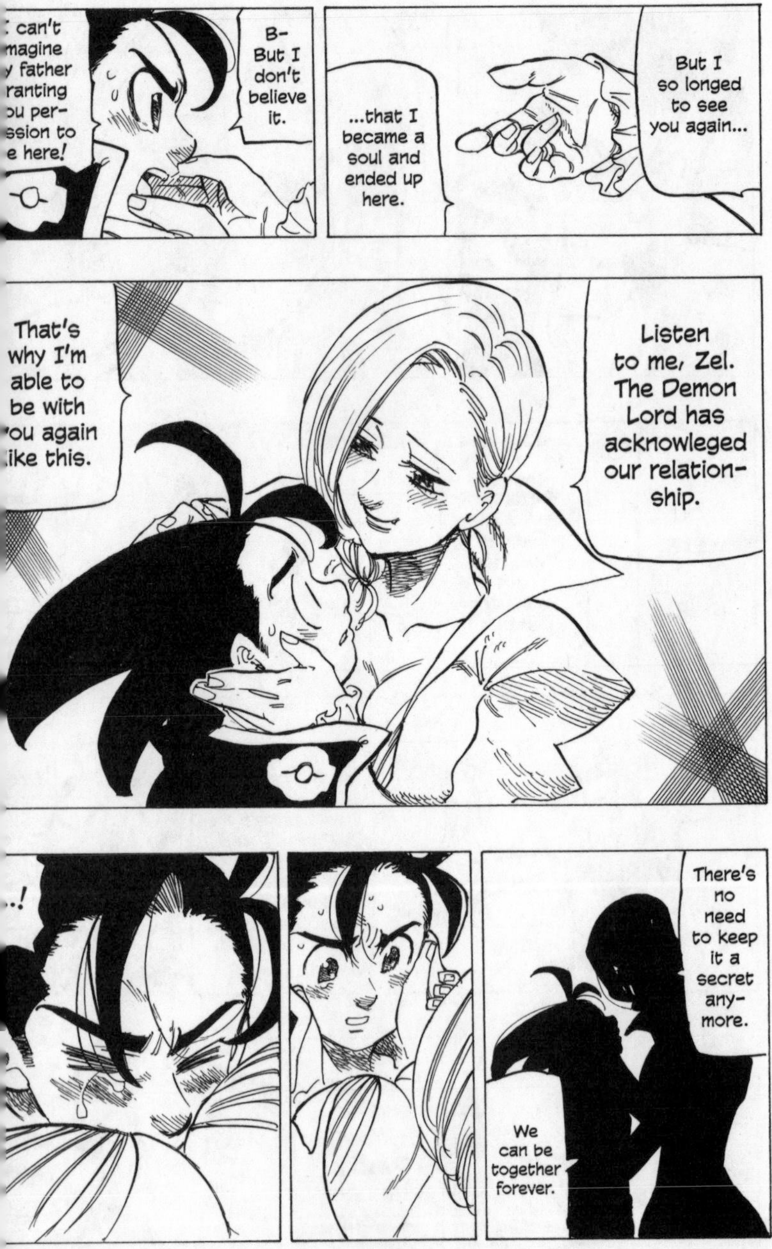
But I so longed to see you again...
...that I became a soul and ended up here.
B- But I don't believe it.
can't magine y father ranting ou per- ssion to e here!
Listen to me, Zel. The Demon Lord has acknowleged our relationship.
That's why I'm able to be with ou again ike this.
There's no need to keep it a secret anymore.
We can be together forever.
..!

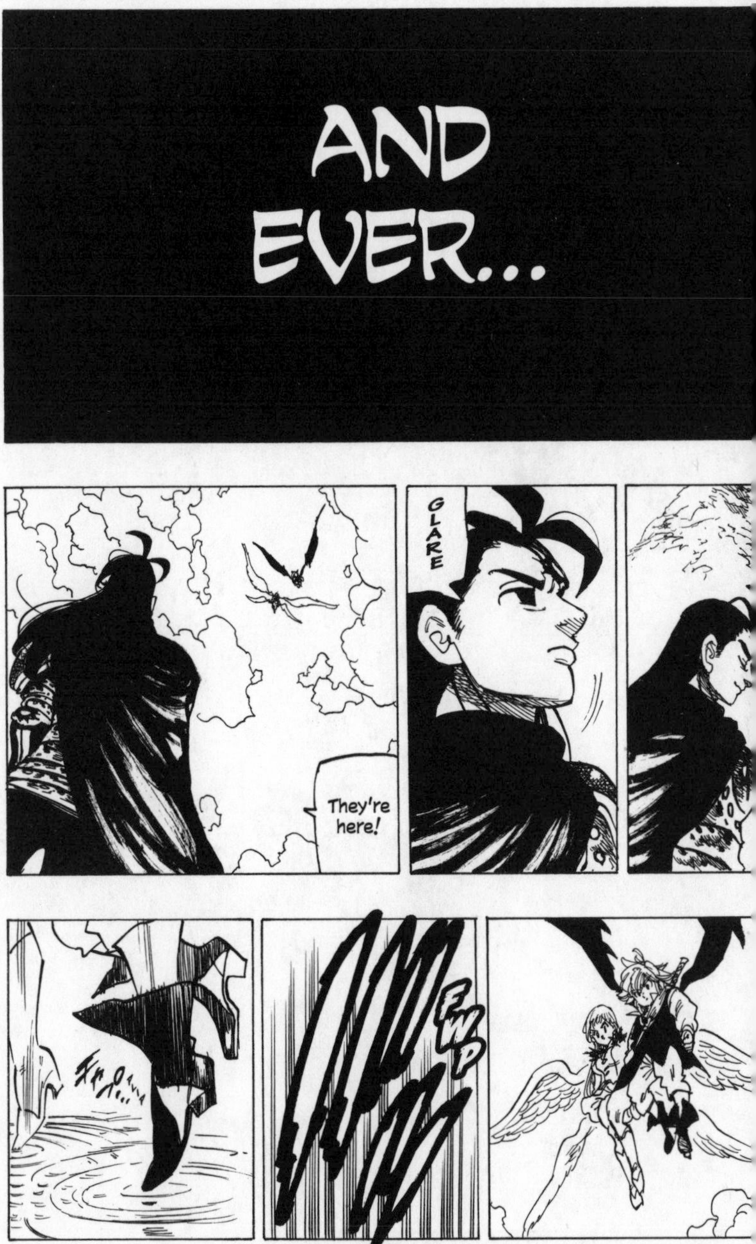
AND EVER...
GLARE
They're here!
FWP

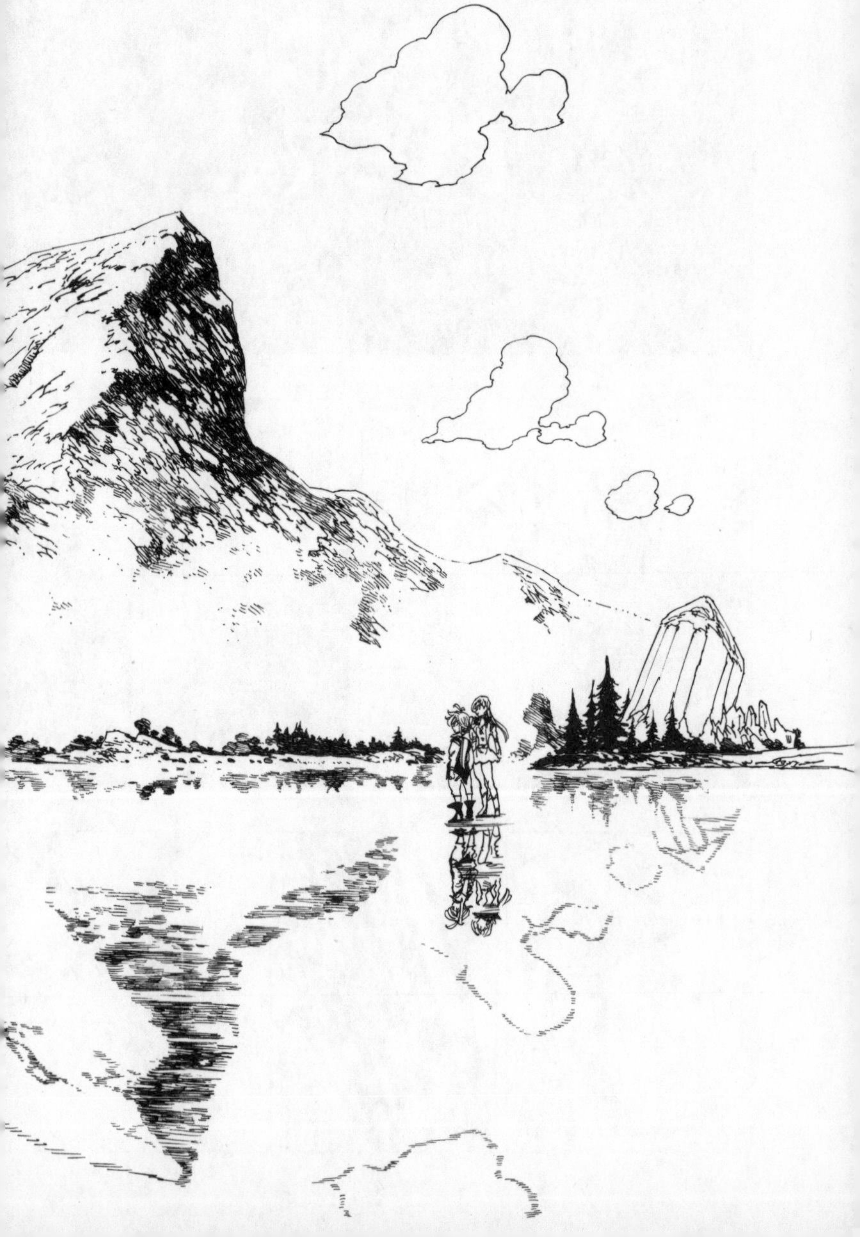

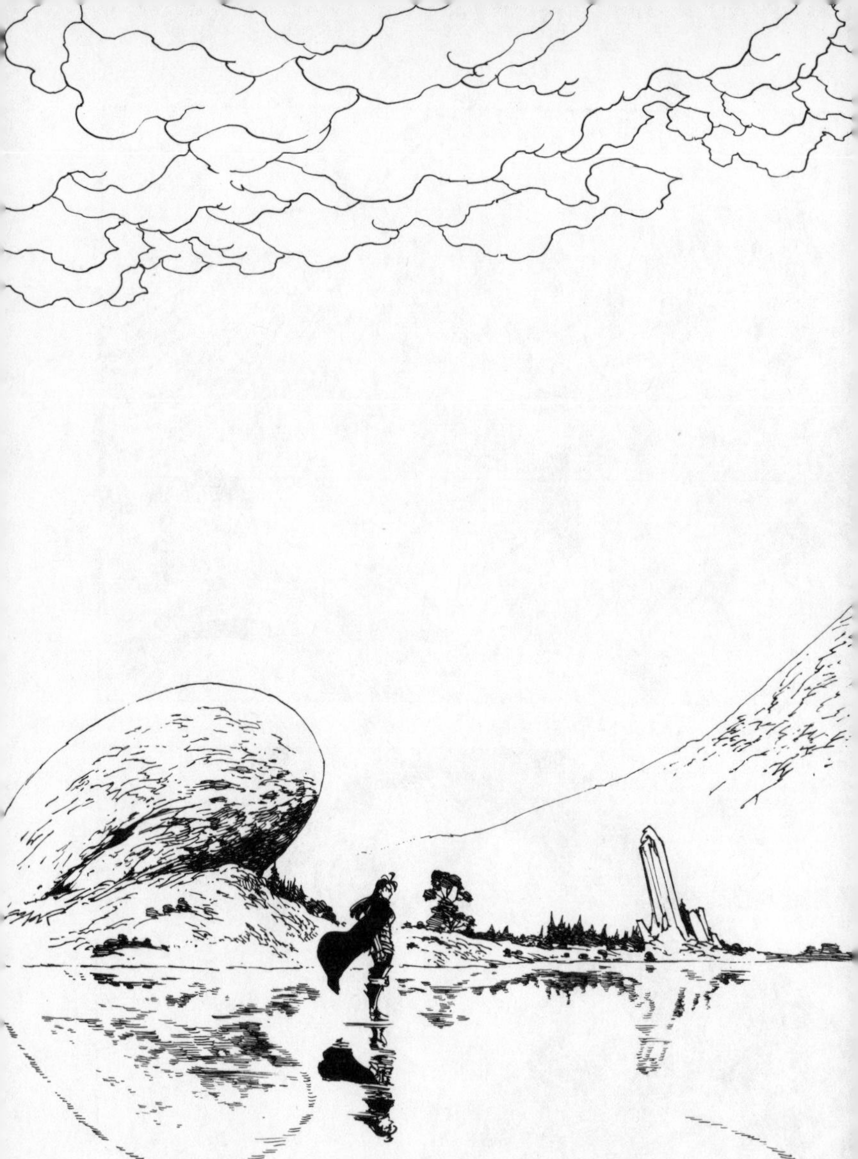

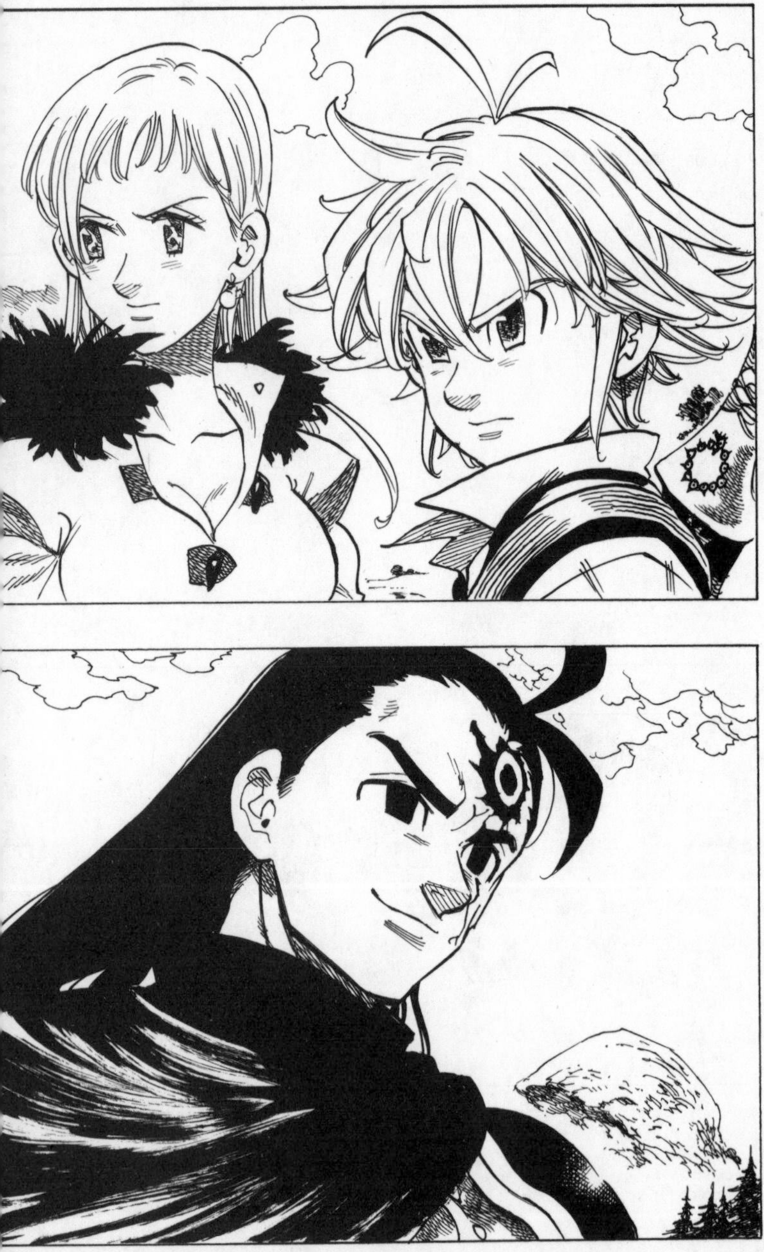

Chapter 314 - Their Demon L

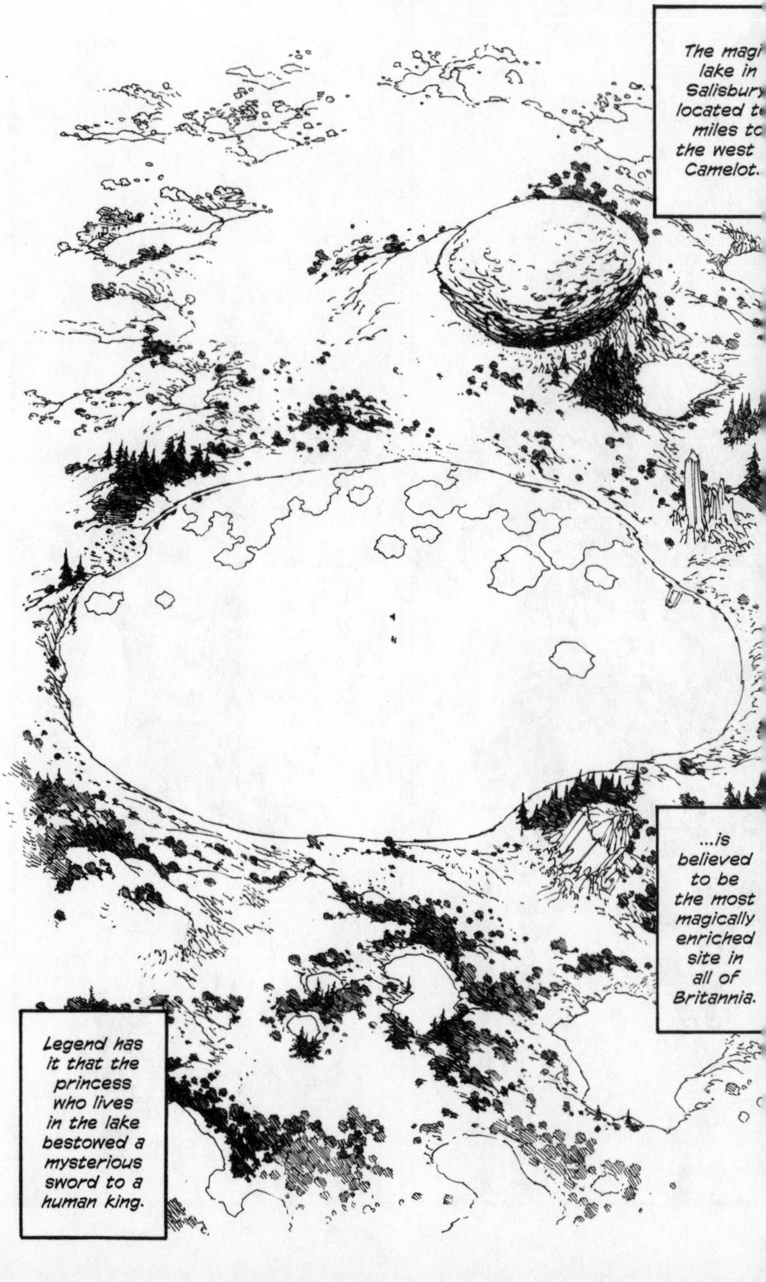
The magi
lake in
Salisbur
located t
miles to
the west
Camelot.
...is believed to be the most magically enriched site in all of Britannia.
Legend has it that the princess who lives in the lake bestowed a mysterious sword to a human king.

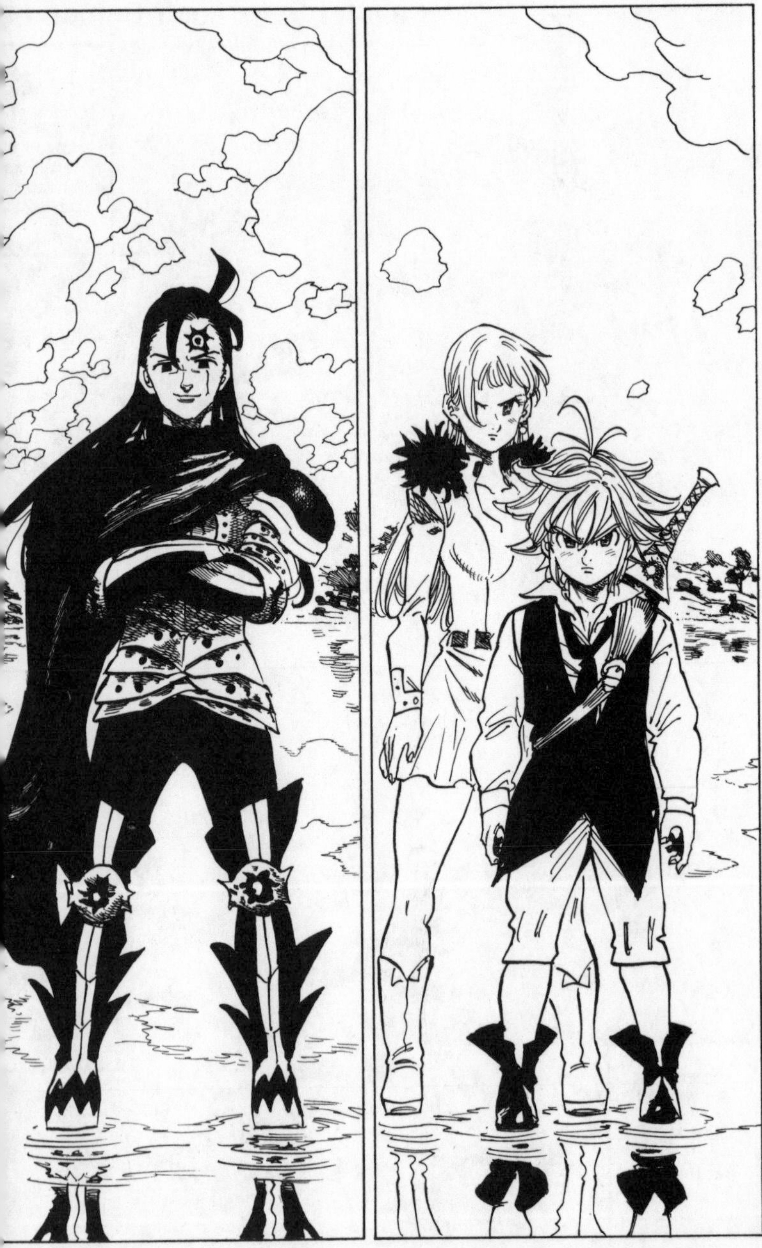

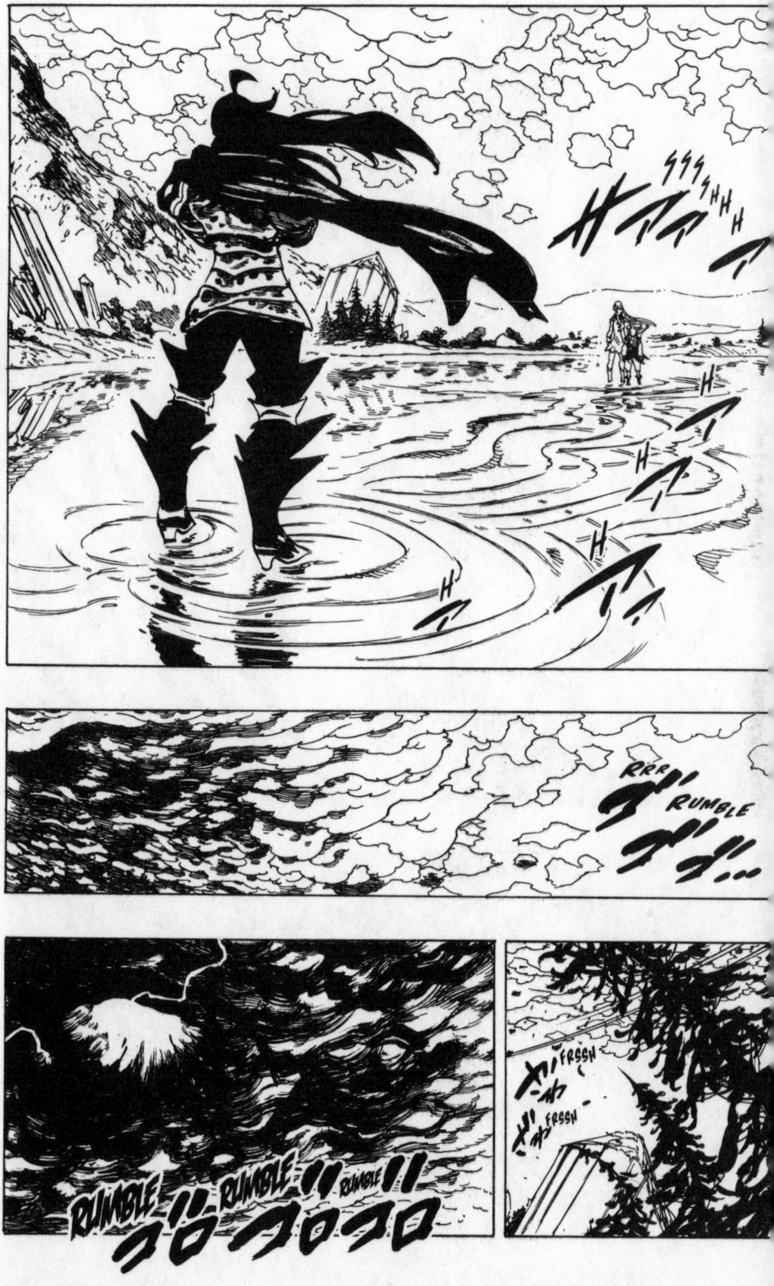
SSSSHHH
H
H
H
H
RRR
RUMBLE
FRSSH
FRSSH
RUMBLE!!
RUMBLE!!
RUMBLE!!

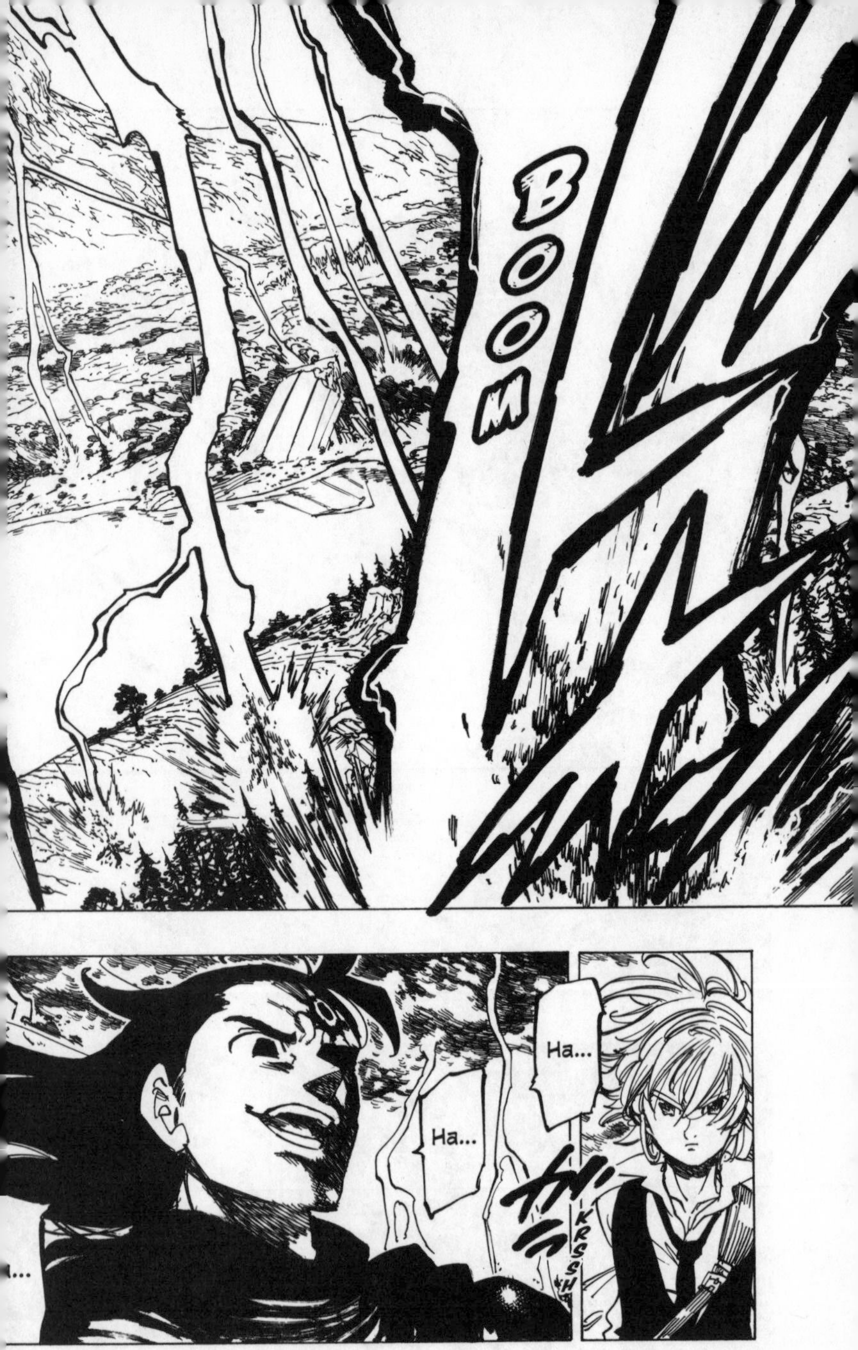
BOOOM
Ha...
KRSSH
Ha...

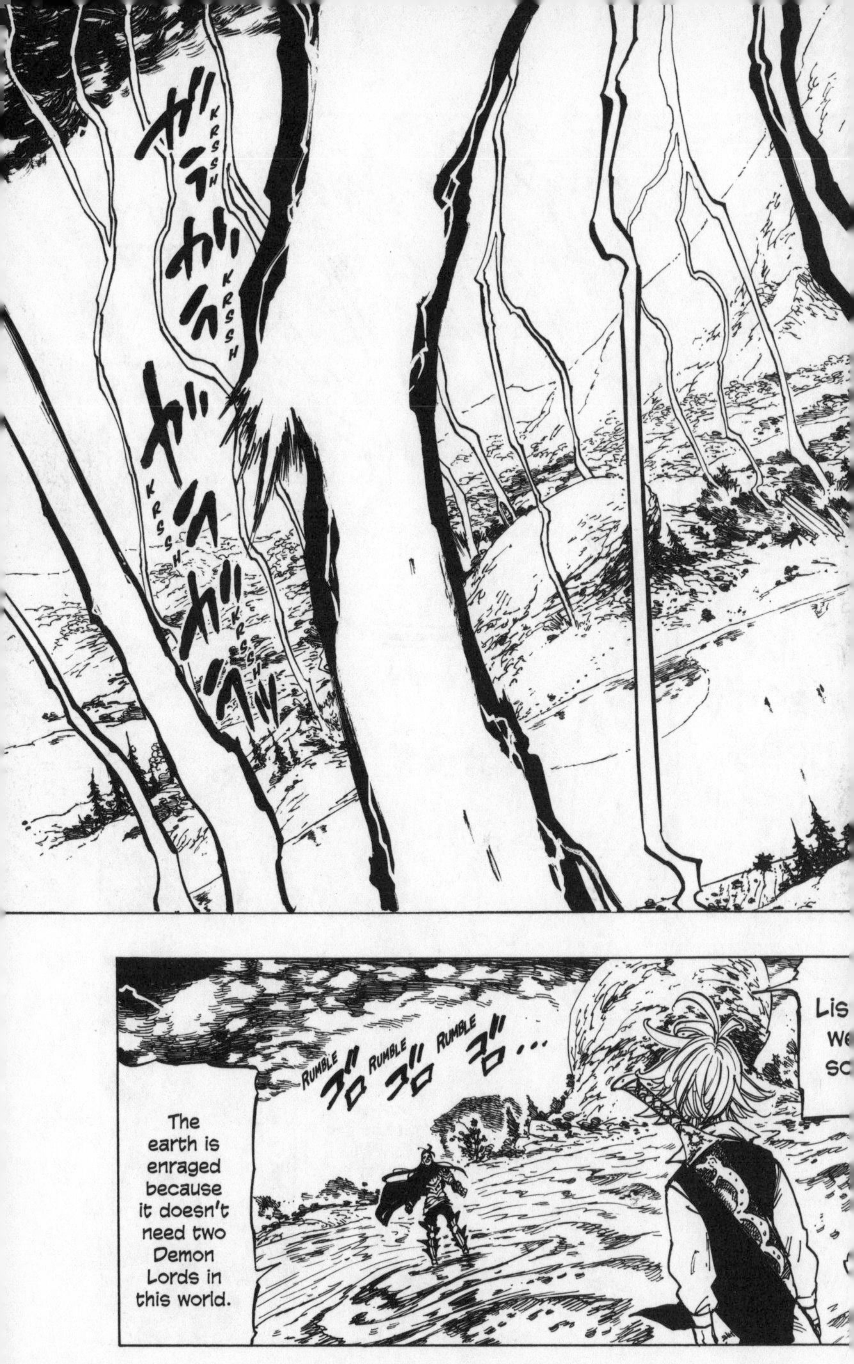
KRSSH
KRSSH
KRSSH
KRSSH
RUMBLE
RUMBLE
RUMBLE
The earth is enraged because it doesn't need two Demon Lords in this world.

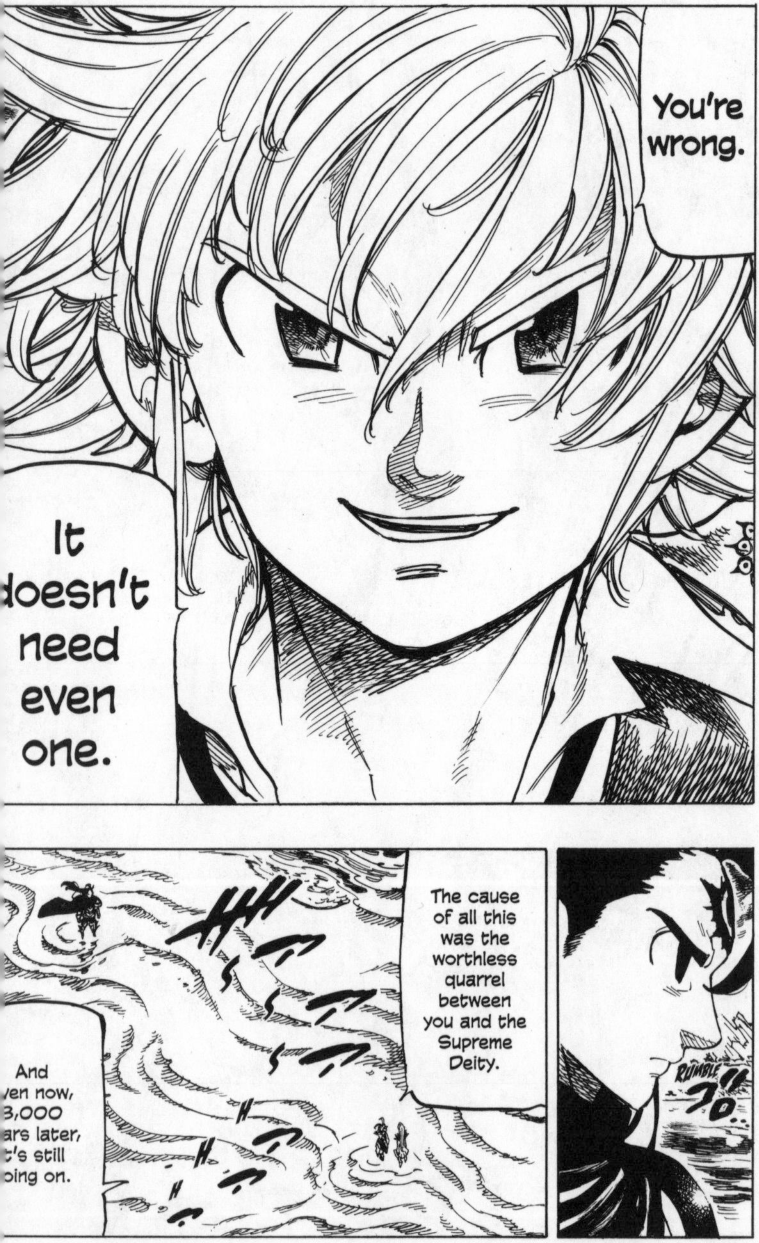
You're wrong.
It doesn't need even one.
RUMBLE
The cause of all this was the worthless quarrel between you and the Supreme Deity.
And ven now, 3,000 ars later, t's still oing on.

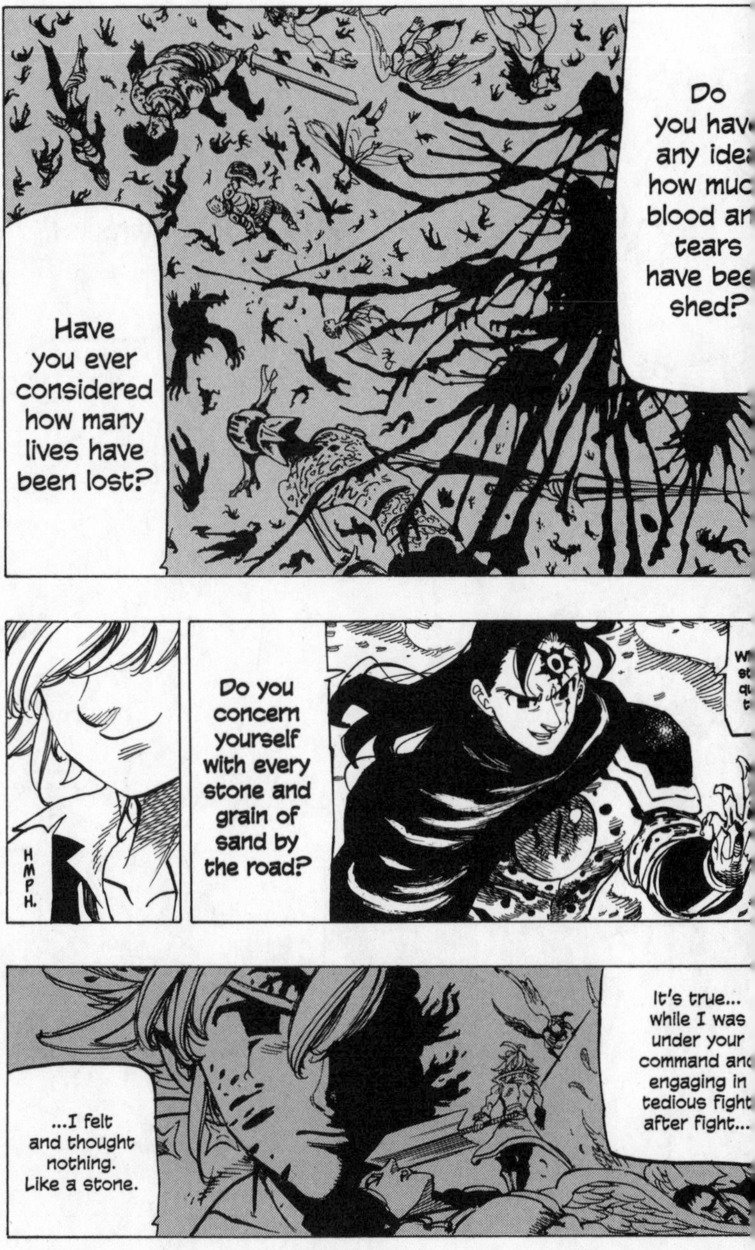
Do you hav any ide how muc blood an tears have bee shed?
Have you ever considered how many lives have been lost?
Do you concern yourself with every stone and grain of sand by the road?
HMPH.
It's true... while I was under your command an engaging in tedious fight after fight...
...I felt and thought nothing. Like a stone.

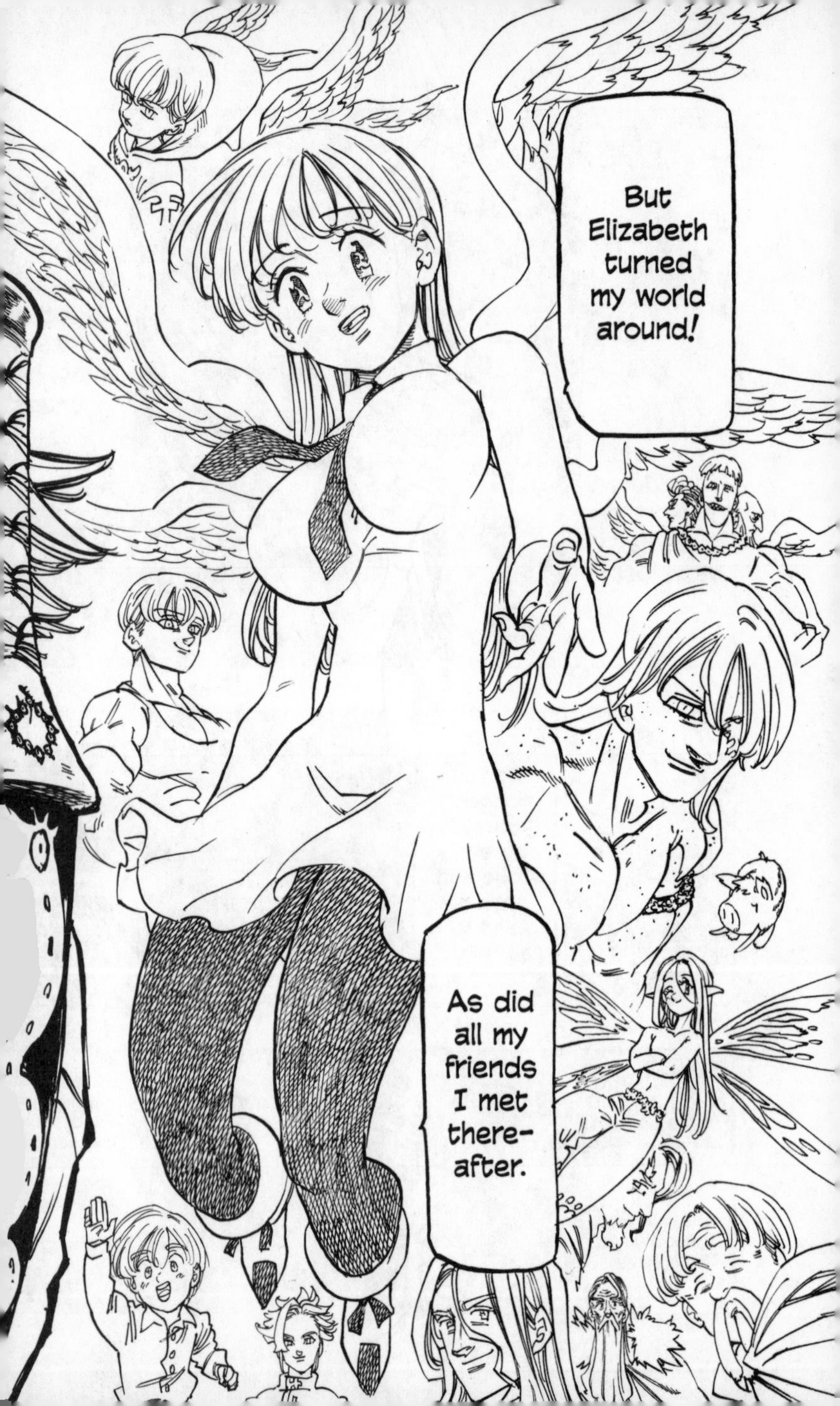
But Elizabeth turned my world around!
As did all my friends I met there-after.

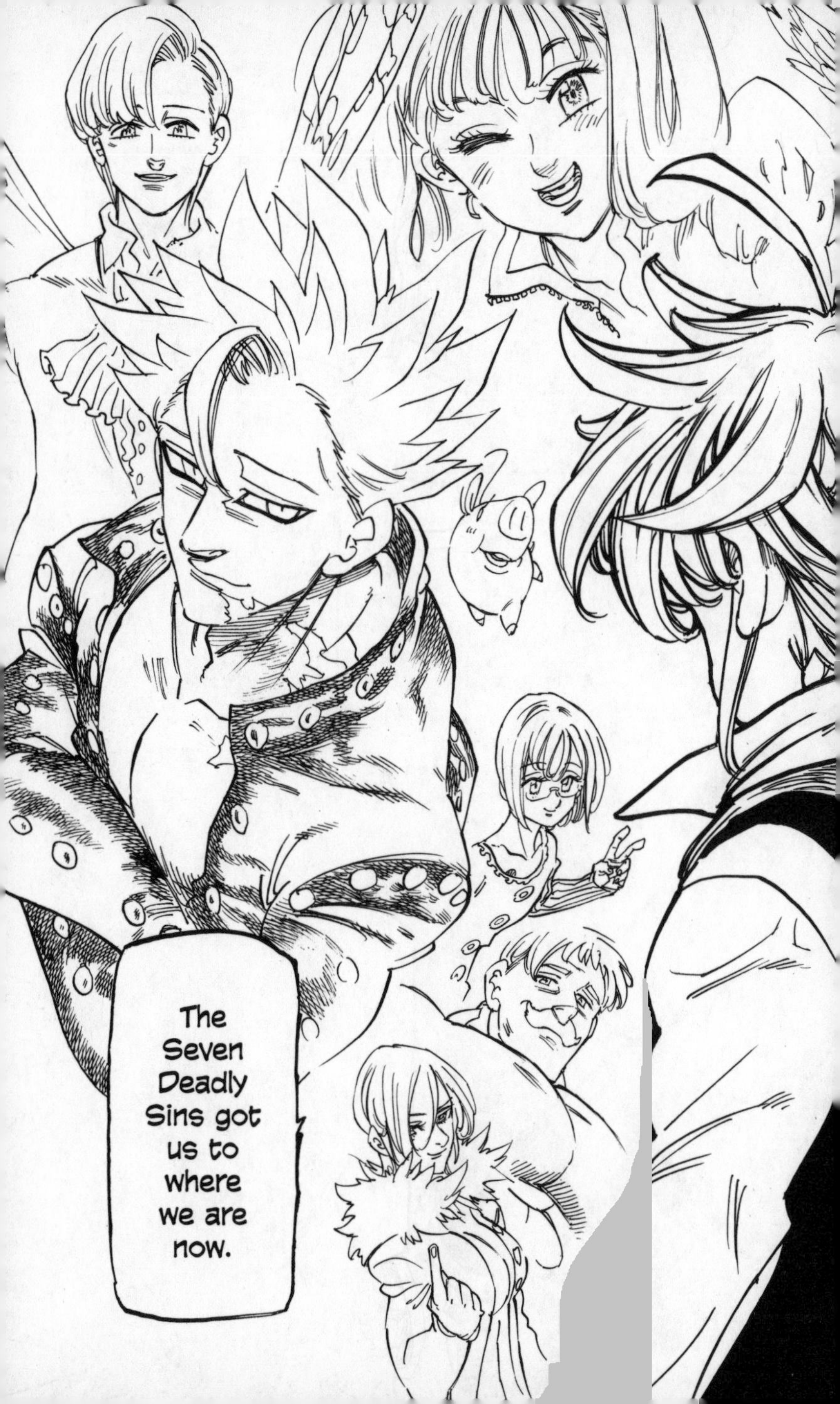
The Seven Deadly Sins got us to where we are now.

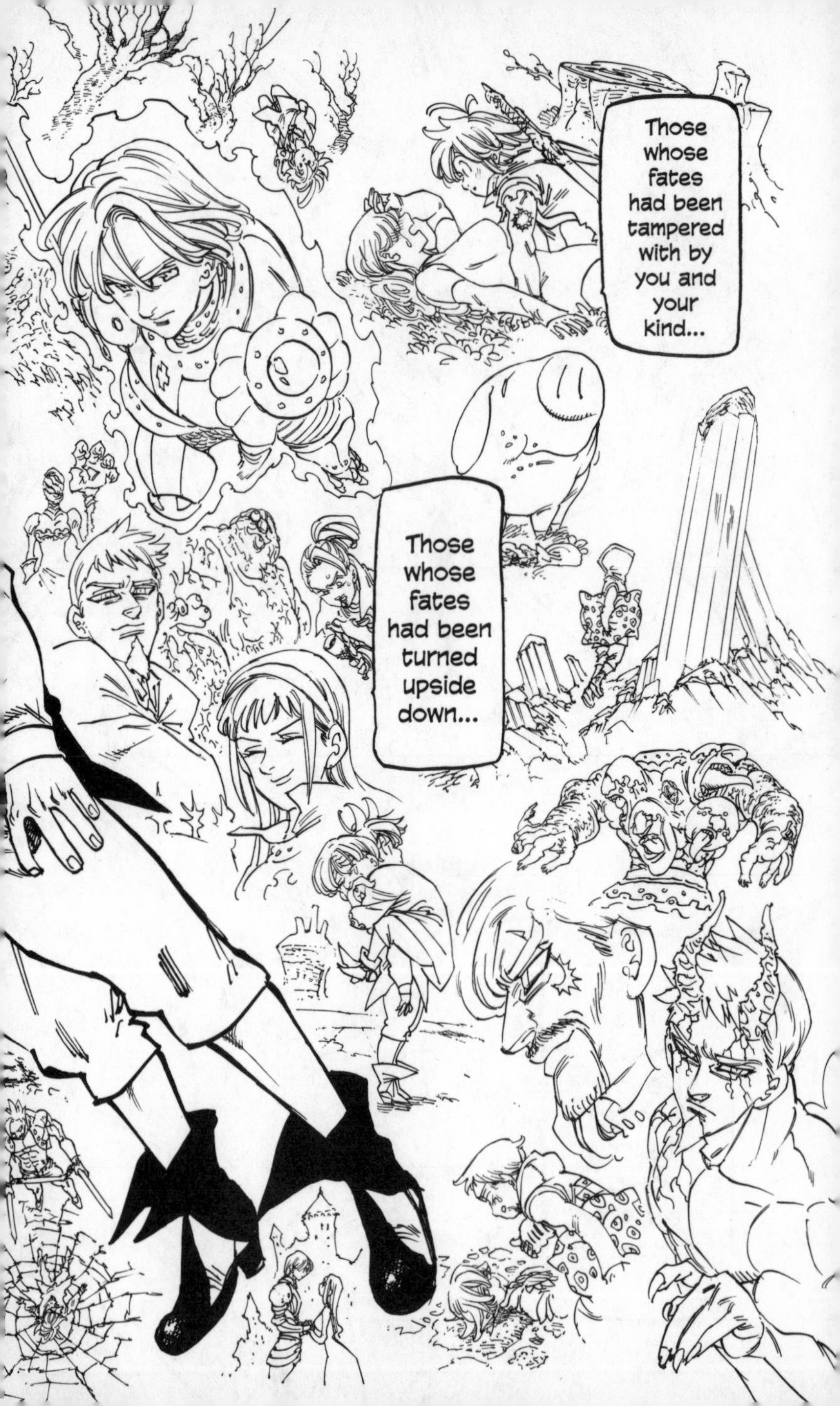
Those whose fates had been tampered with by you and your kind...
Those whose fates had been turned upside down...

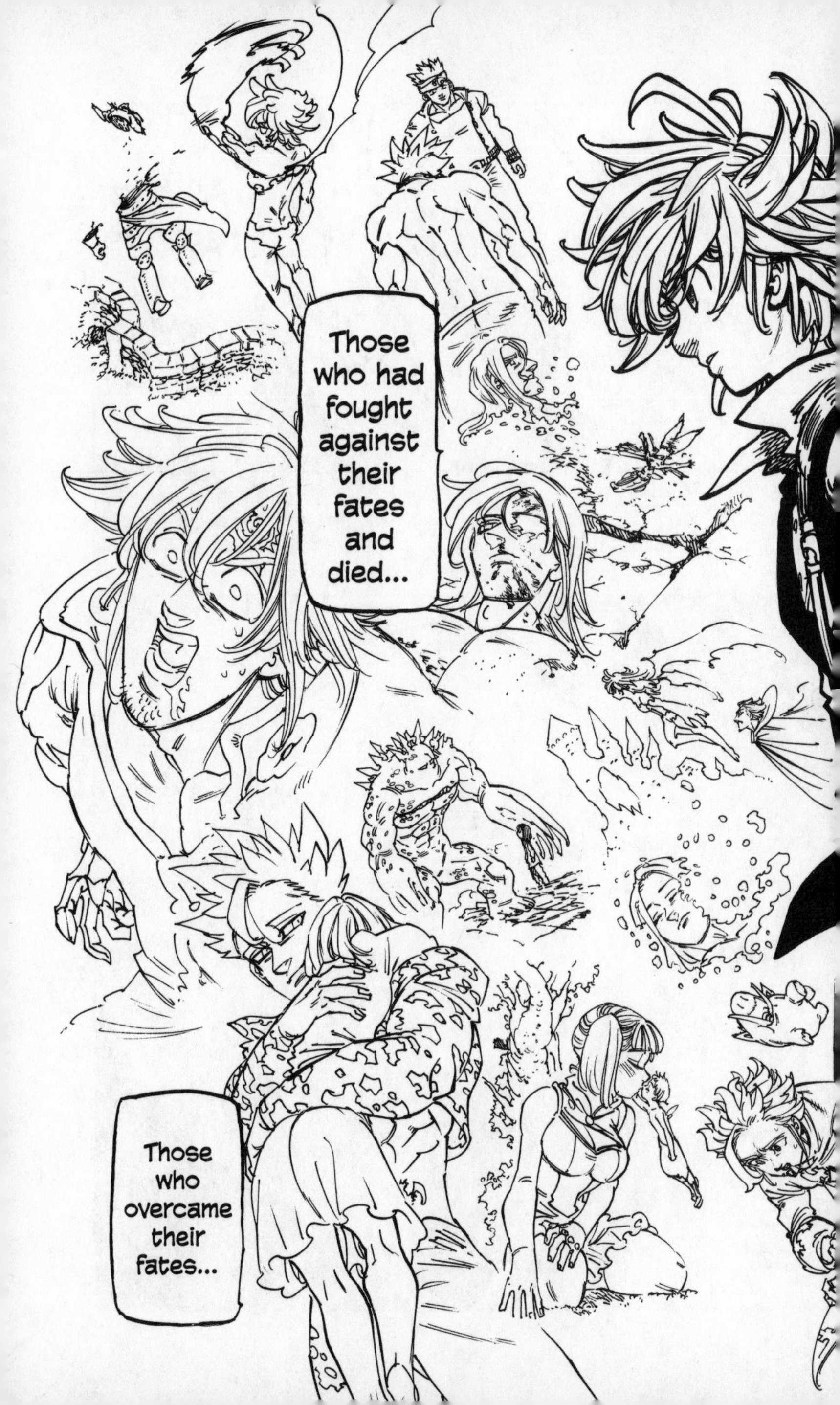
Those who had fought against their fates and died...
Those who overcame their fates...

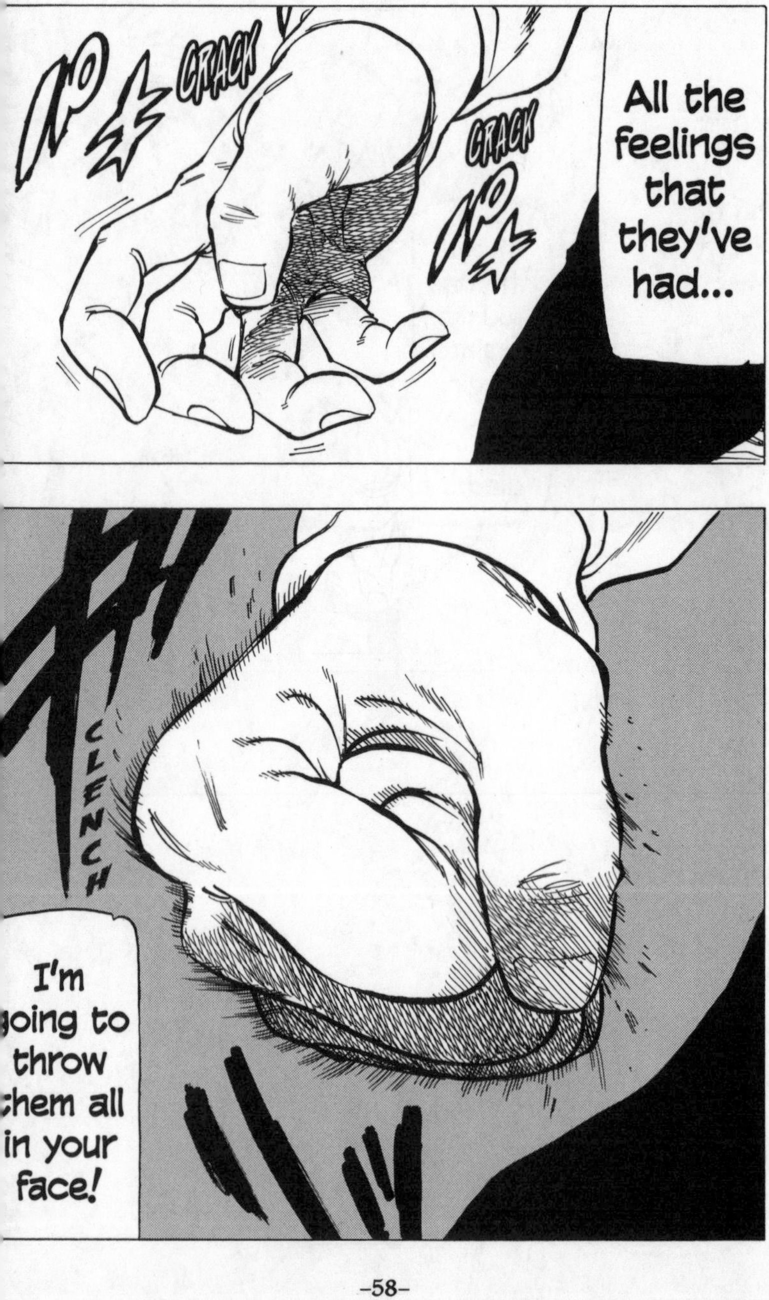
All the feelings that they've had...
CRACK
CRACK
CLENCH
I'm going to throw them all in your face!

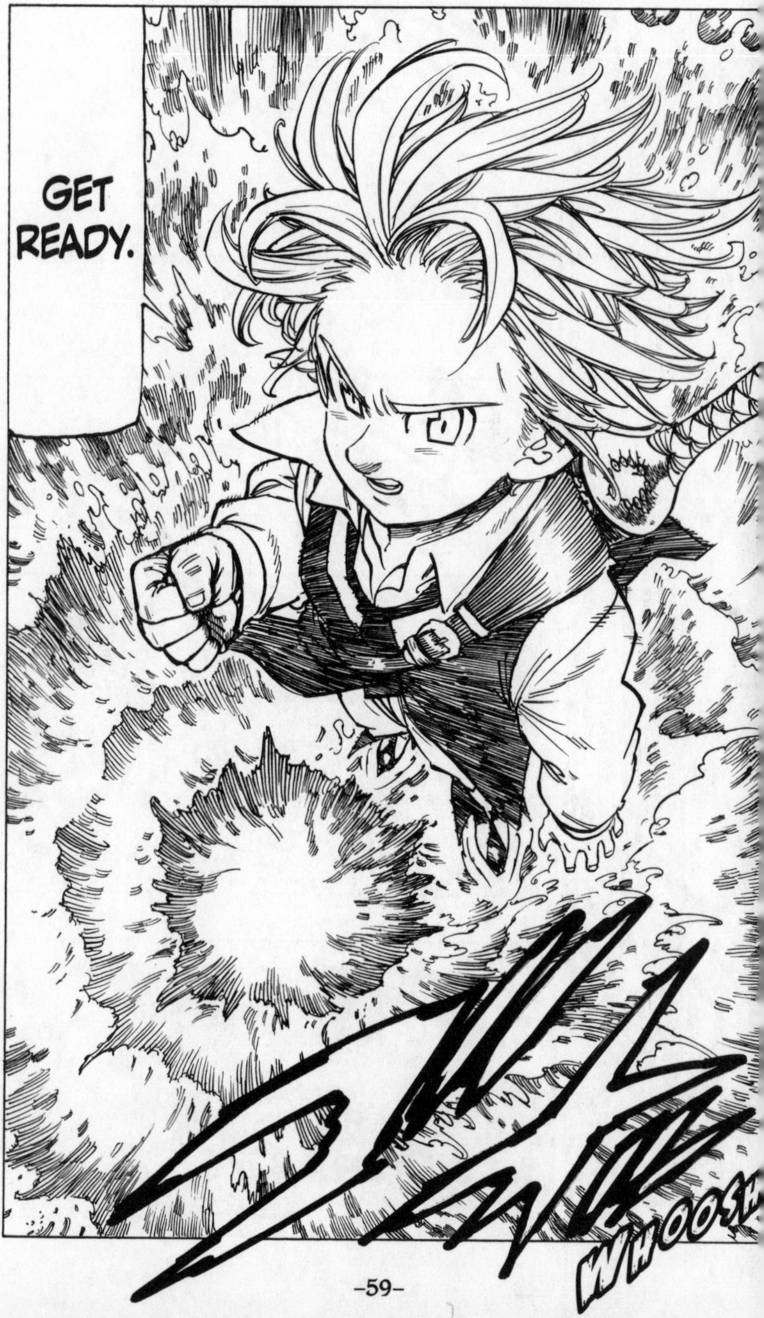
GET READY.
WHOOSH

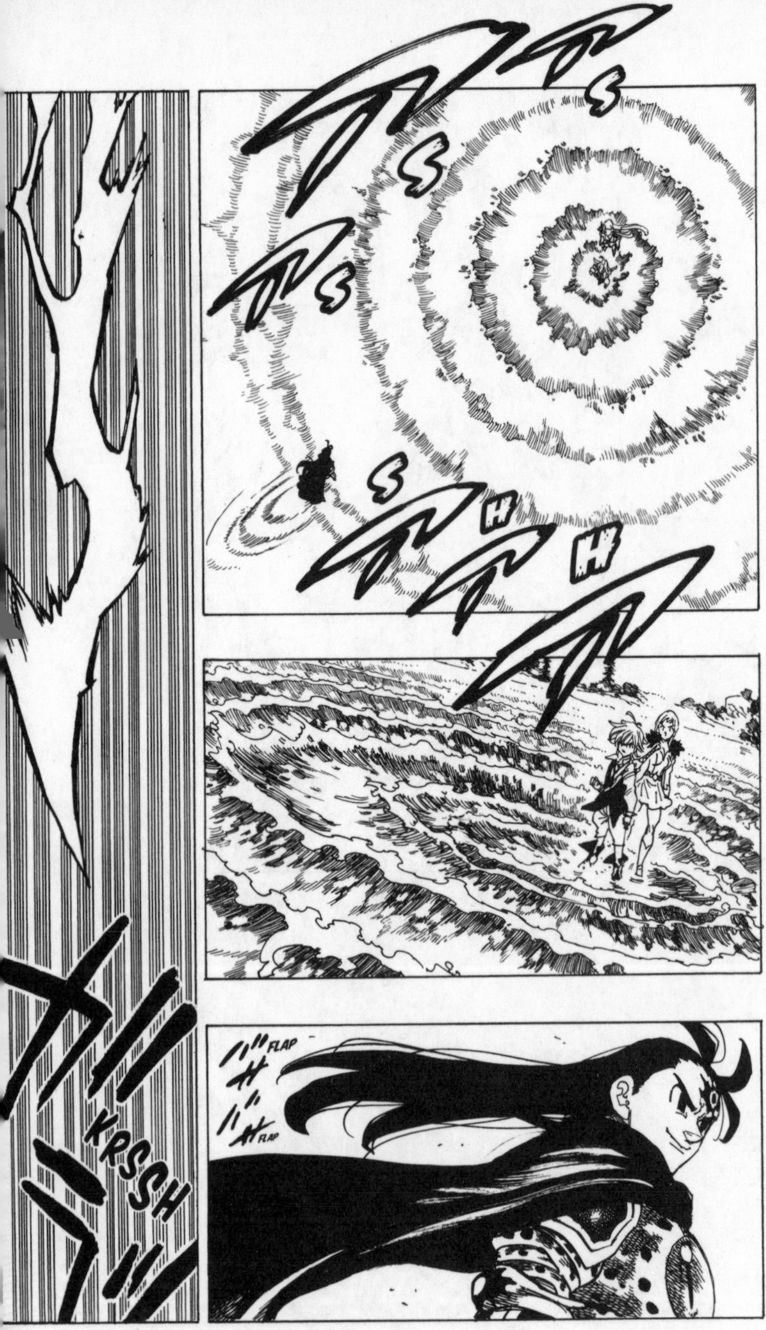
SSSSHH
FLAP
FLAP
KRSSH

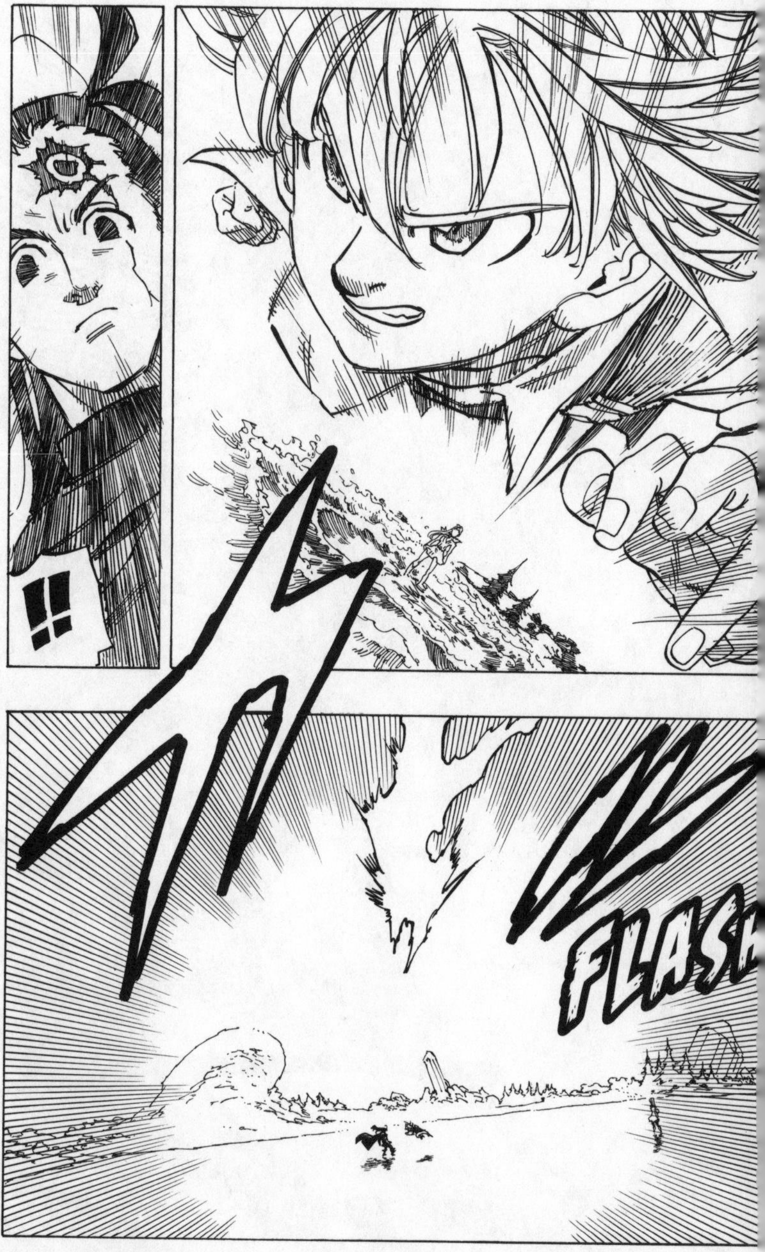
!!
FLASH

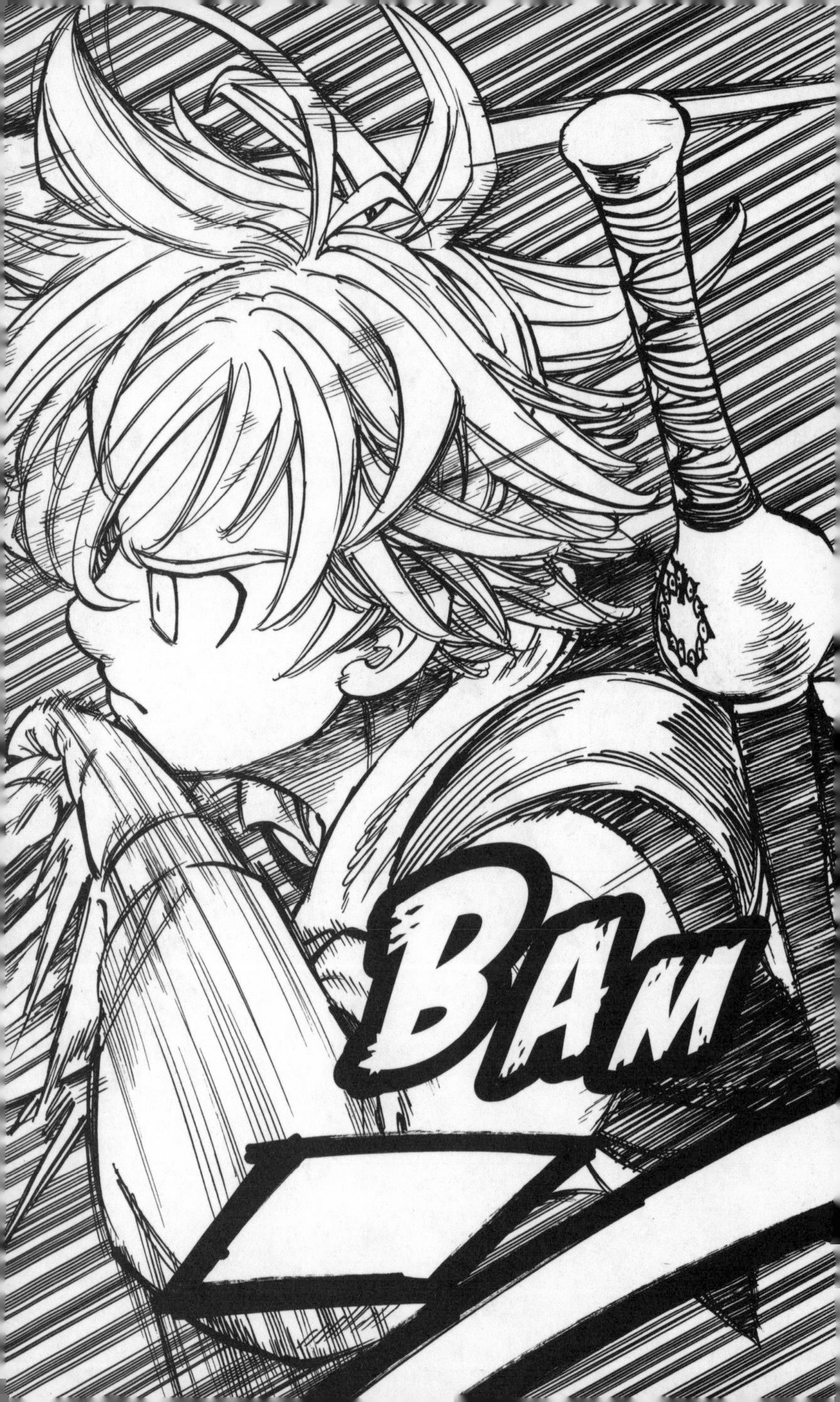
BAM

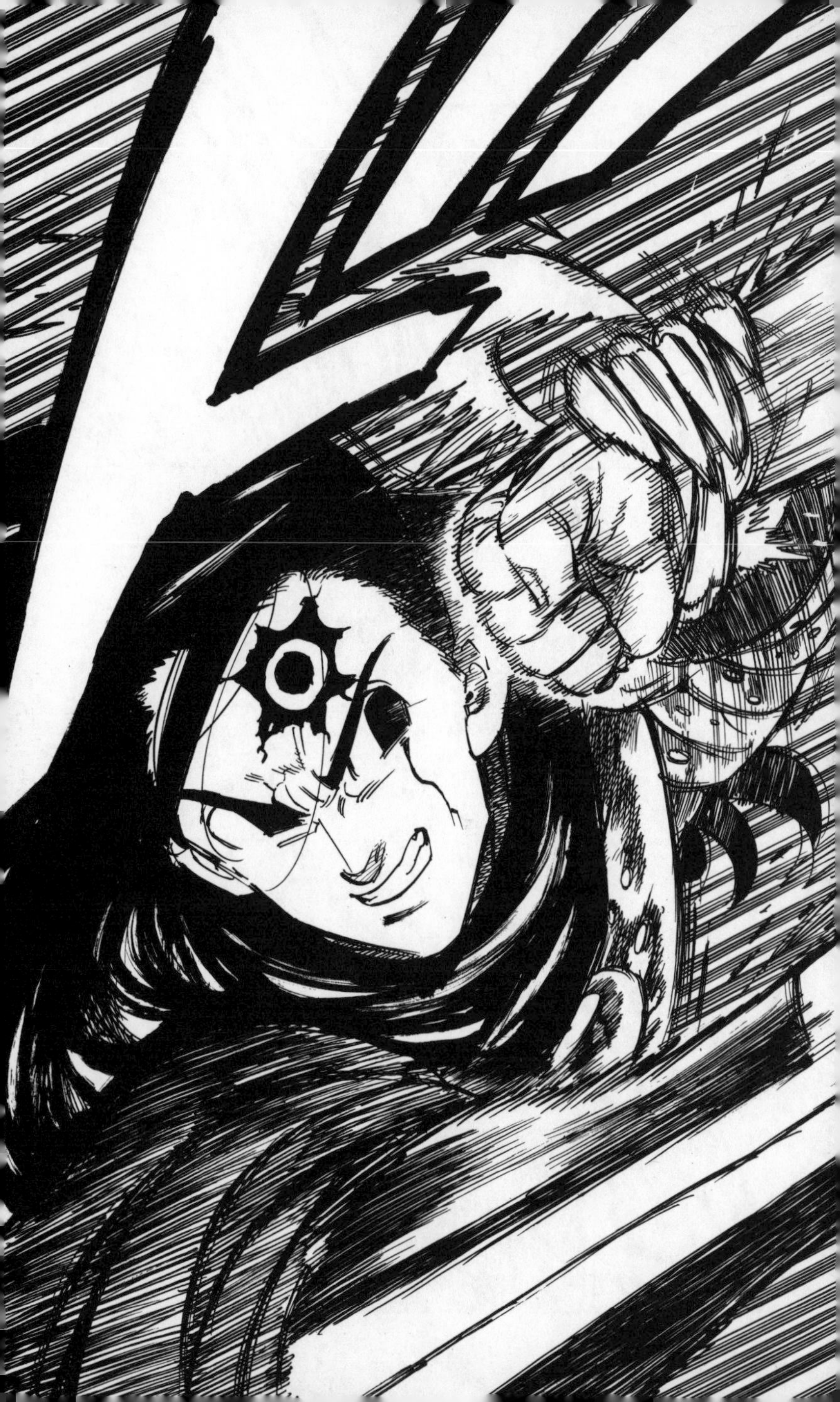

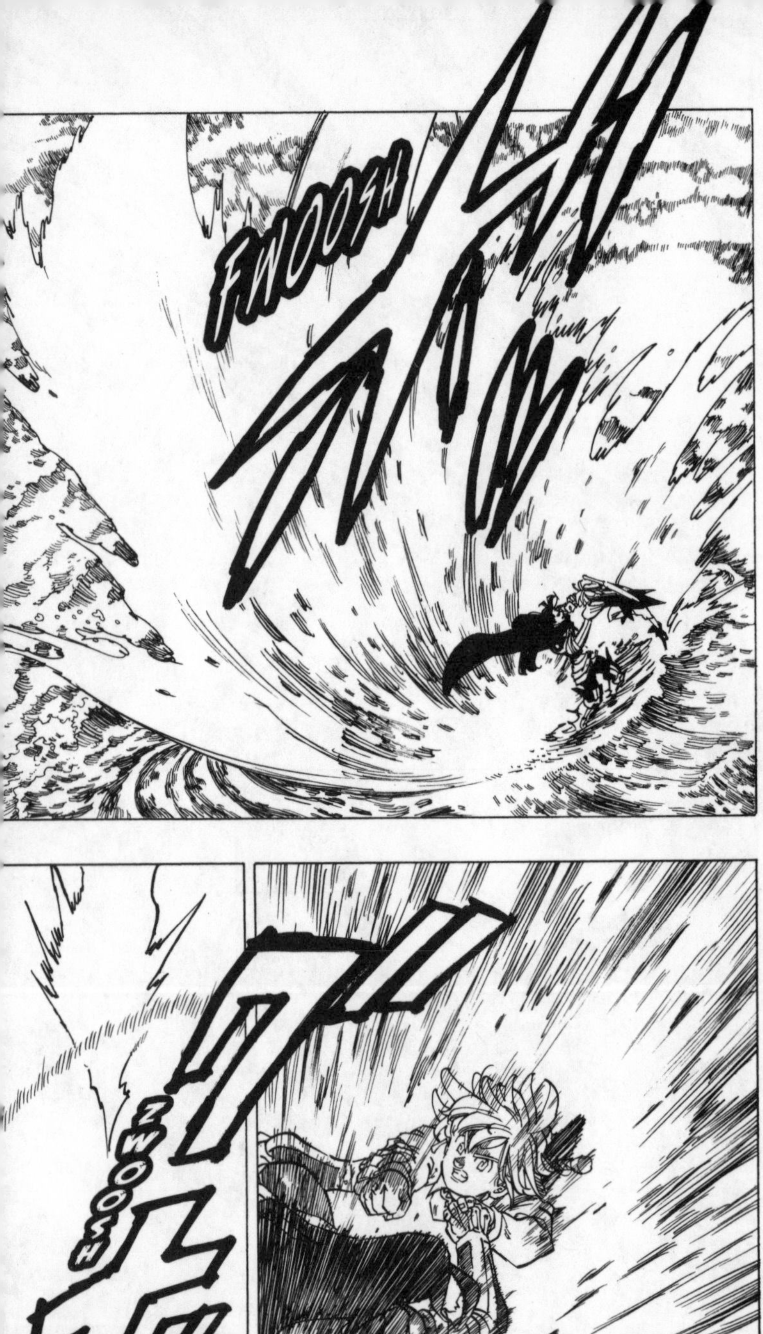
FWOOSH
ZWOOSH

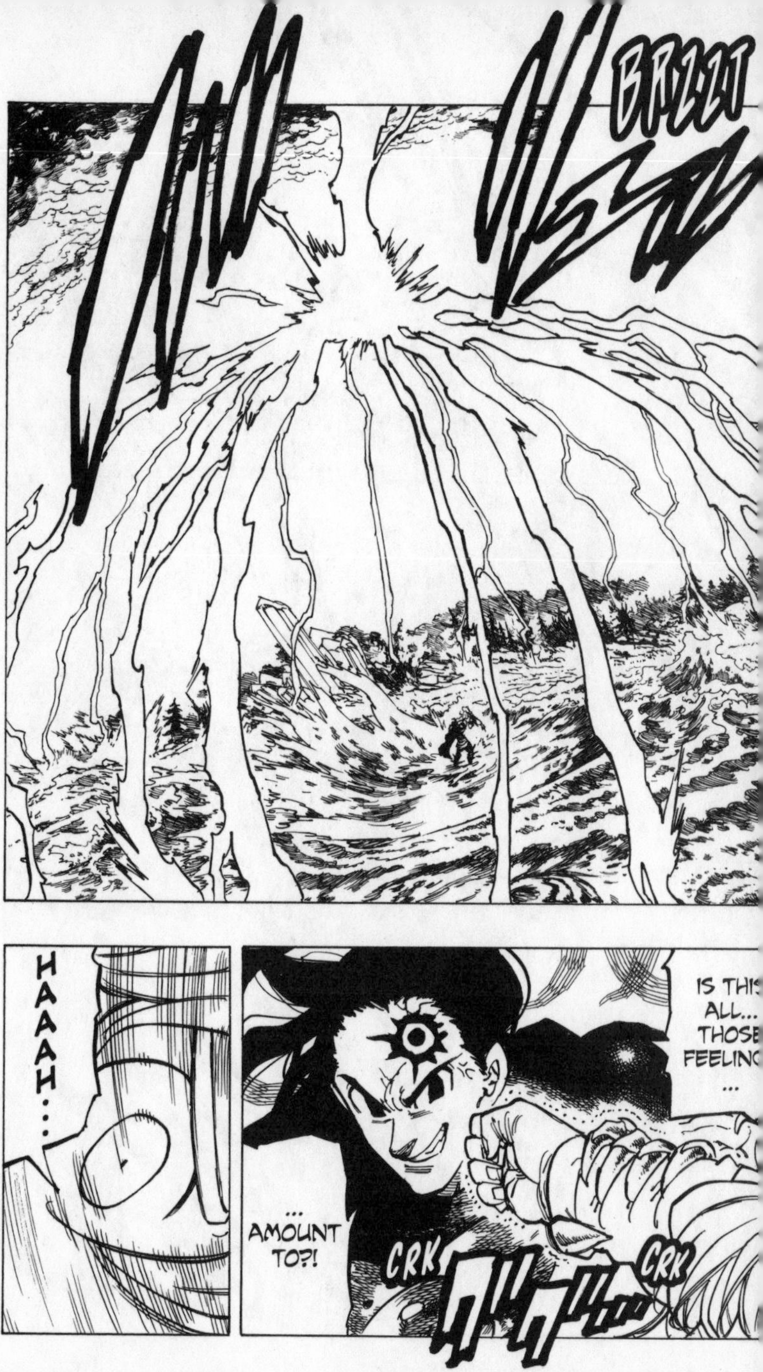
BRZZT
IS THI
ALL...
THOSE
FEELIN
...
...
AMOUNT
TO?!
CRK
CRK
HAAAH...

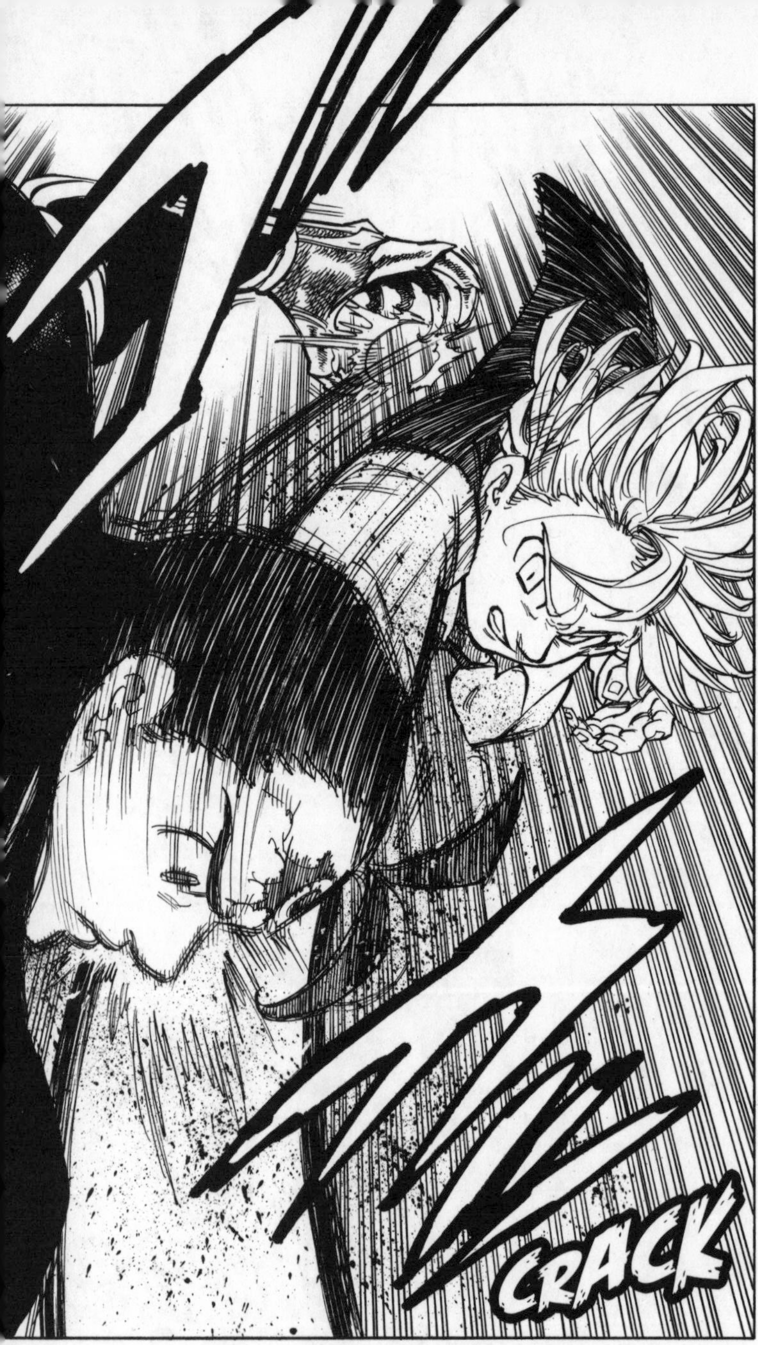
CRACK

The Seven Deadly Sins

Chapter 315 - The Final Battle

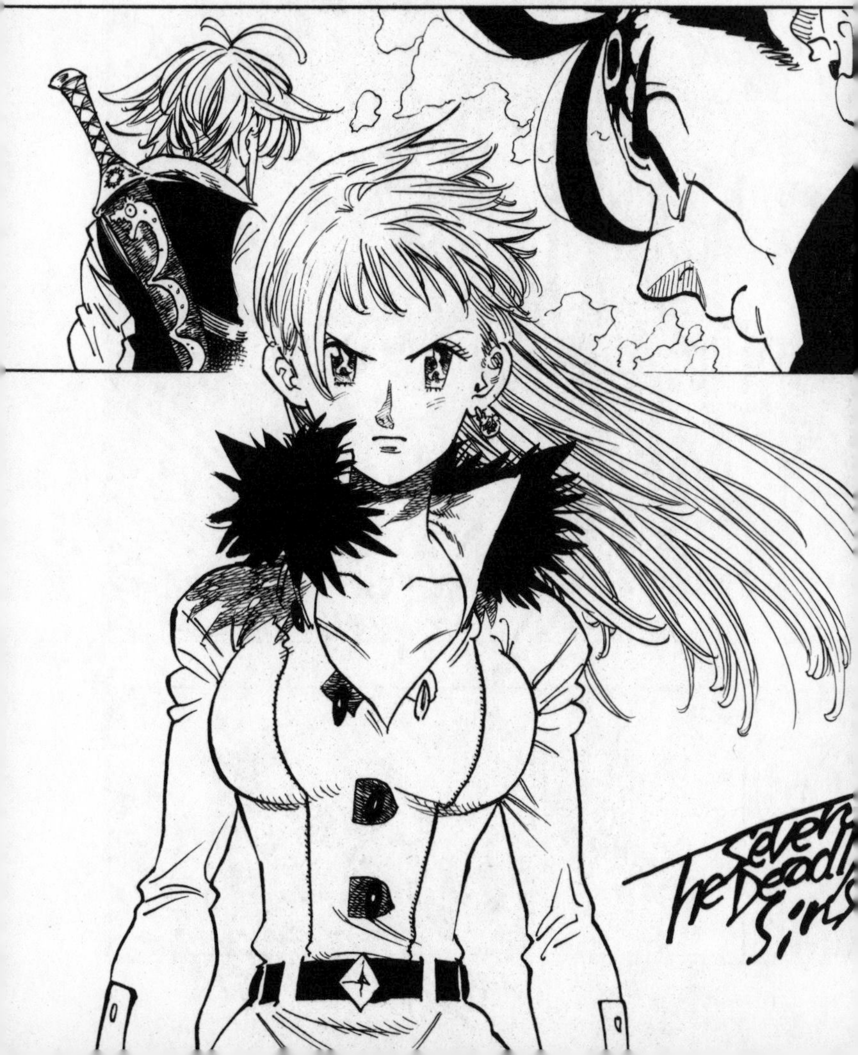

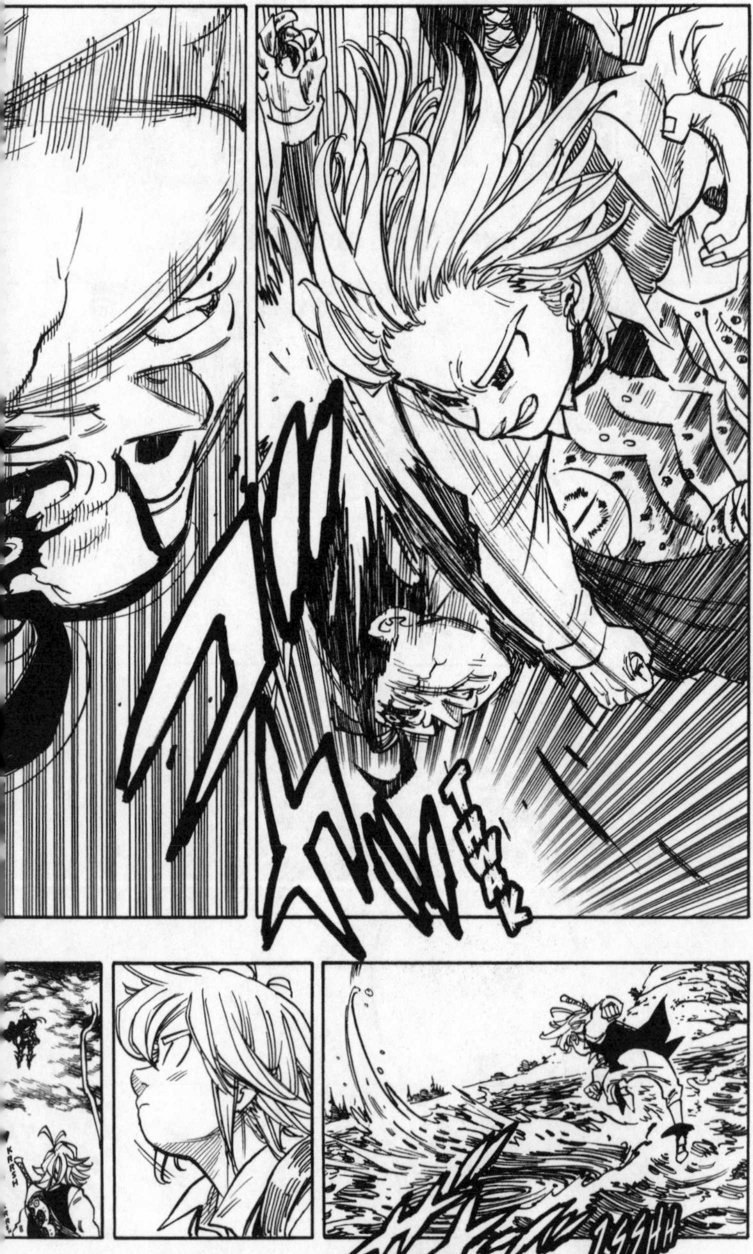
THWAK
ZSSHH
KRRSH

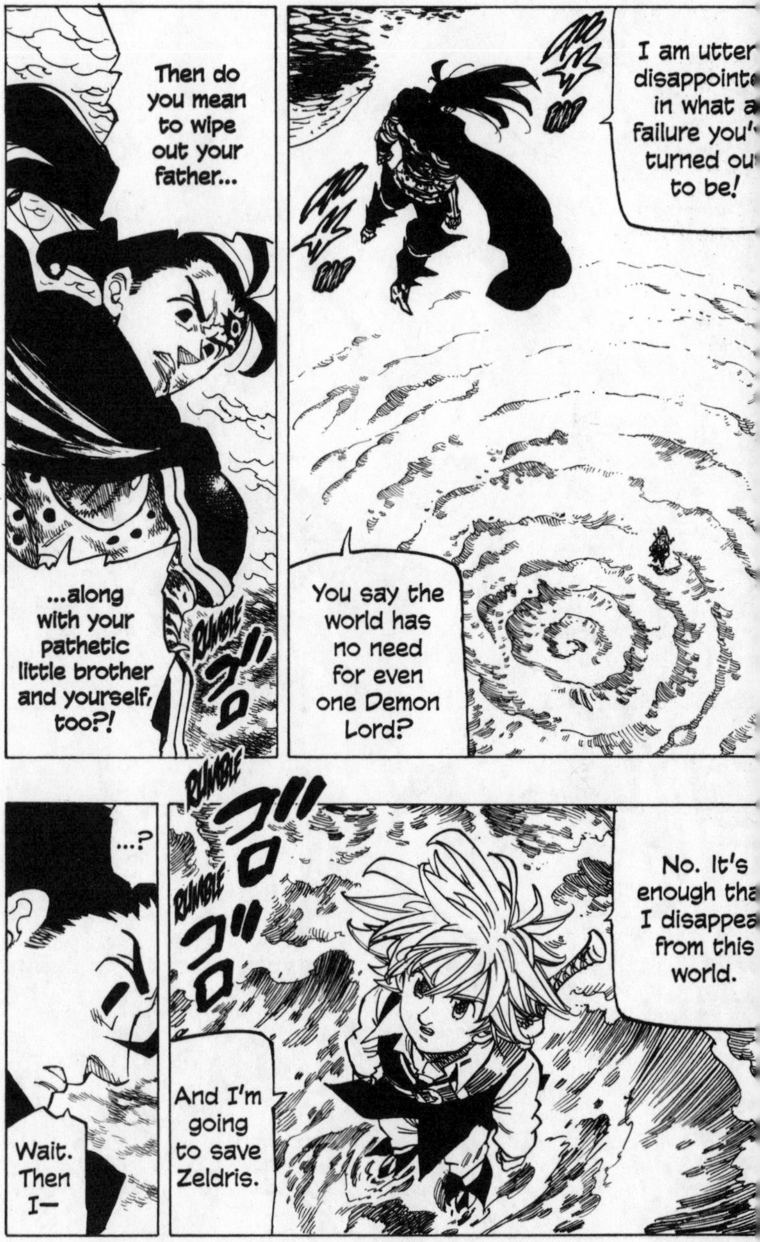

I am utter disappointe in what a failure you' turned ou to be!
You say the world has no need for even one Demon Lord?
Then do you mean to wipe out your father...
...along with your pathetic little brother and yourself, too?!
RUMBLE
RUMBLE
No. It's enough tha I disappea from this world.
RUMBLE
And I'm going to save Zeldris.
...?
Wait. Then I—

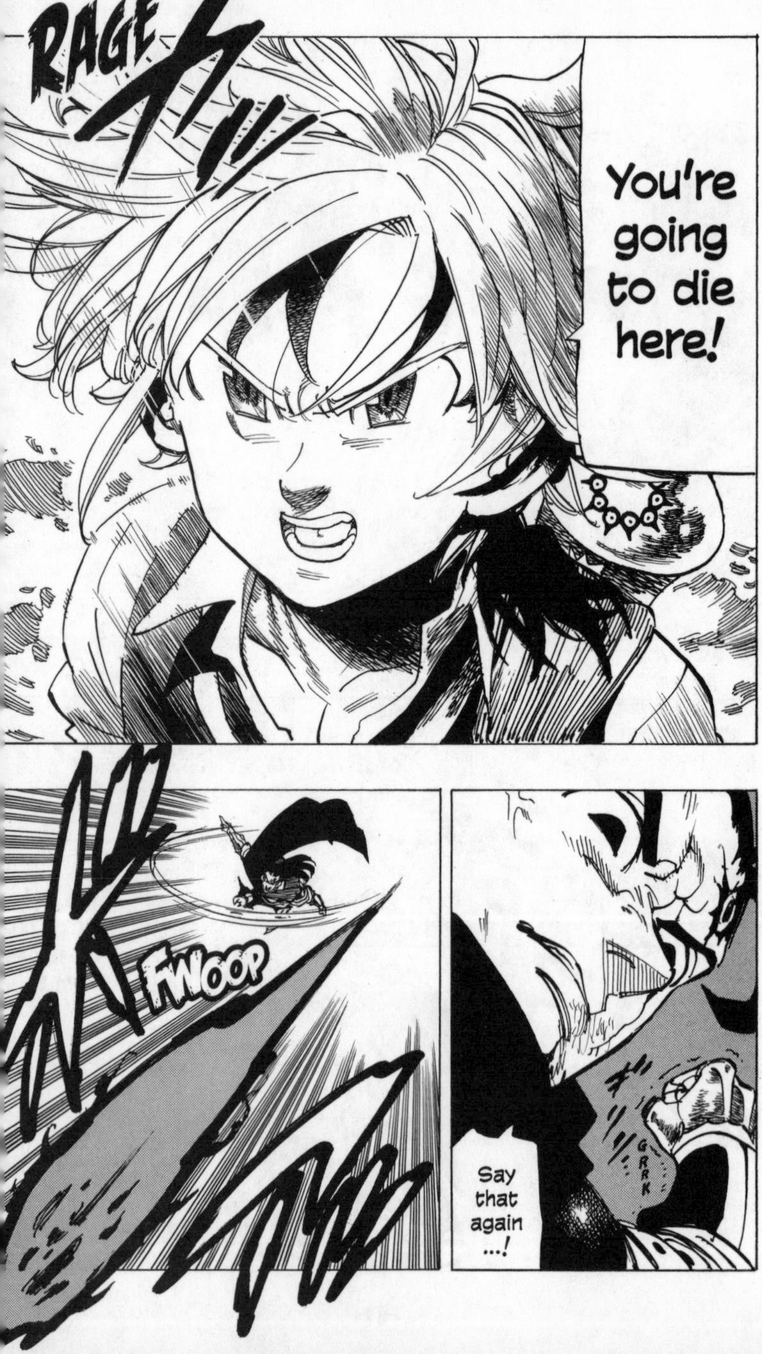
RAGE
You're going to die here!
GRRK
Say that again ...!
FWOOP

FWOOO

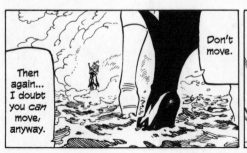

Then again... I doubt you *can* move, anyway.

Don't move.

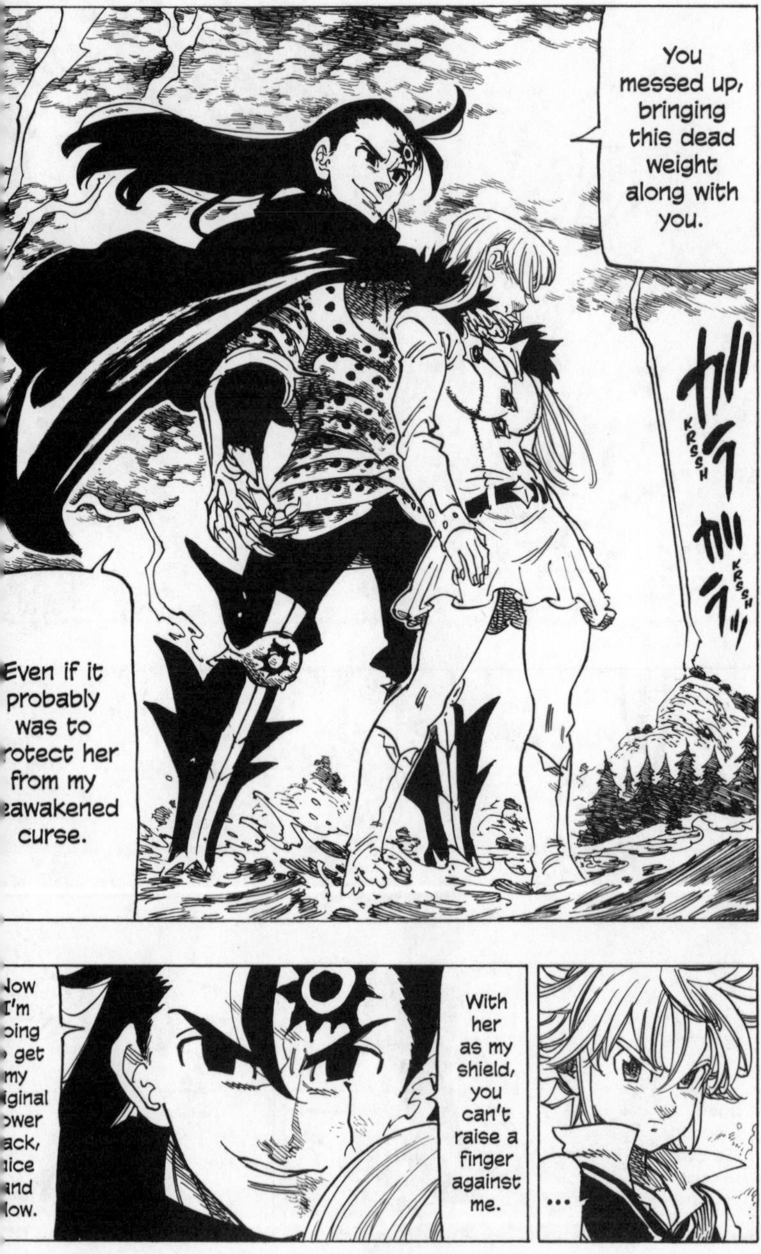
You messed up, bringing this dead weight along with you.
KRSSH
KRSSH
Even if it probably was to protect her from my reawakened curse.
...
With her as my shield, you can't raise a finger against me.
ow I'm oing get my iginal ower ack, ice and low.

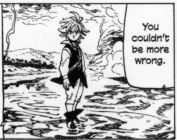

...Pf
What's so funny ?!
You couldn't be more wrong.
I didn't come here to be dead weight for him.
I came to defeat you.

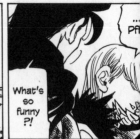

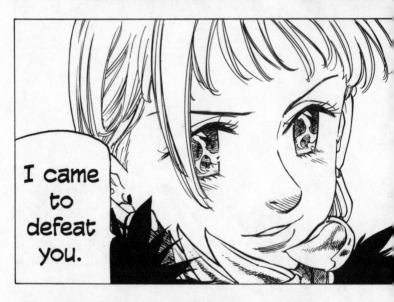

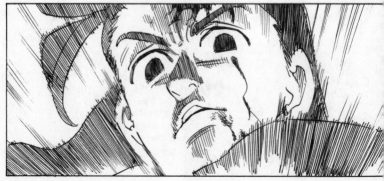

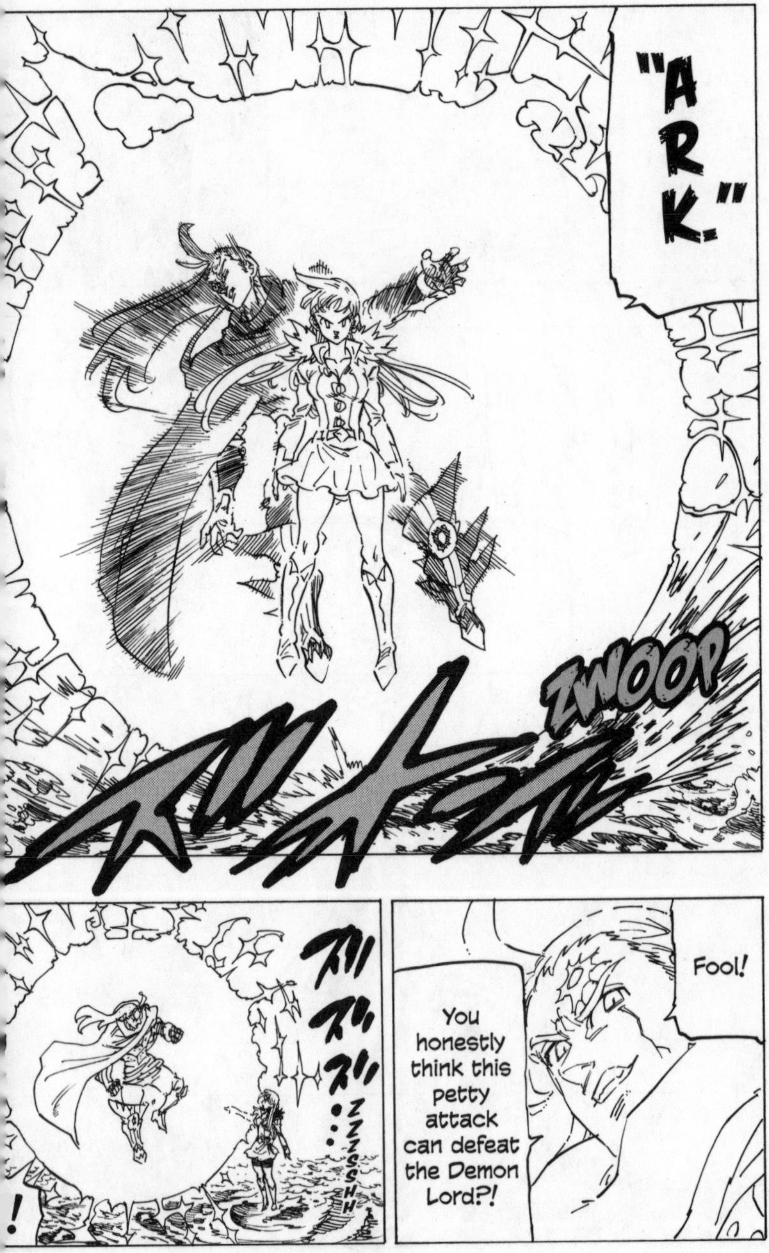
"ARK."
ZWOOP
Fool!
You honestly think this petty attack can defeat the Demon Lord?!
ZZZSSHH...
!

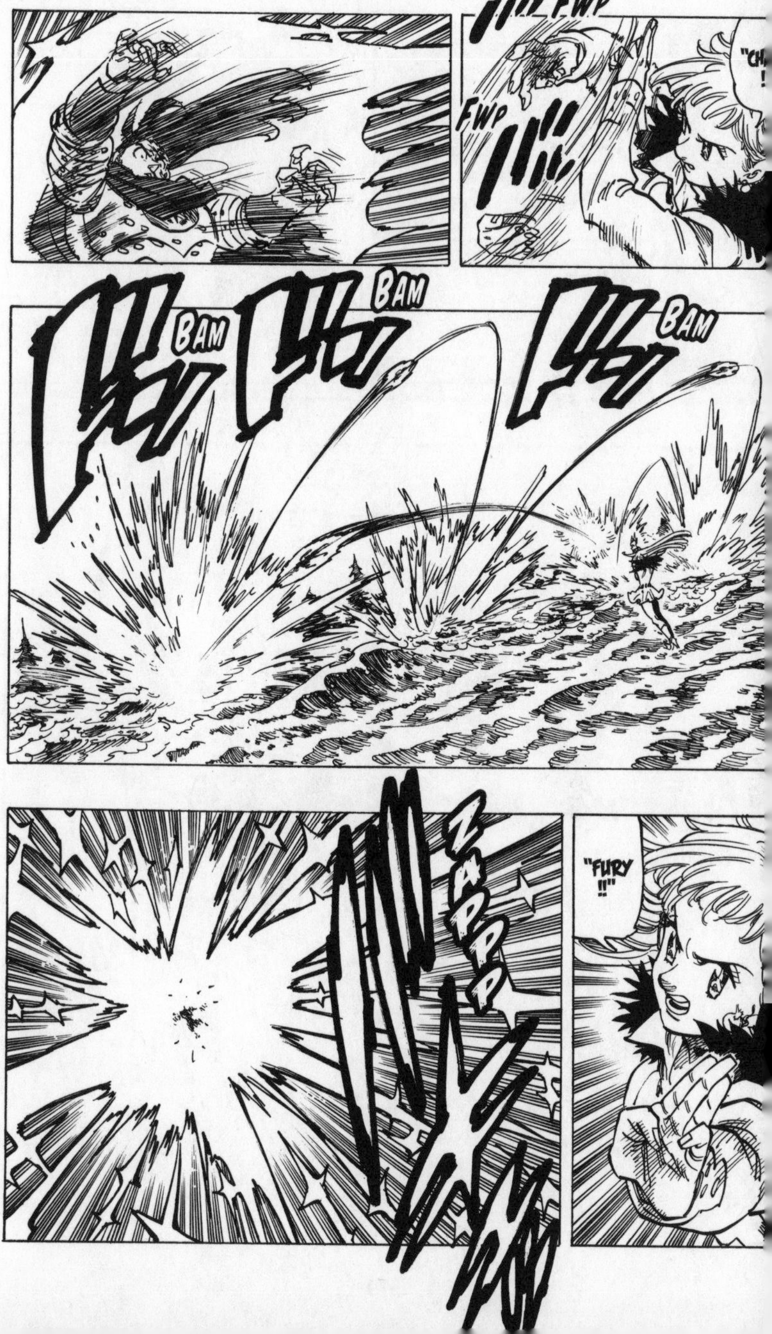
FWP
FWP
BAM
BAM
BAM
"FURY!!"
ZAPPP

If you underestimate her, you're cruising for a bruising. I've been there, too. As Lord of the Demon World, you must know what they call her there.

YOU... LITTLE...

...HUSSY ...!

"Bloody Ellie."

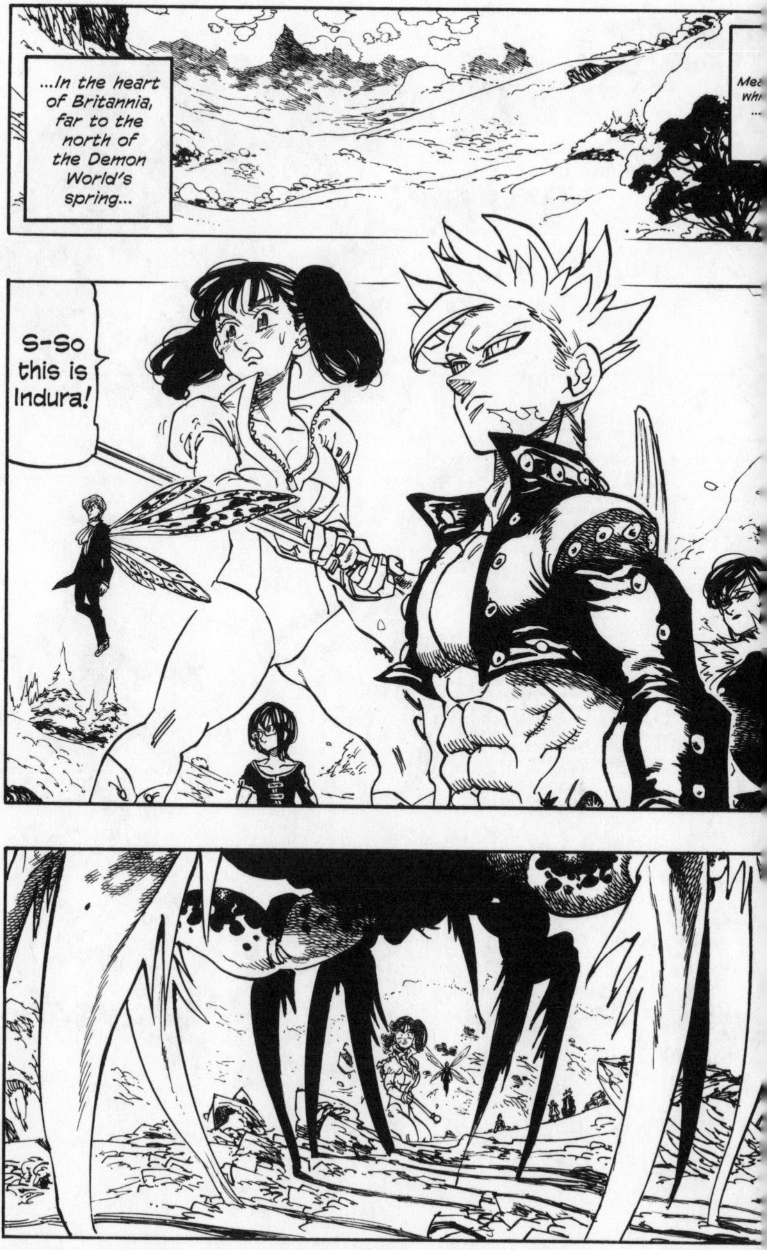
...In the heart of Britannia, far to the north of the Demon World's spring...
S-So this is Indura!

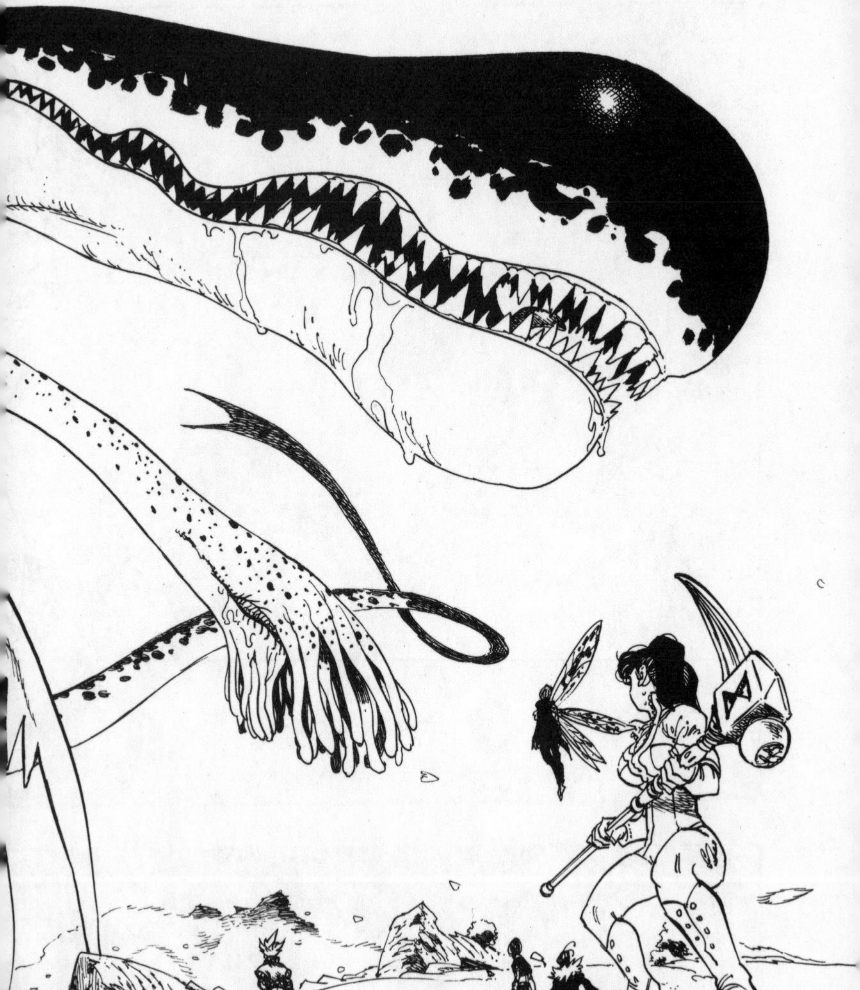

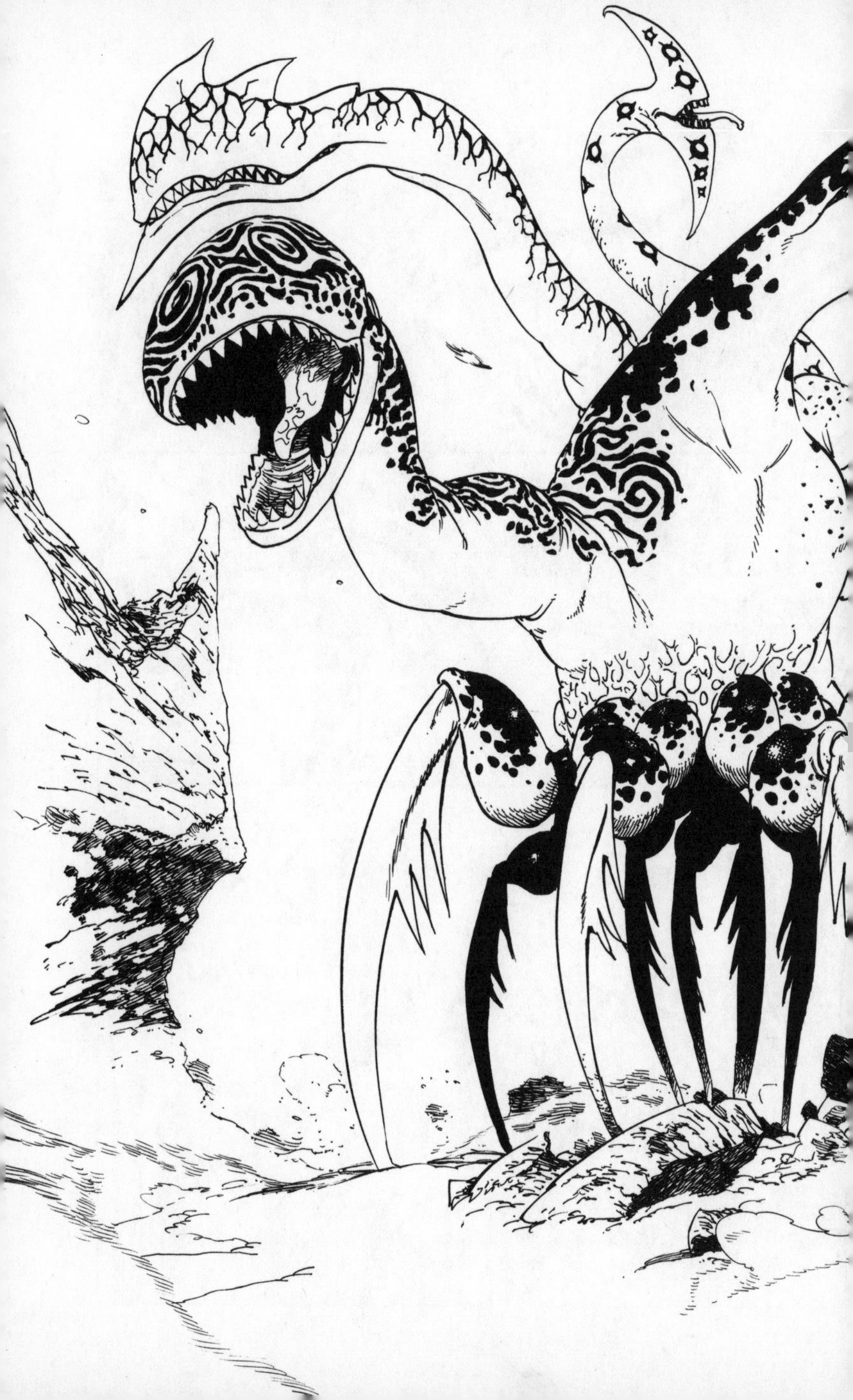

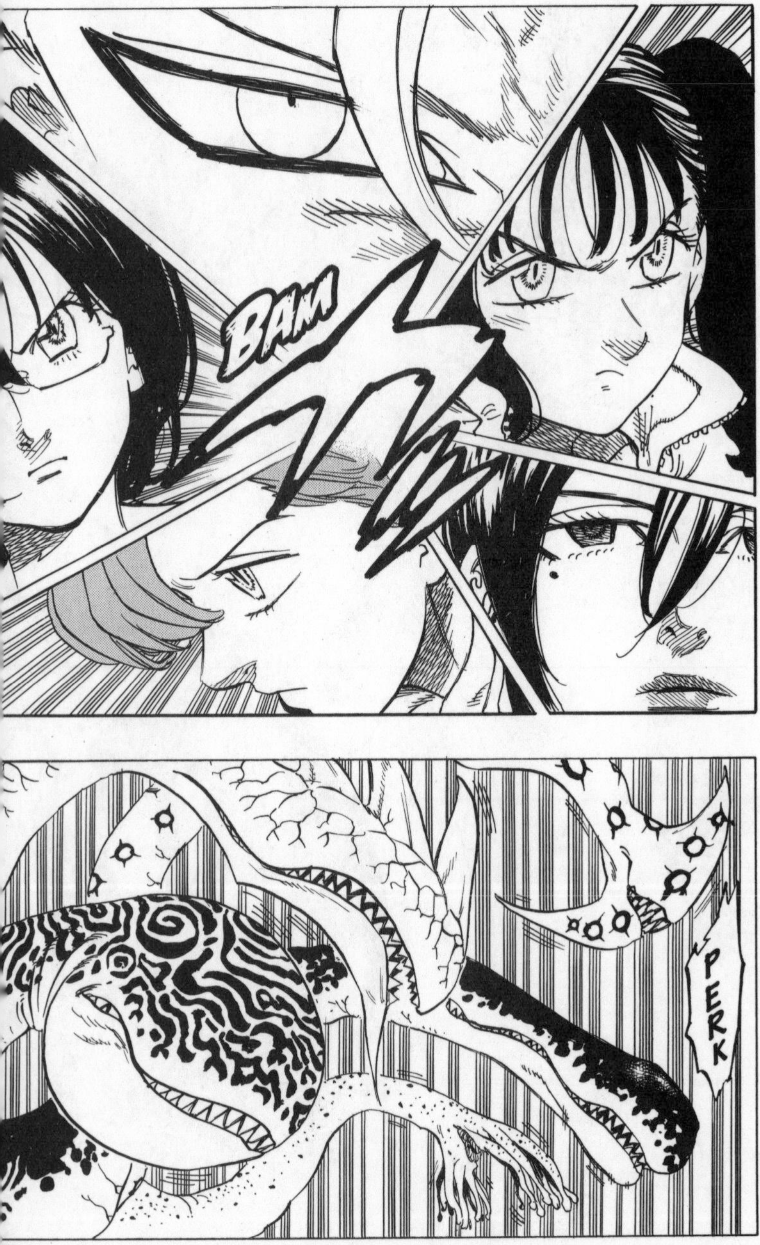
BAM
PERK

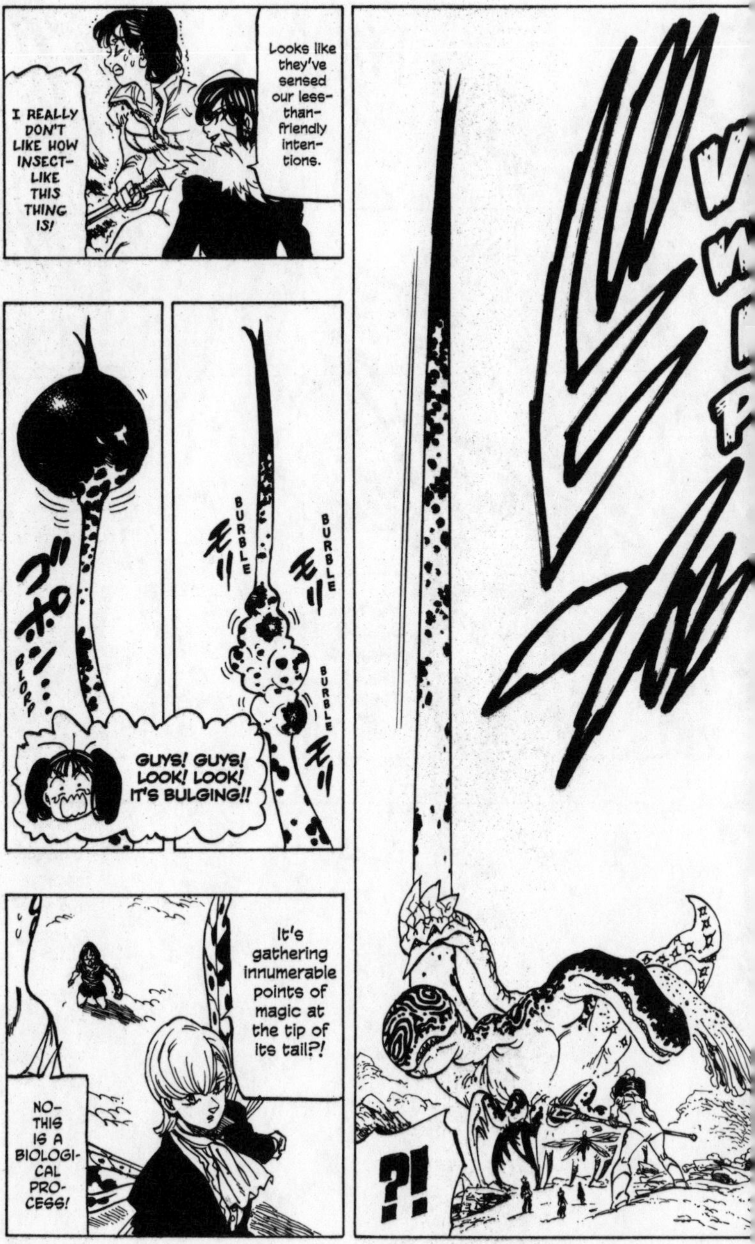
?!
Looks like they've sensed our less-than-friendly intentions.
I REALLY DON'T LIKE HOW INSECT-LIKE THIS THING IS!
BURBLE
BURBLE
BURBLE
BLORP
GUYS! GUYS! LOOK! LOOK! IT'S BULGING!!
It's gathering innumerable points of magic at the tip of its tail?!
NO—THIS IS A BIOLOGICAL PROCESS!

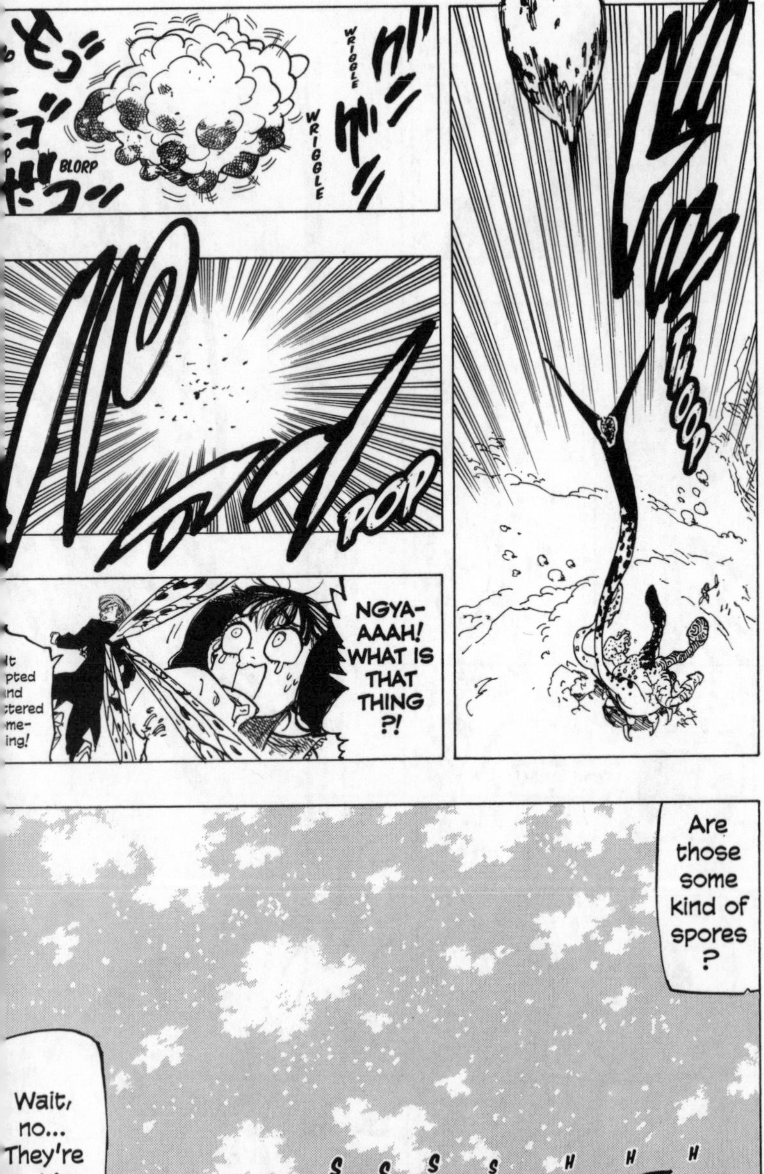

THOOP
WRIGGLE
WRIGGLE
BLORP
POP
NGYA-AAAH! WHAT IS THAT THING?!
Are those some kind of spores?
Wait, no... They're oo big...
SSSSHHH

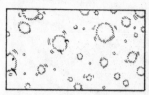
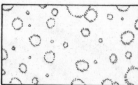

That's ...!

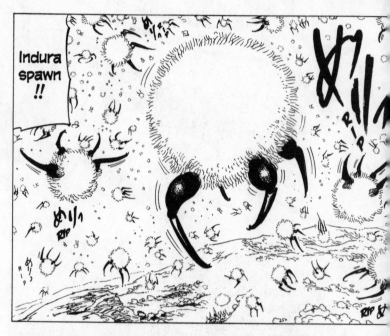

Indura spawn!!

We have to stop them!!

They're going to spread throughout Britannia!

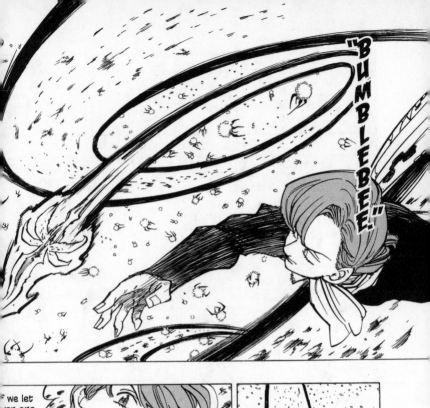

"BUMBLEBEE!"

f we let ven one of them escape, 'll cause emendous ama—

!!

WWOOSH

"EXTER-MINATE RAY!"

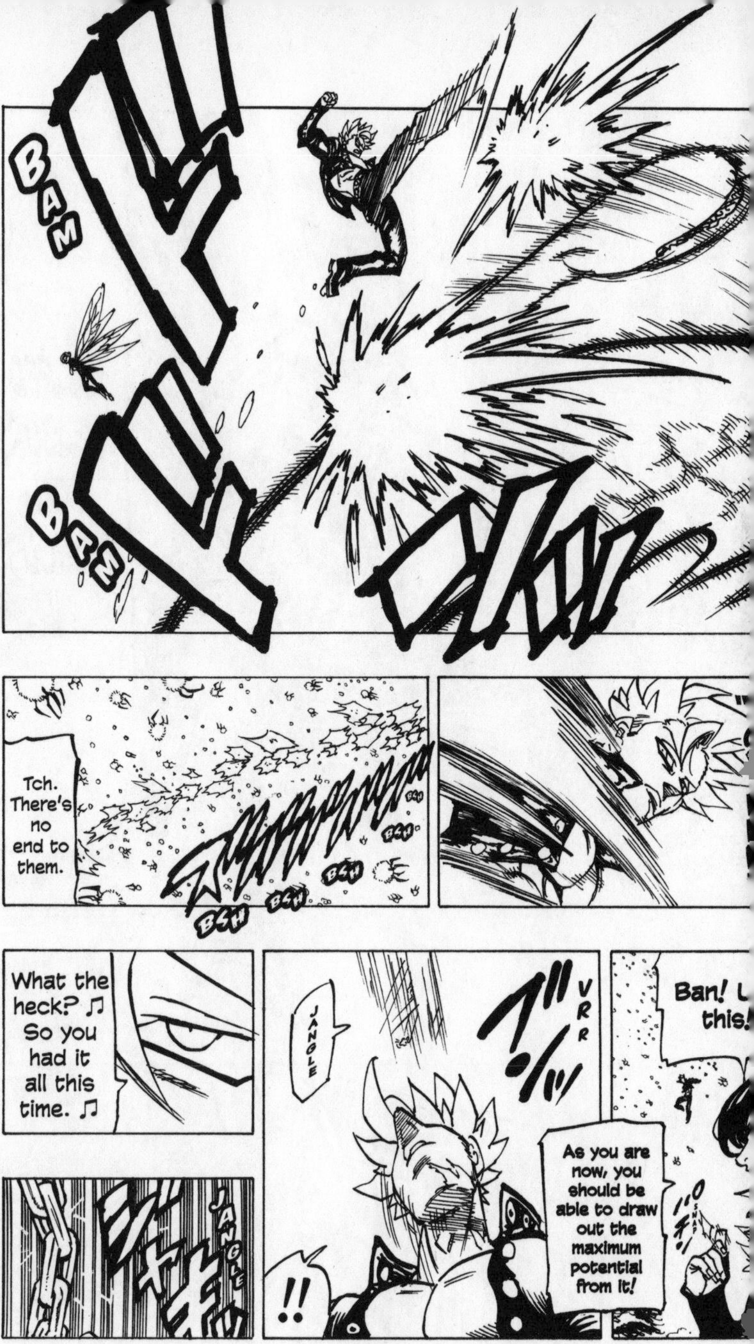
BAM
BAM
Tch. There's no end to them.
BSH
BSH
BSH
BSH
BSH
Ban! U
this!
SNAP
VRR
JANGLE
As you are now, you should be able to draw out the maximum potential from it!
!!
What the heck? ♫ So you had it all this time. ♫
JANGLE

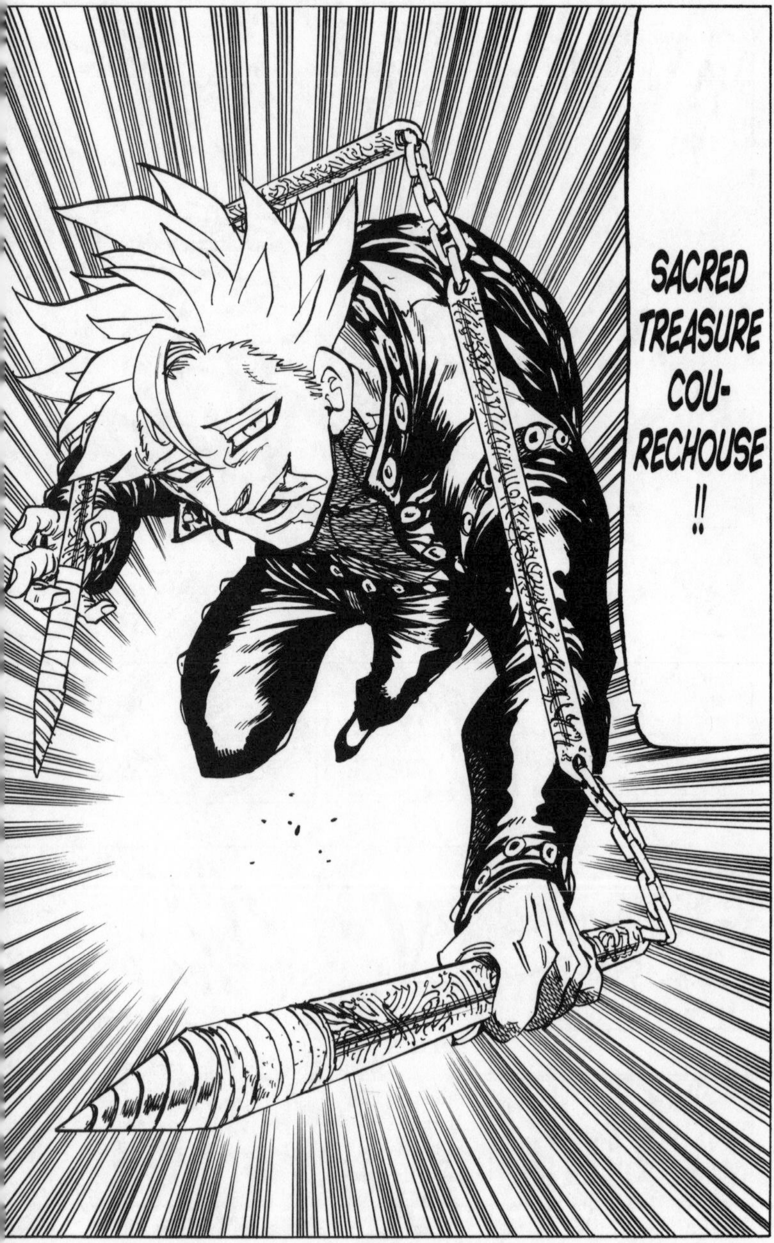
SACRED TREASURE COU-RECHOUSE !!

Chapter 316 - The Lord's Grace Indura

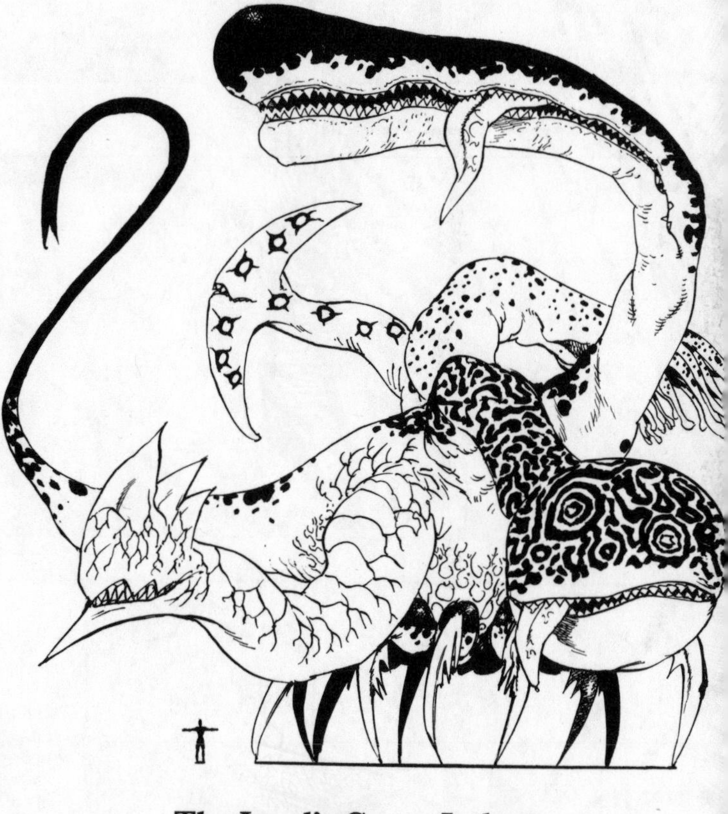

The Lord's Grace Indura

A legendary beast that high-ranking Demons turn into when they've sacrificed six of their seven hearts to darkness. Unlike other Indura that go by different names, the Lord's Grace Indura is the form taken by a member of The Ten Commandments who is loyal to the Demon Lord. It's the most powerful of its kind and said to have a Combat Class higher than all other Indura.

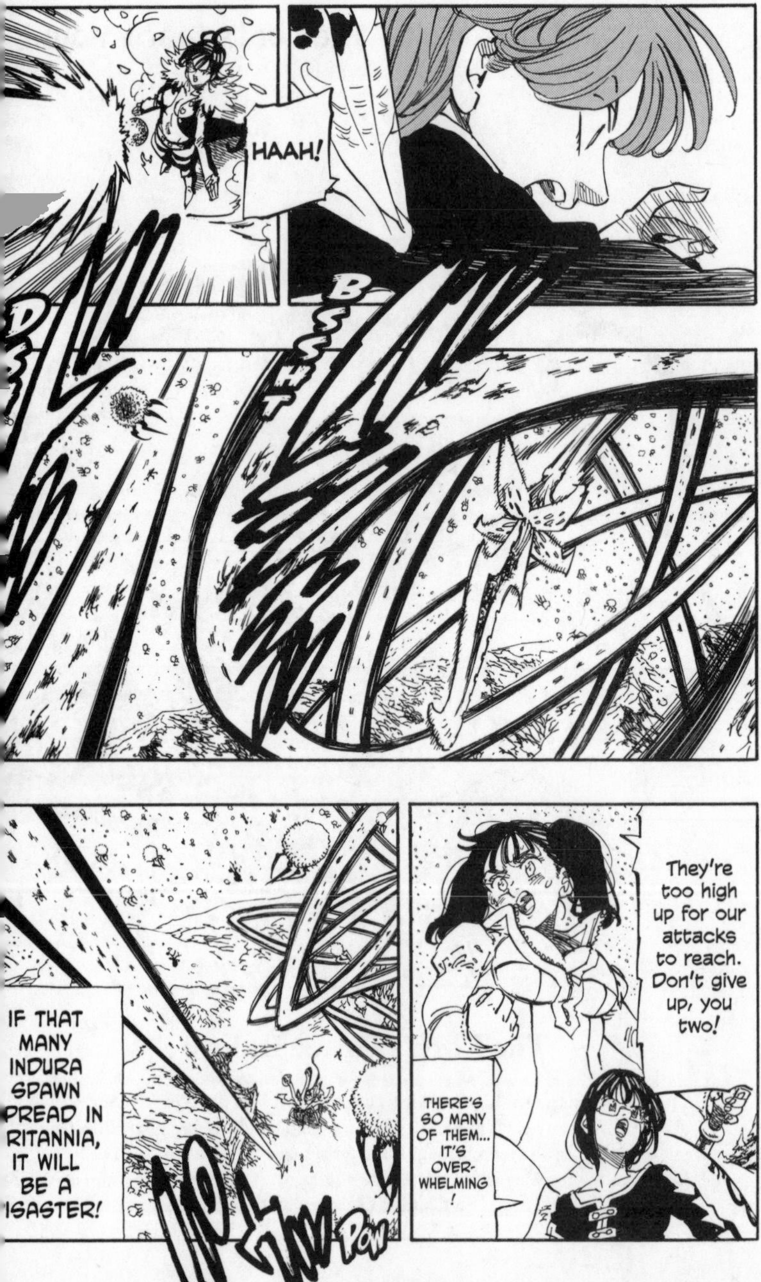
HAAH!
BSSHT
They're too high up for our attacks to reach. Don't give up, you two!
THERE'S SO MANY OF THEM... IT'S OVER-WHELMING!
IF THAT MANY INDURA SPAWN PREAD IN RITANNIA, IT WILL BE A ISASTER!
POW

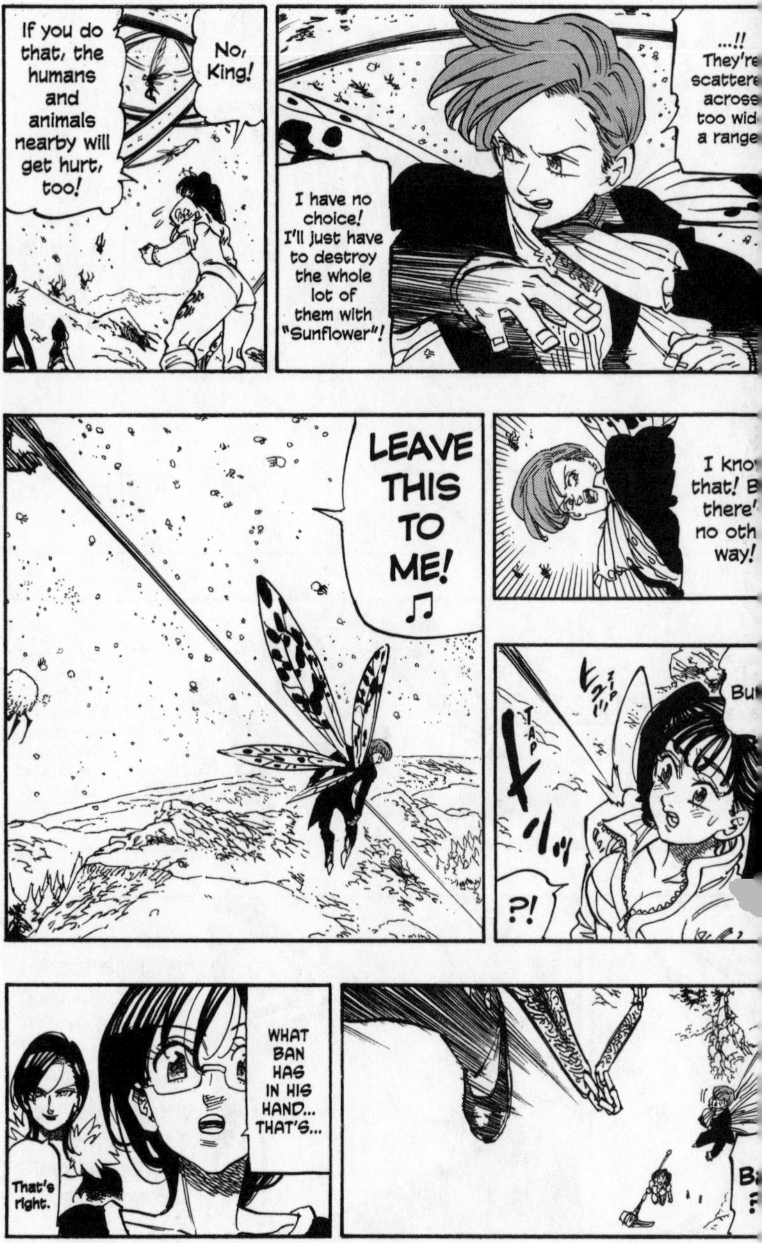

...!! They'r scatter across too wid a range
I have no choice! I'll just have to destroy the whole lot of them with "Sunflower"!
No, King!
If you do that, the humans and animals nearby will get hurt, too!
I kno that! B there' no oth way!
Bu
TAP
?!
LEAVE THIS TO ME! ♫
B ??
WHAT BAN HAS IN HIS HAND... THAT'S...
That's right.

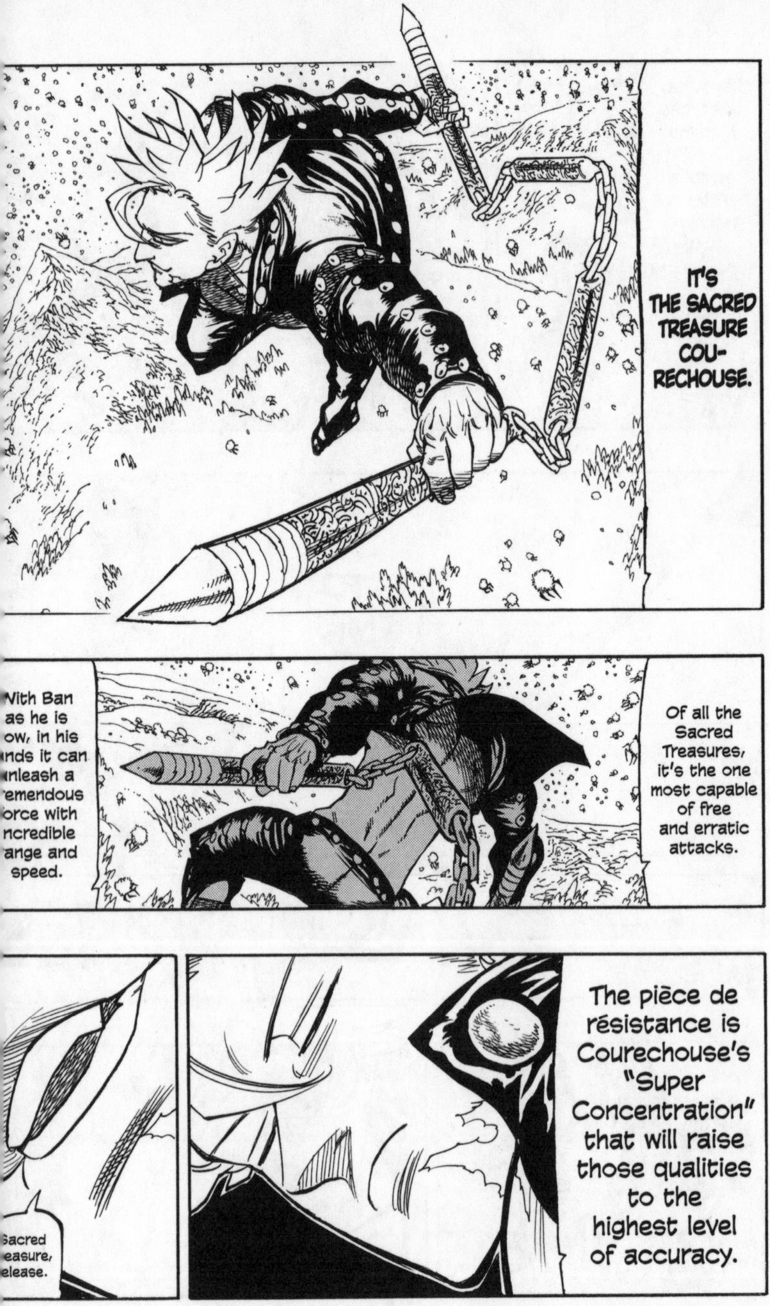
IT'S THE SACRED TREASURE COU-RECHOUSE.
Of all the Sacred Treasures, it's the one most capable of free and erratic attacks.
With Ban as he is ow, in his nds it can nleash a remendous orce with ncredible ange and speed.
The pièce de résistance is Courechouse's "Super Concentration" that will raise those qualities to the highest level of accuracy.
Sacred easure, elease.

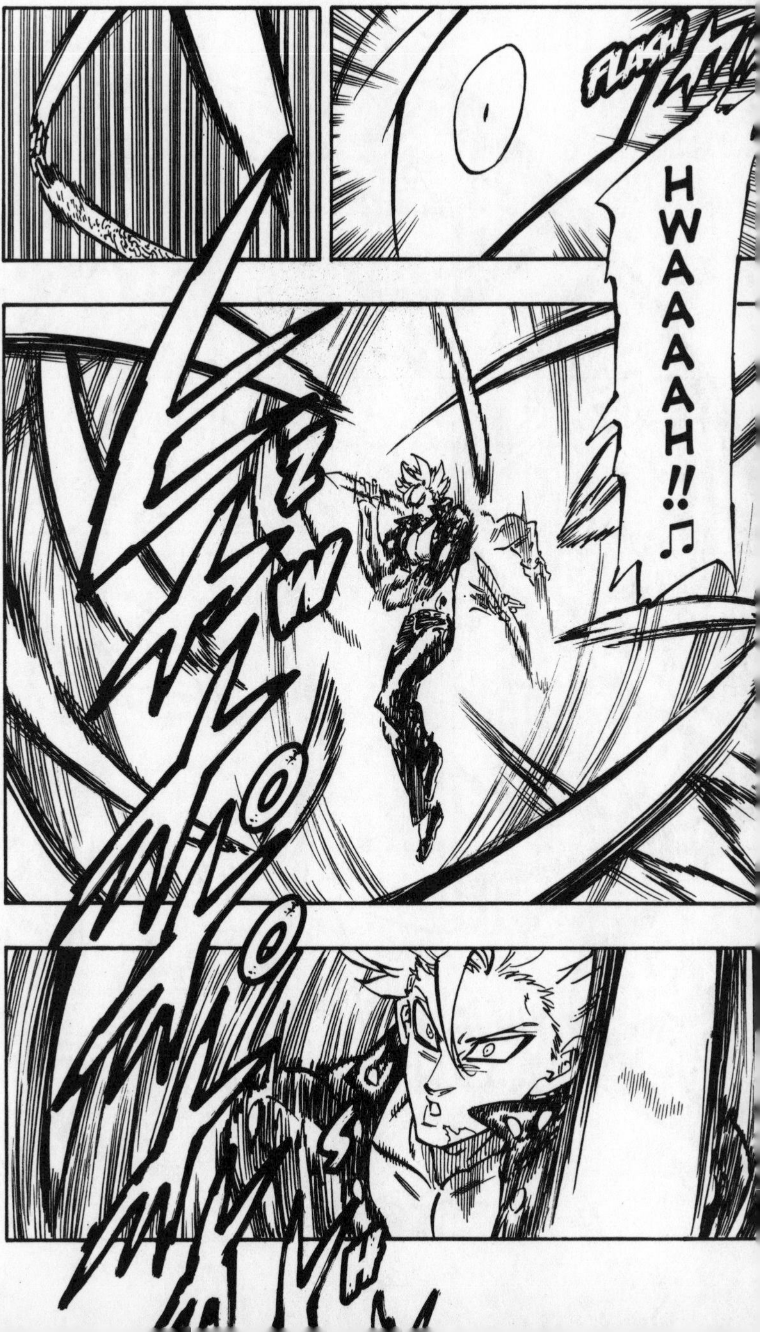
FLASH
HWAAAAAH!!♫

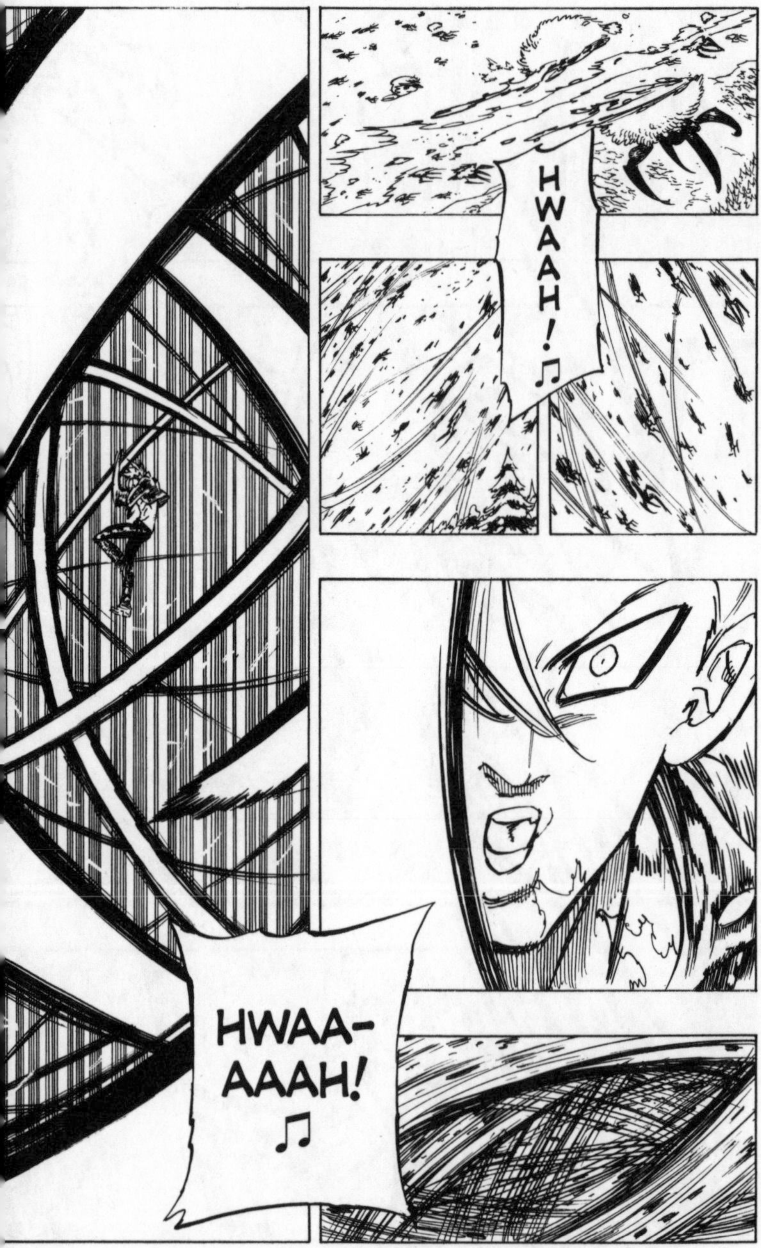
HWAAH!♫
HWAA-AAAH!♫

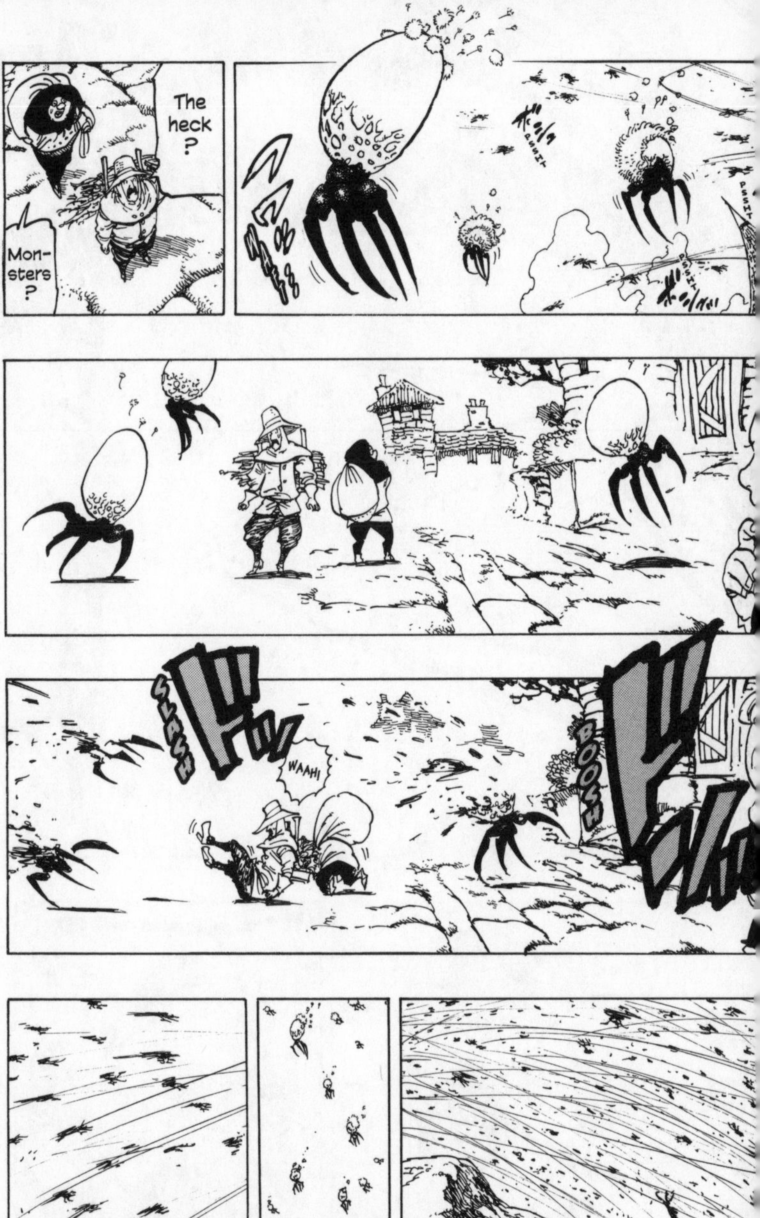
PSSHT
PSSHT
The heck?
Monsters?
BOOSH
WAAH!
SLASH

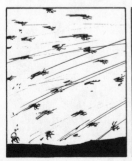

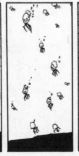

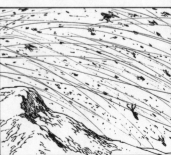

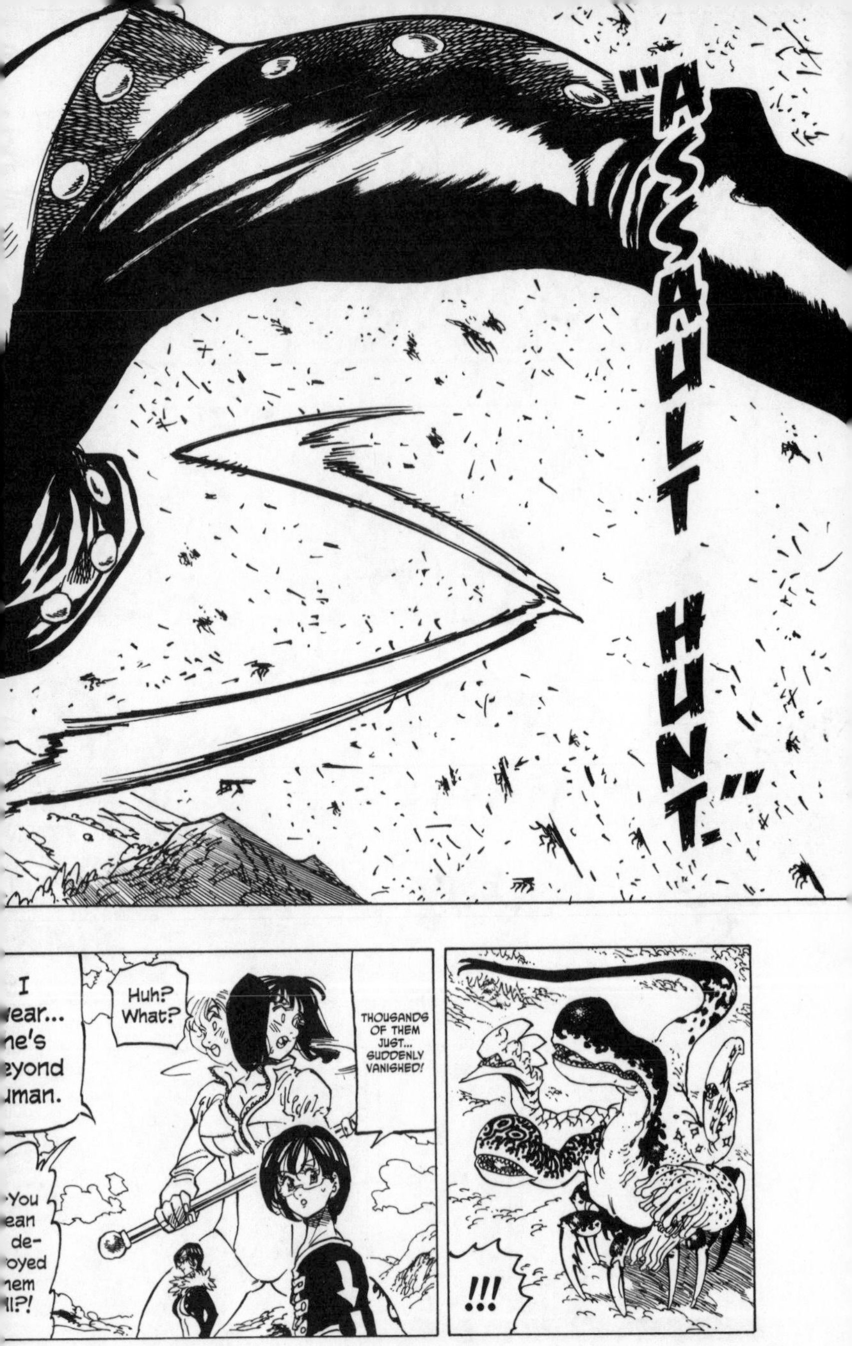
"ASSAULT HUNT..."
!!!
THOUSANDS OF THEM JUST... SUDDENLY VANISHED!
Huh? What?
I ear... e's eyond uman.
You ean de- oyed hem ll?!

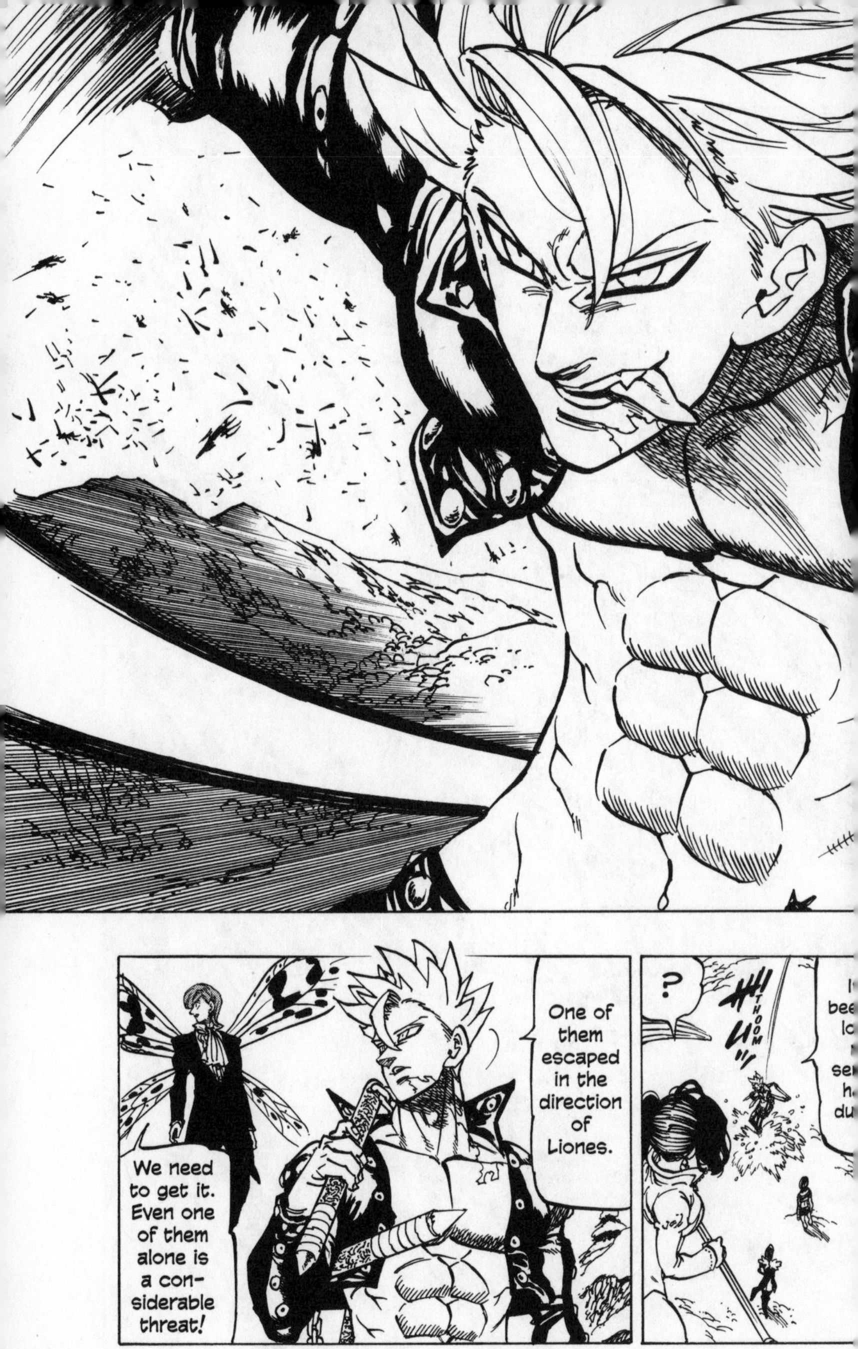
?
THOOM
One of them escaped in the direction of Liones.
We need to get it. Even one of them alone is a considerable threat!

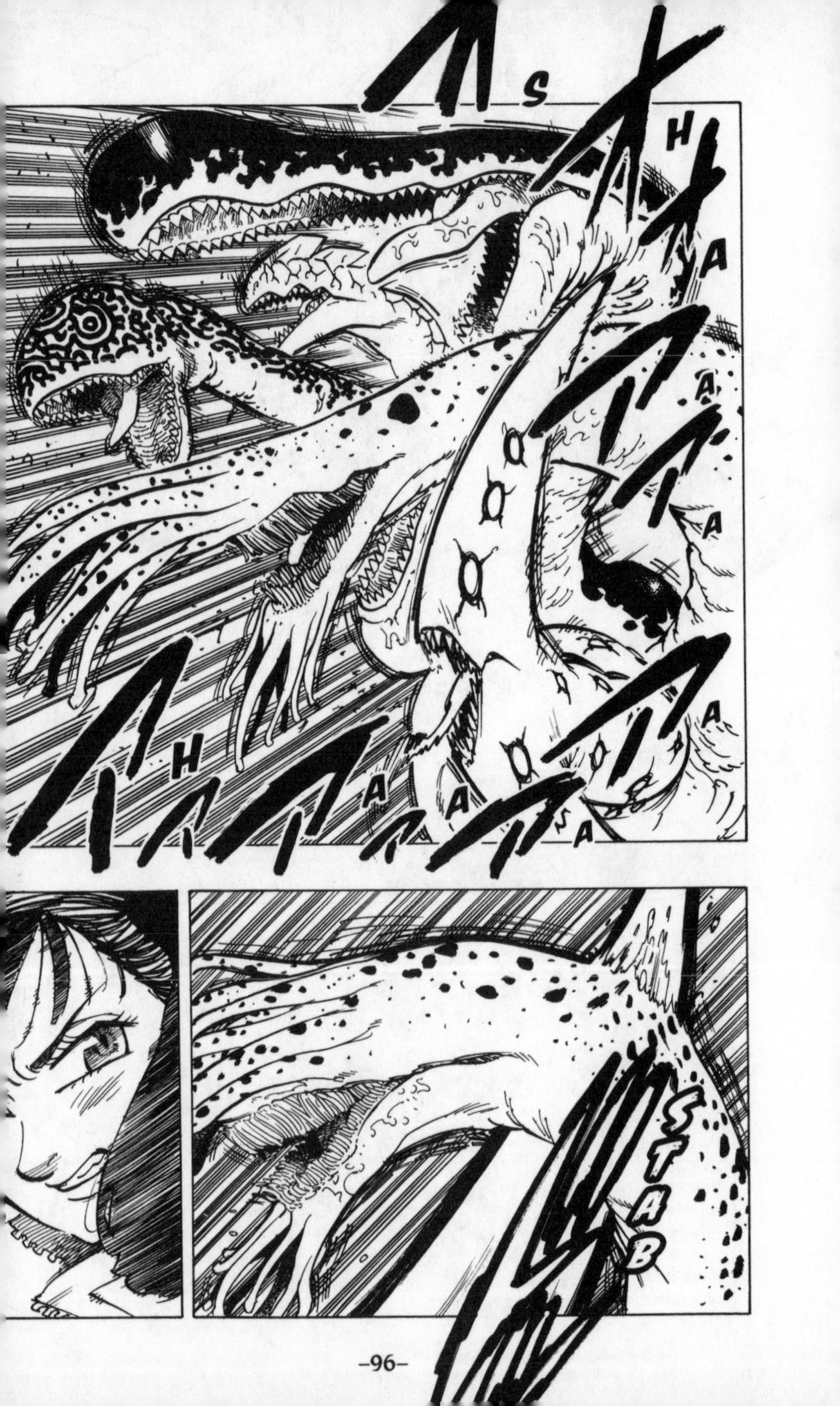
SHAAAA
HAAAAA
STAB

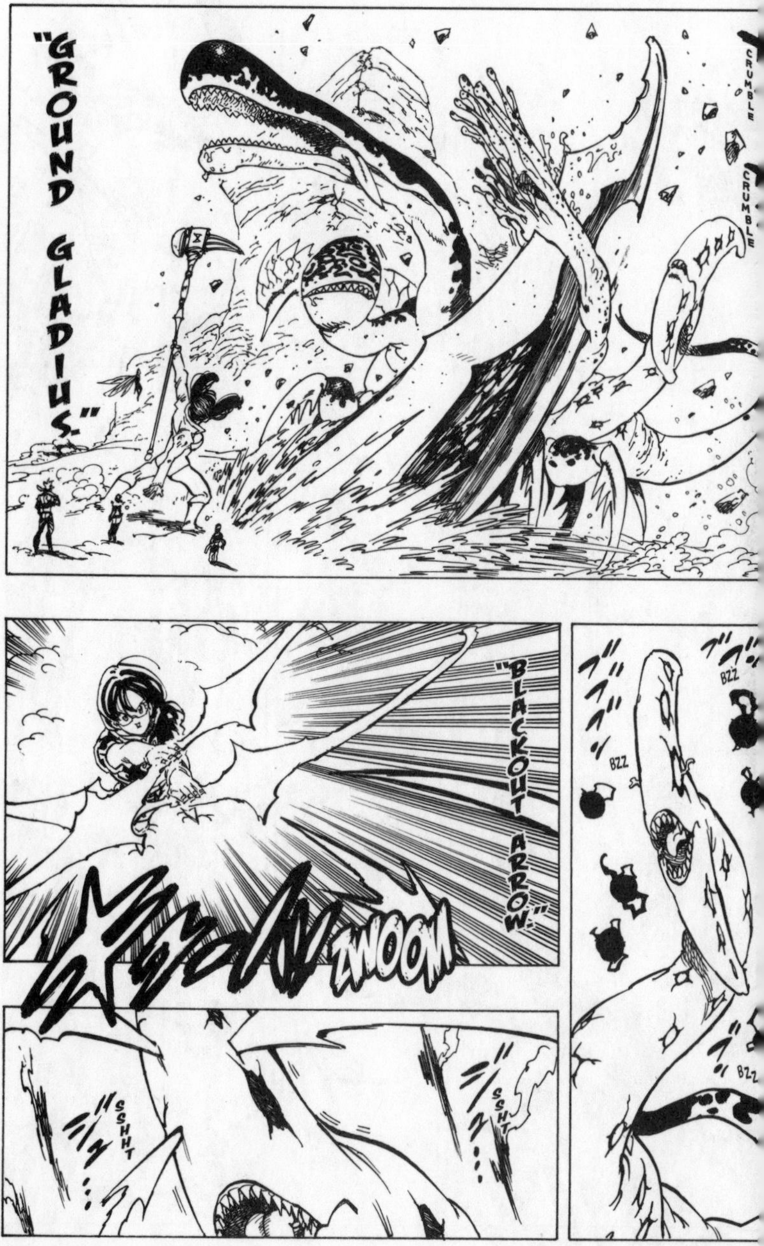
CRUMBLE
CRUMBLE
"GROUND GLADIUS."
BZZ
BZZ
BZZ
"BLACKOUT ARROW."
ZWOOM
SSHT
SSHT

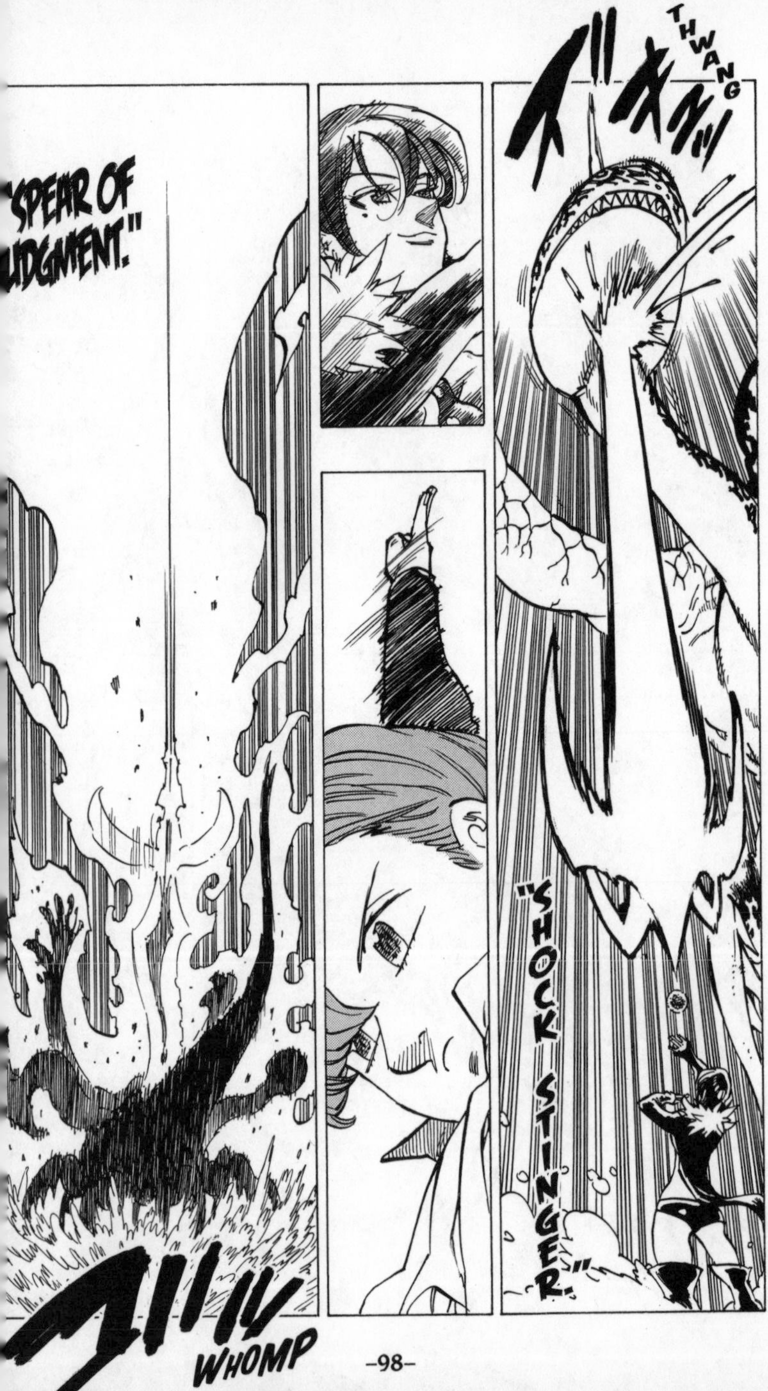
THWANG
"SHOCK STINGER."
"SPEAR OF JUDGMENT."
WHOMP

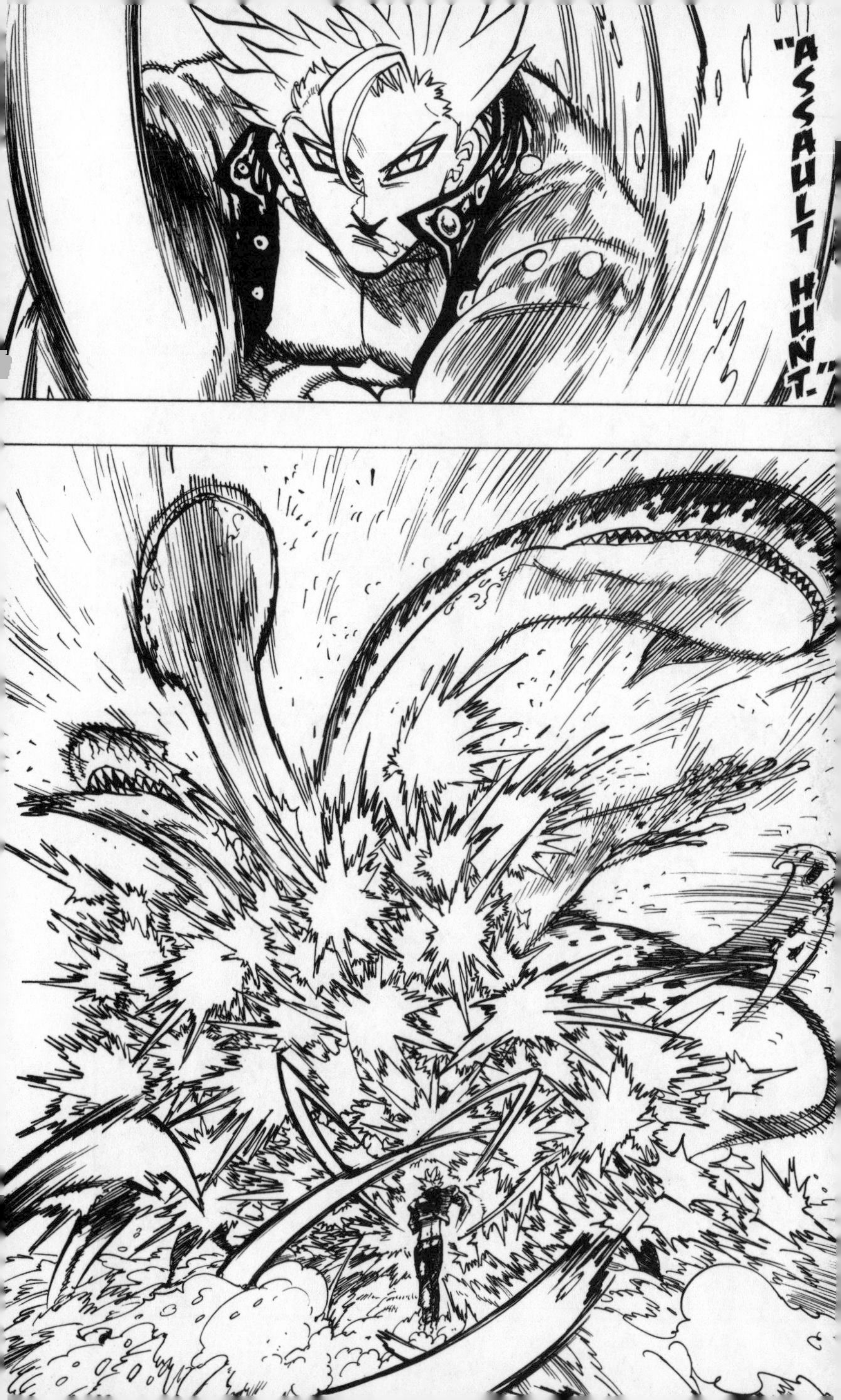
"ASSAULT HUNT."

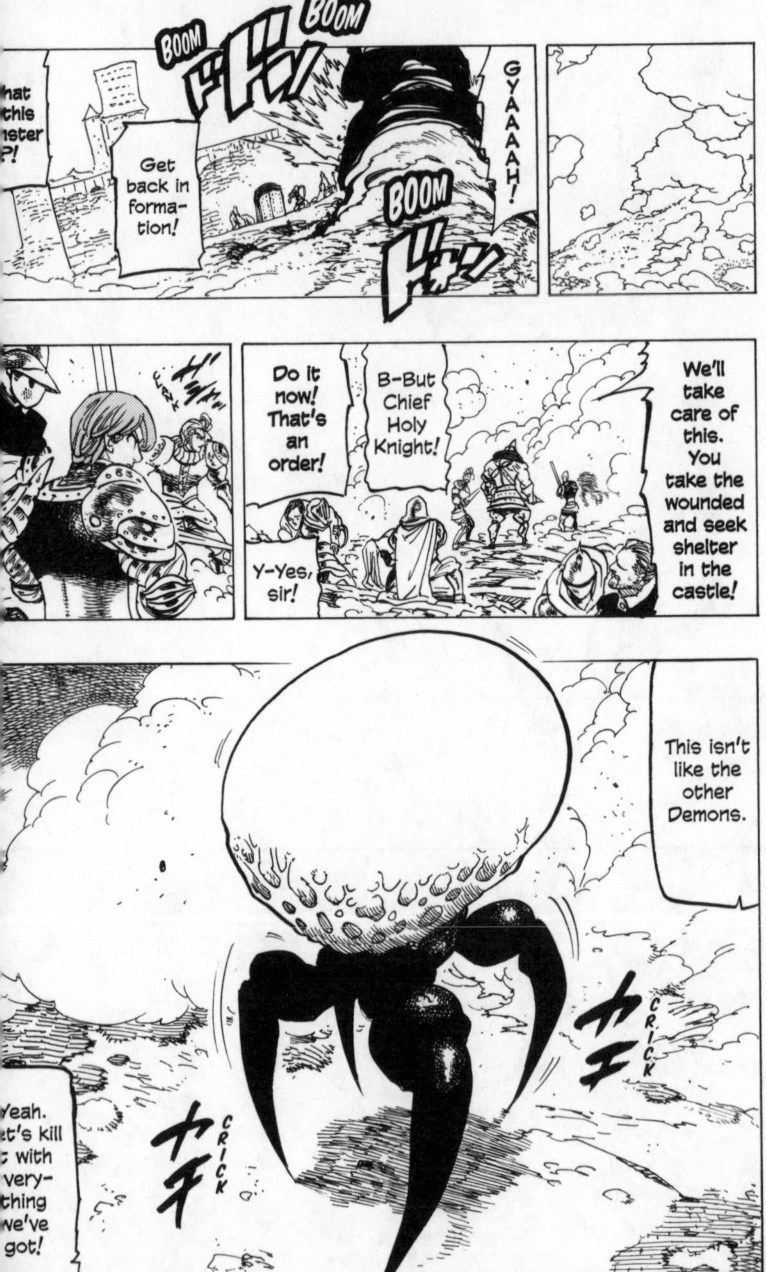

GYAAAAH!
BOOM
BOOM
Get back in forma-tion!
BOOM
hat this nster ?!
We'll take care of this. You take the wounded and seek shelter in the castle!
B-But Chief Holy Knight!
Do it now! That's an order!
Y-Yes, sir!
CLANK
This isn't like the other Demons.
CRICK
CRICK
Yeah. t's kill with very-thing we've got!

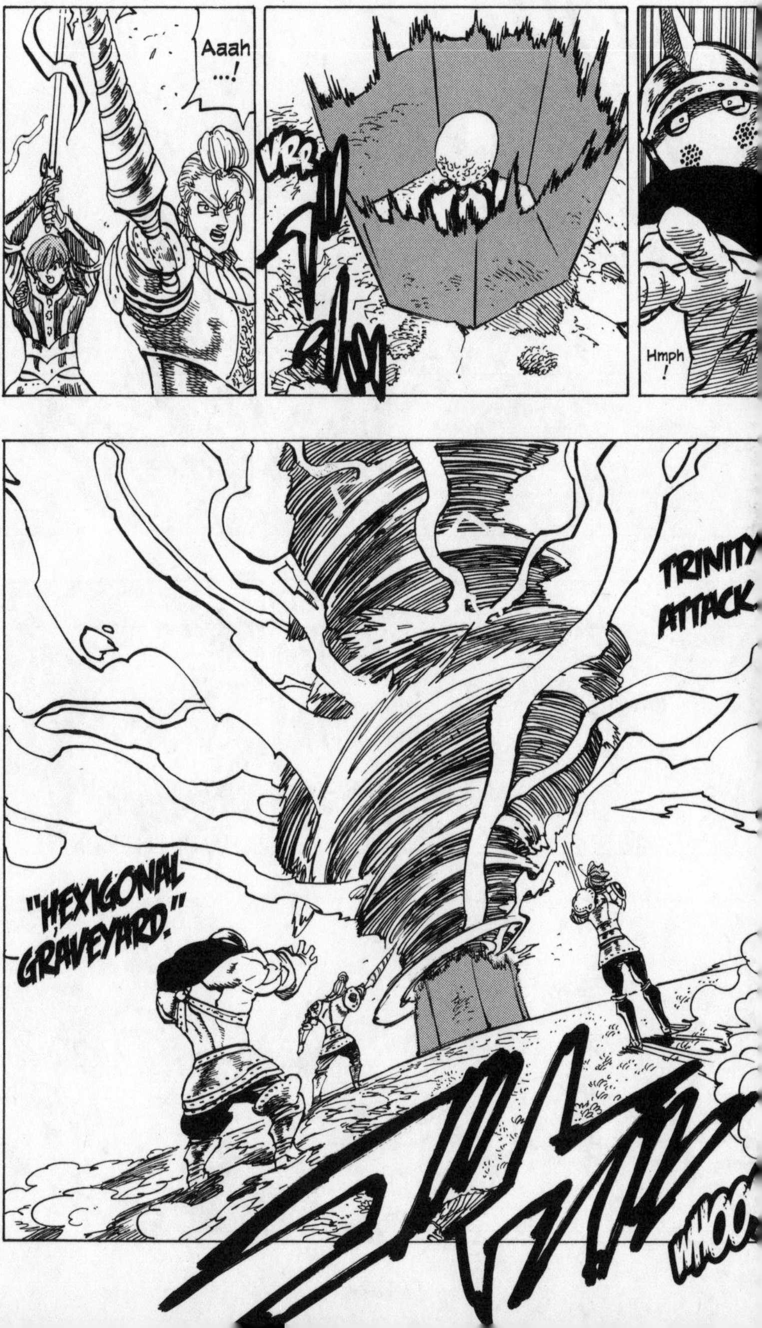
Hmph
!
VRR
Aaah
...!
TRINITY
ATTACK
"HEXIGONAL
GRAVEYARD."
WHOO

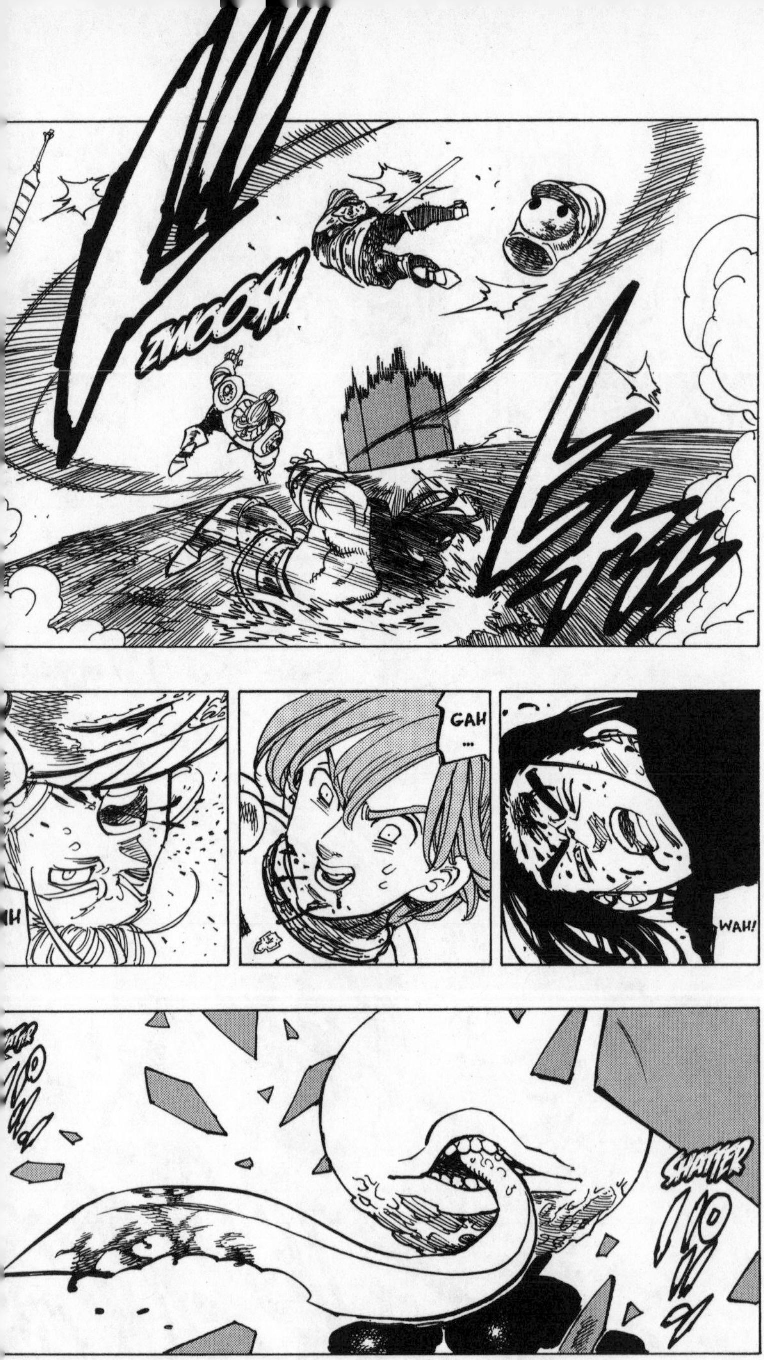
ZWOOOM
WAH!
GAH ...
SHATTER
SHATTER

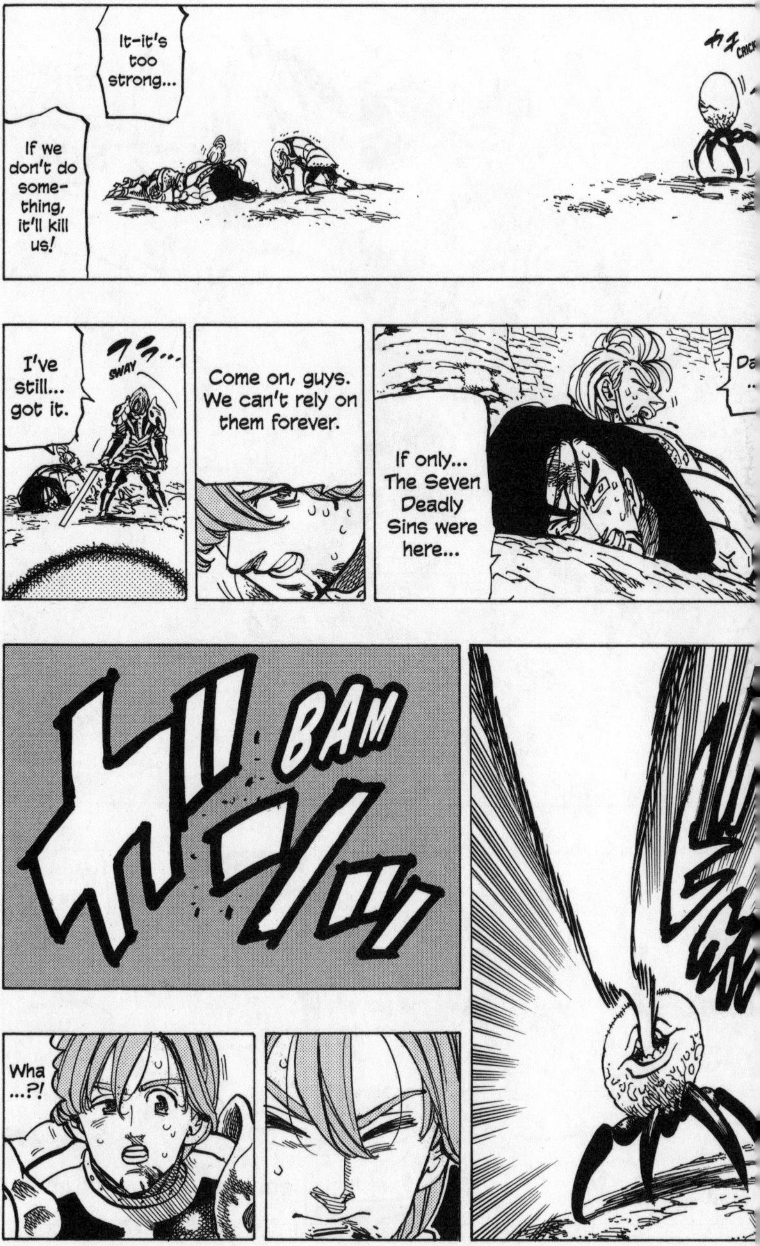
CRICK
It-it's too strong...
If we don't do something, it'll kill us!
Da
...
If only... The Seven Deadly Sins were here...
Come on, guys. We can't rely on them forever.
SWAY
I've still... got it.
BAM
Wha ...?!

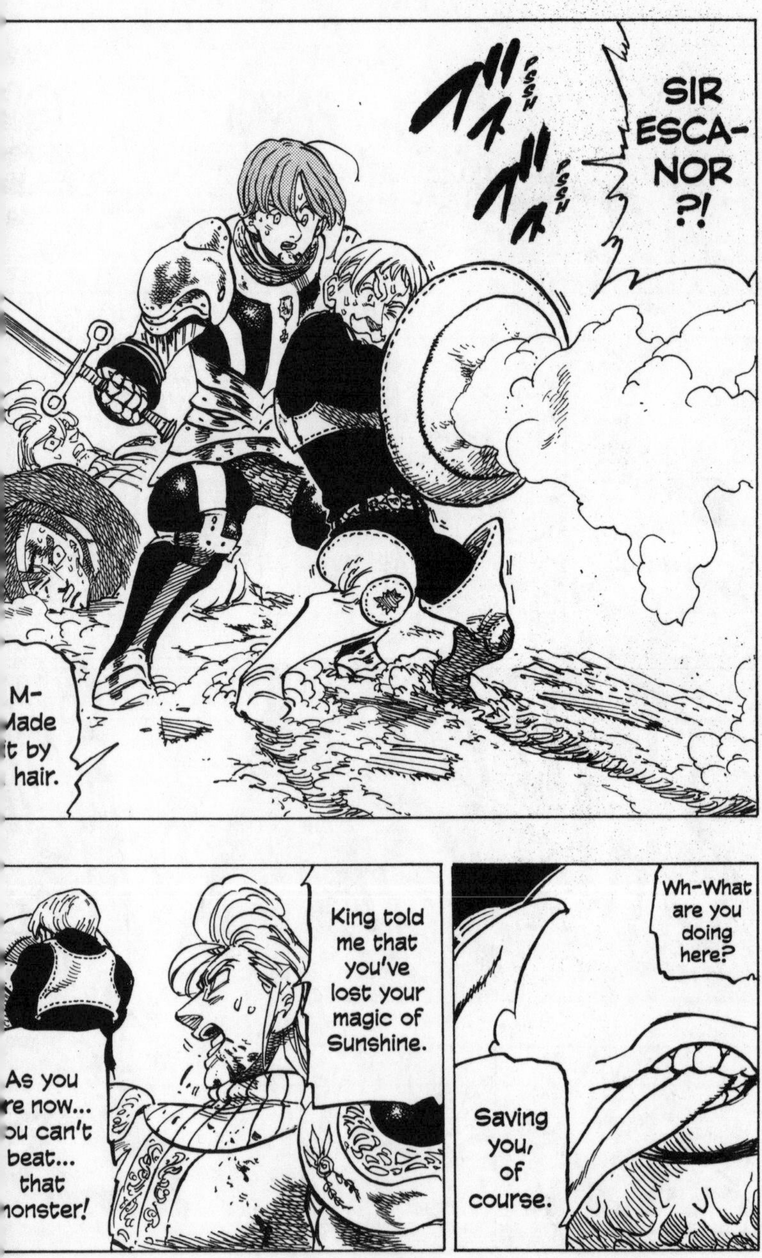
PSSH
PSSH
SIR ESCA-NOR?!
M- ade t by hair.
Wh-What are you doing here?
Saving you, of course.
King told me that you've lost your magic of Sunshine.
As you re now... ou can't beat... that onster!

Sorry if this comes off as impudent...

...but I'm not about to cower and hide to save my skin.

When you shielded us...

Koff!

It's my job as an old soldier to protect that!

But you youngsters have a bright and shining future ahead of you.

It's all right. I don't have much time left anyway.

UF!!!
SHNK

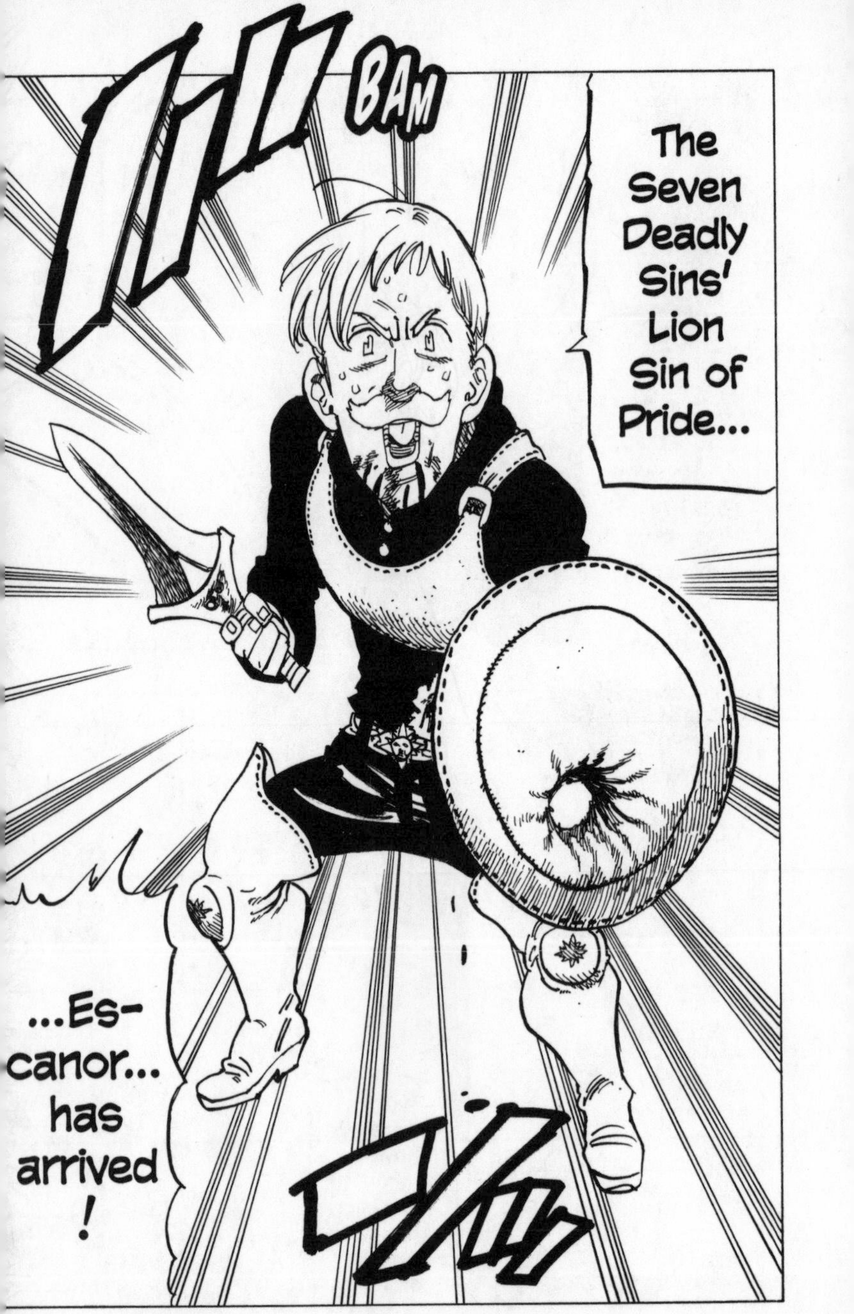
BAM
The Seven Deadly Sins' Lion Sin of Pride...
...Es-canor... has arrived!

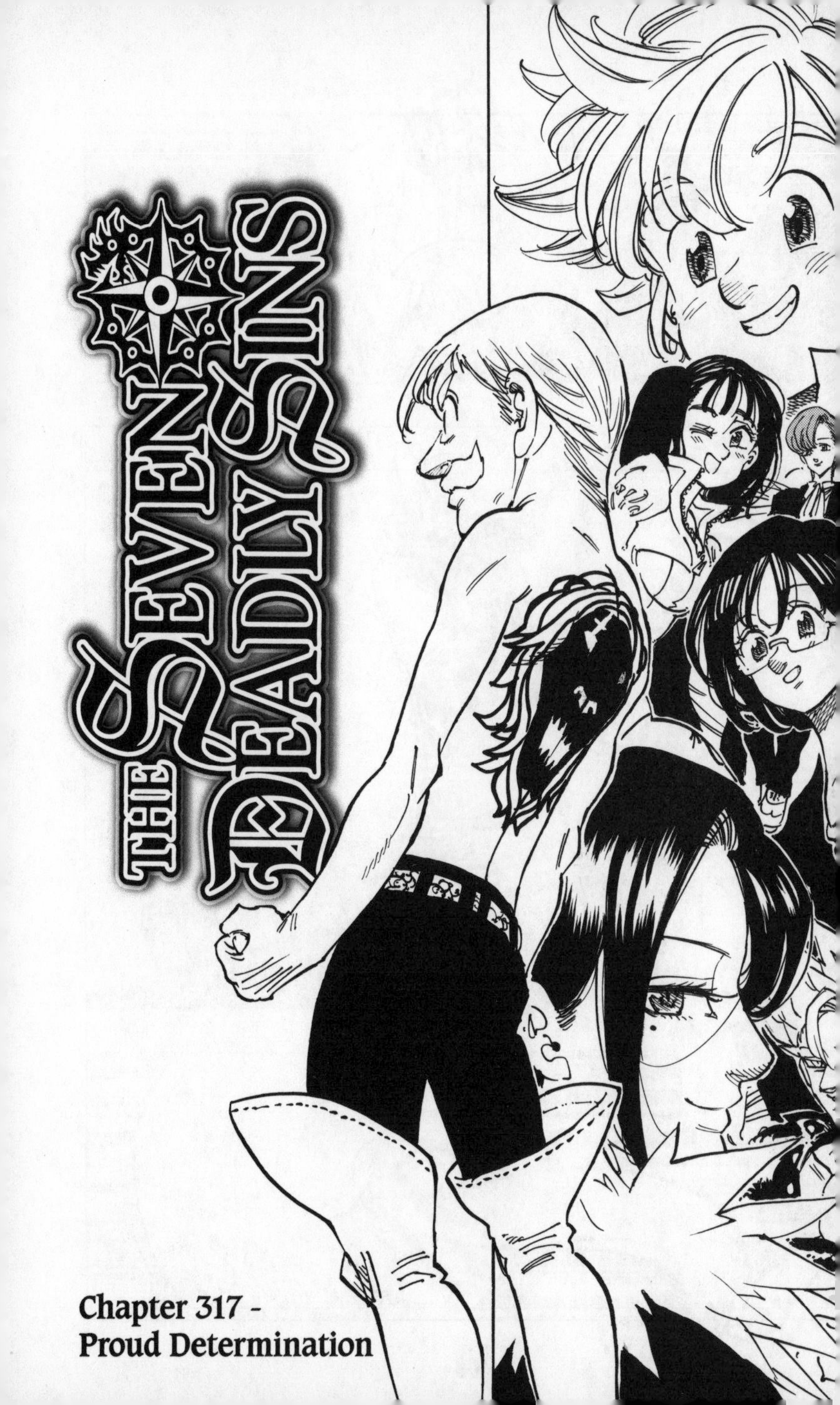
THE SEVEN DEADLY SINS

Chapter 317 - Proud Determination

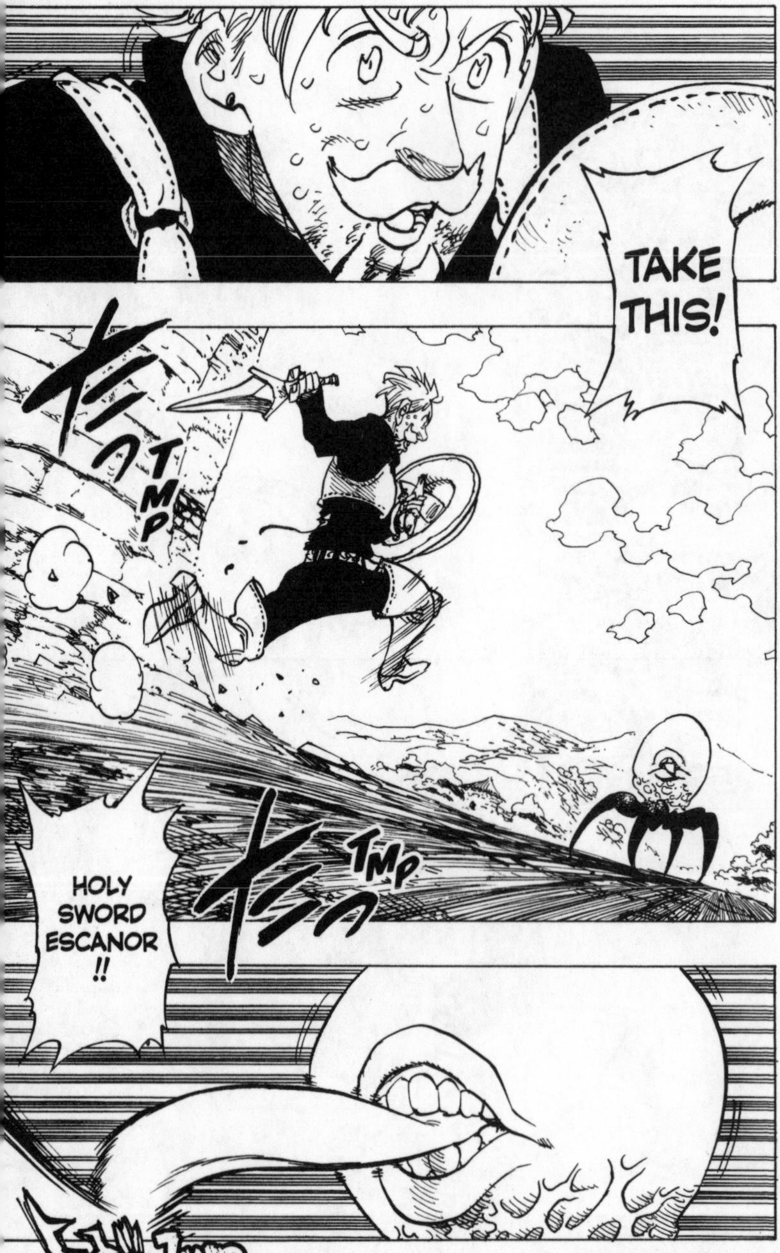
TAKE THIS!
TMP
HOLY SWORD ESCANOR !!
TMP
ZWIP

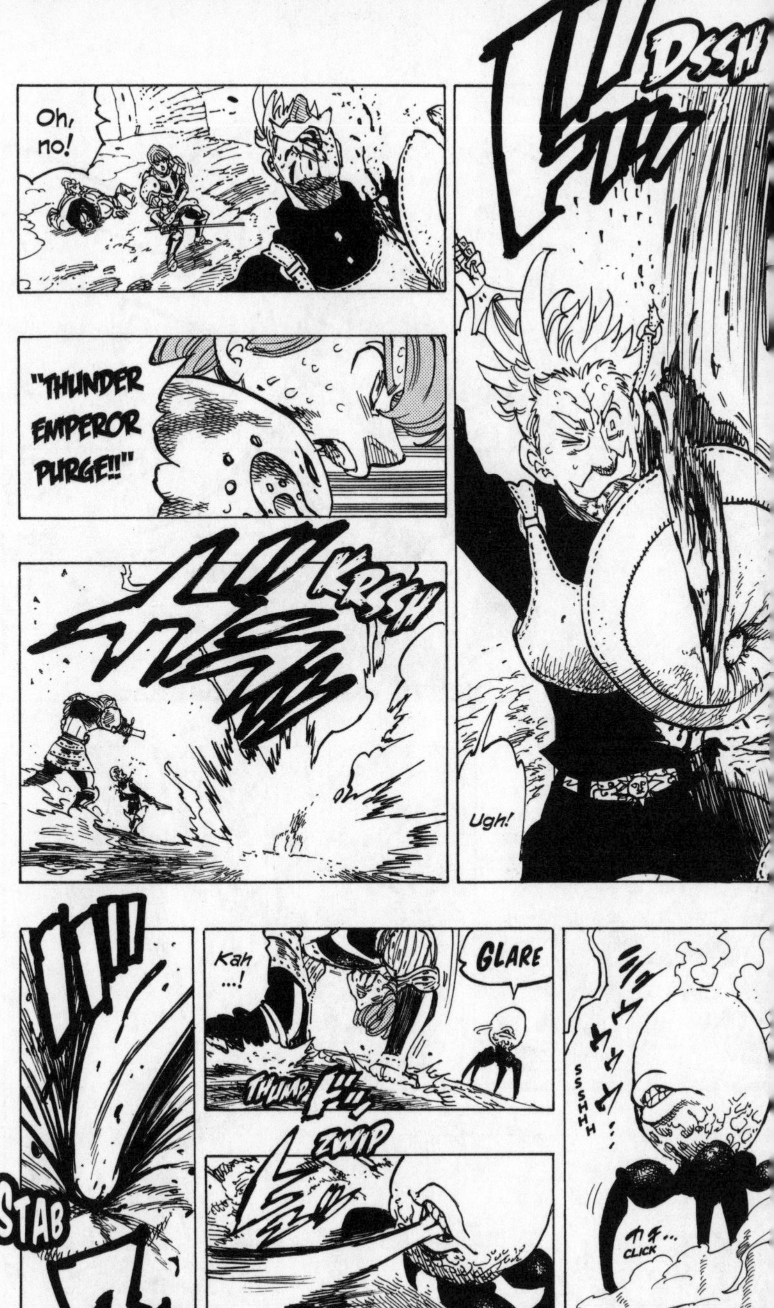
DSSH
Ugh!
Oh, no!
"THUNDER EMPEROR PURGE!!"
KRSSH
SSSHH
カチ...
CLICK
Kah ...!
GLARE
THUMP
ZWIP
STAB

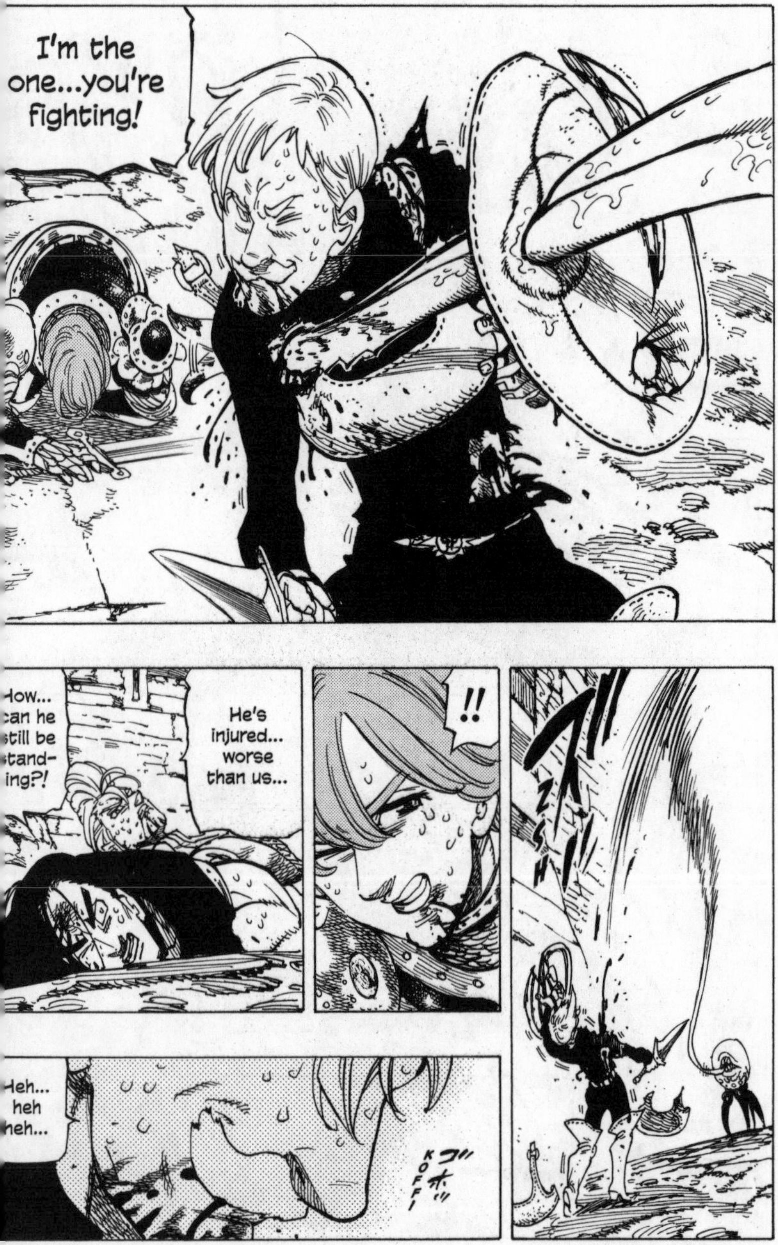

I'm the one...you're fighting!
ZSH
!!
He's injured... worse than us...
How... can he still be standing?!
Heh... heh heh...
KOFF

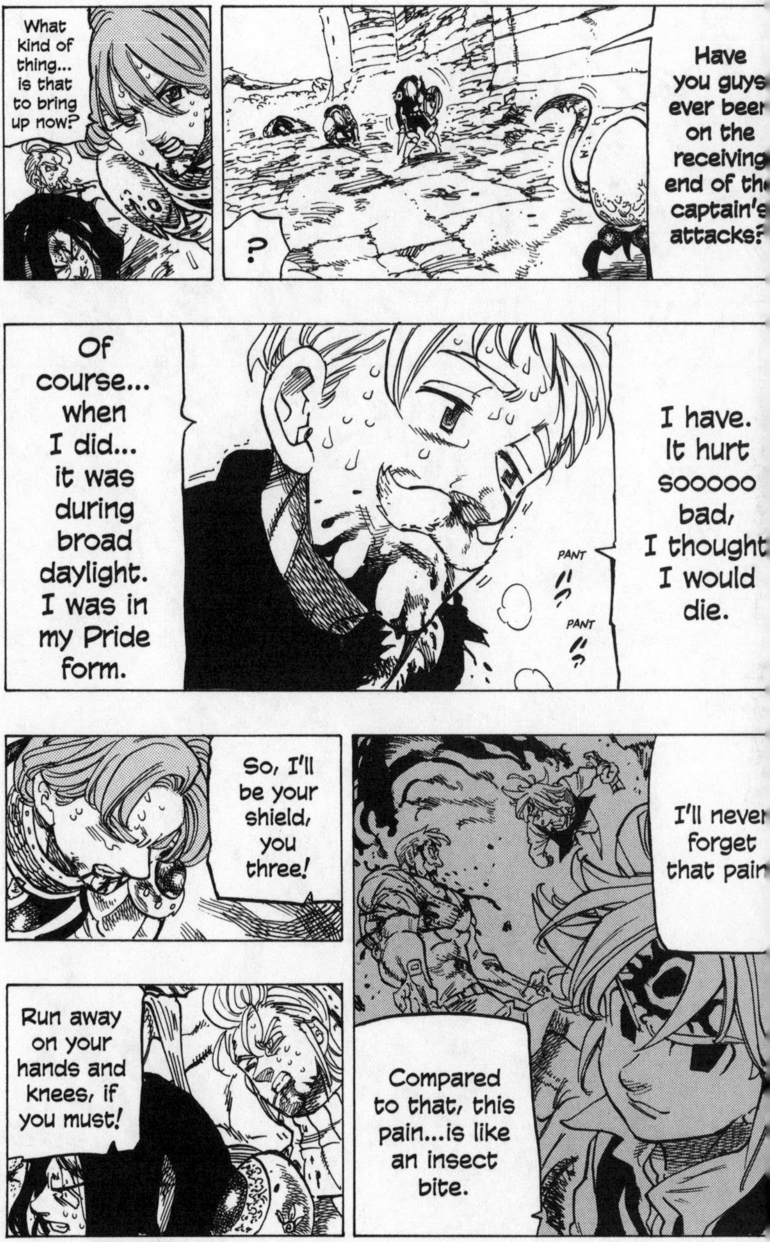
Have you guys ever been on the receiving end of the captain's attacks?
?
What kind of thing... is that to bring up now?
I have. It hurt sooooo bad, I thought I would die.
PANT
PANT
Of course... when I did... it was during broad daylight. I was in my Pride form.
I'll never forget that pain.
Compared to that, this pain...is like an insect bite.
So, I'll be your shield, you three!
Run away on your hands and knees, if you must!

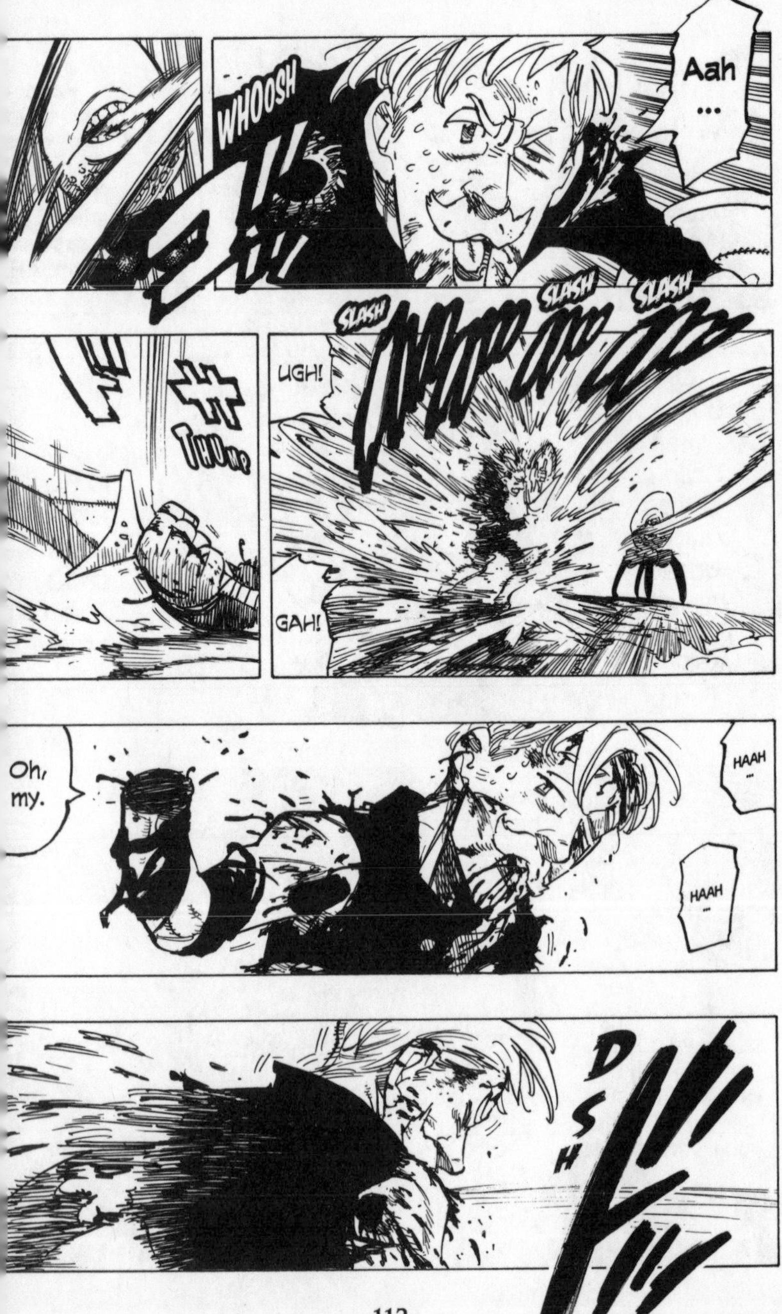
Aah ...
WHOOSH
SLASH
SLASH
SLASH
UGH!
GAH!
THUMP
HAAH ...
HAAH ...
Oh, my.
DSH

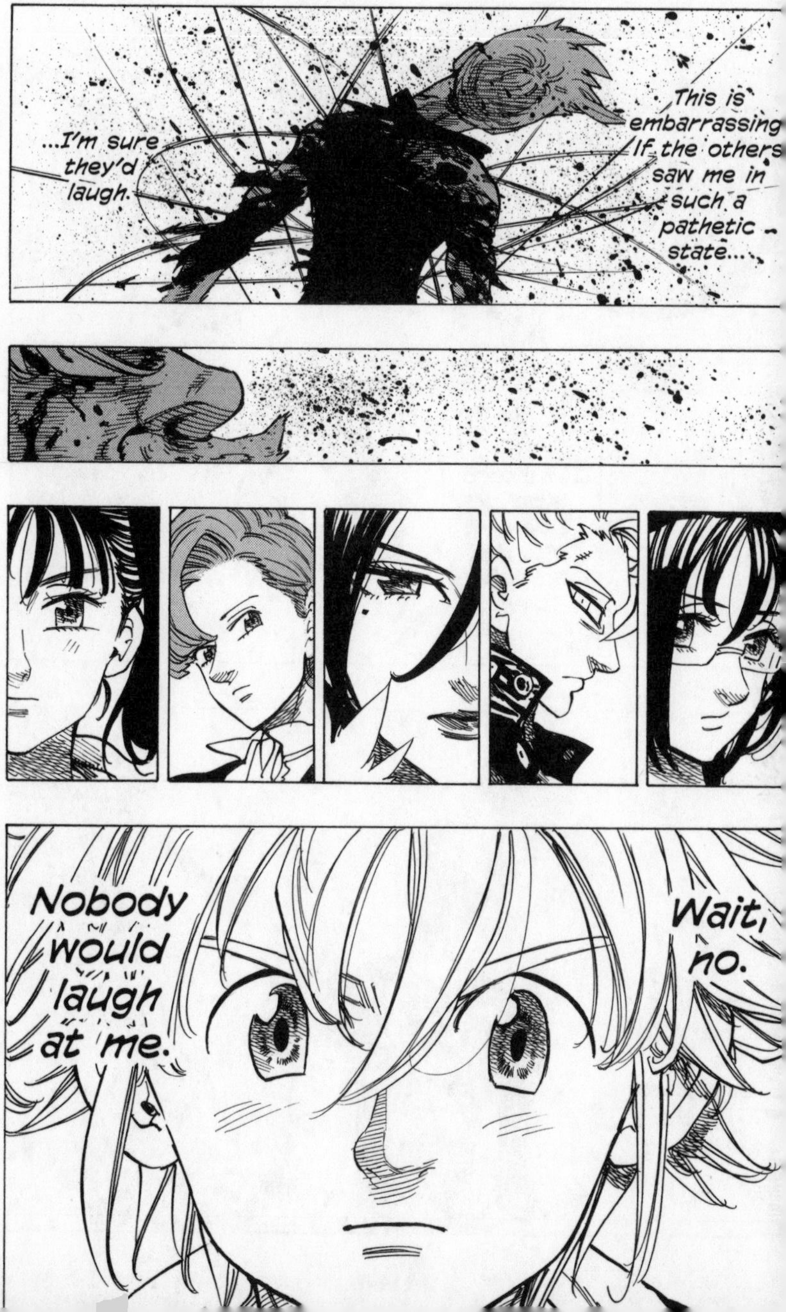
This is embarrassing. If the others saw me in such a pathetic state...
...I'm sure they'd laugh.
Wait, no.
Nobody would laugh at me.

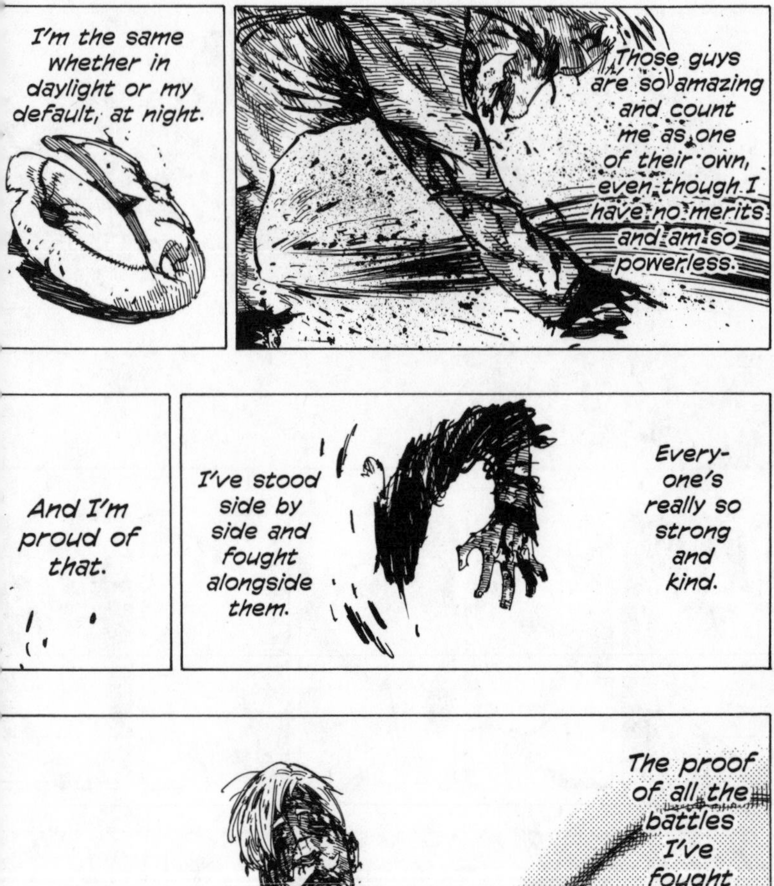
Those guys are so amazing and count me as one of their own, even though I have no merits and am so powerless.
I'm the same whether in daylight or my default, at night.
Every-one's really so strong and kind.
I've stood side by side and fought alongside them.
And I'm proud of that.
The proof of all the battles I've fought with them lives in my heart.
So, even if it's only in spirit, I want to be with everyone to the very end.

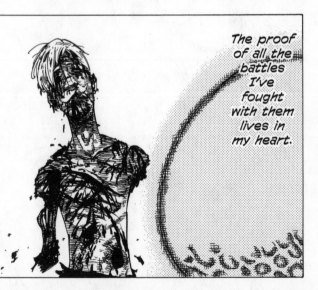

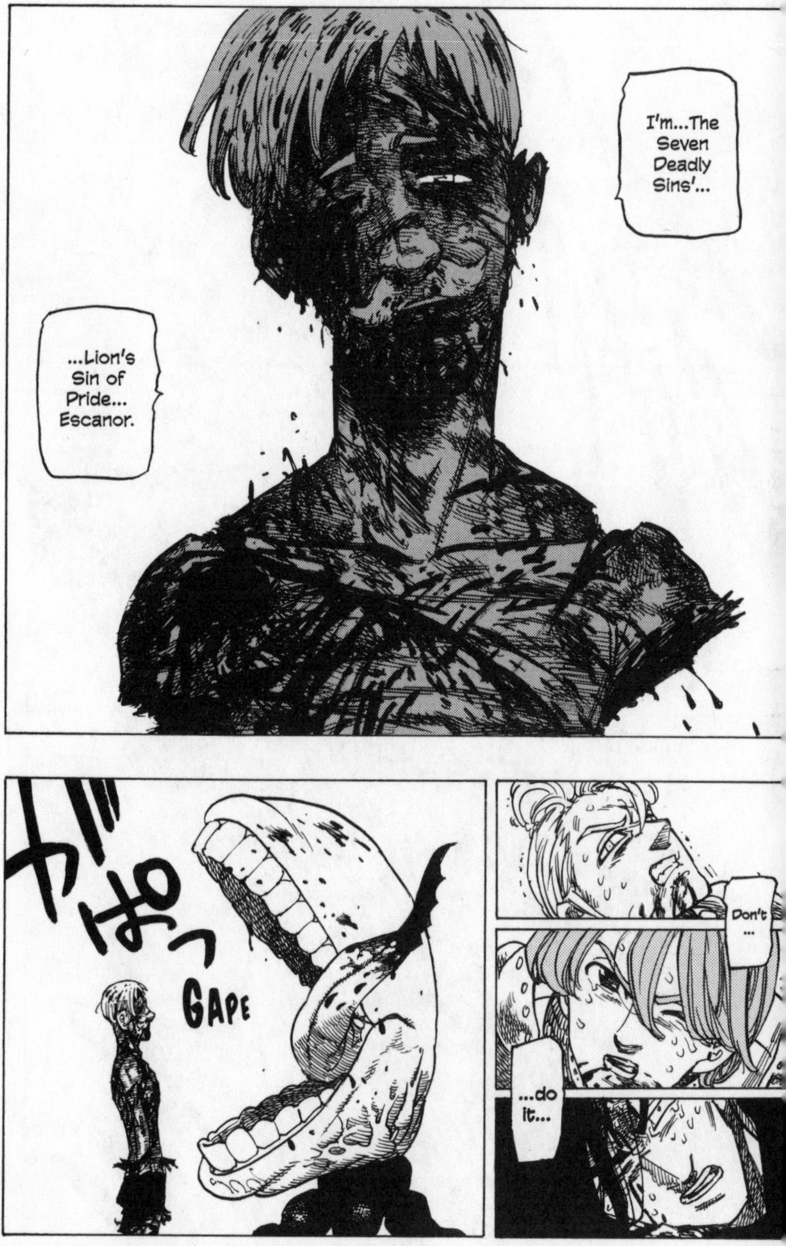
I'm...The Seven Deadly Sins'...
...Lion's Sin of Pride... Escanor.
Don't ...
...do it...
がぱっ
GAPE

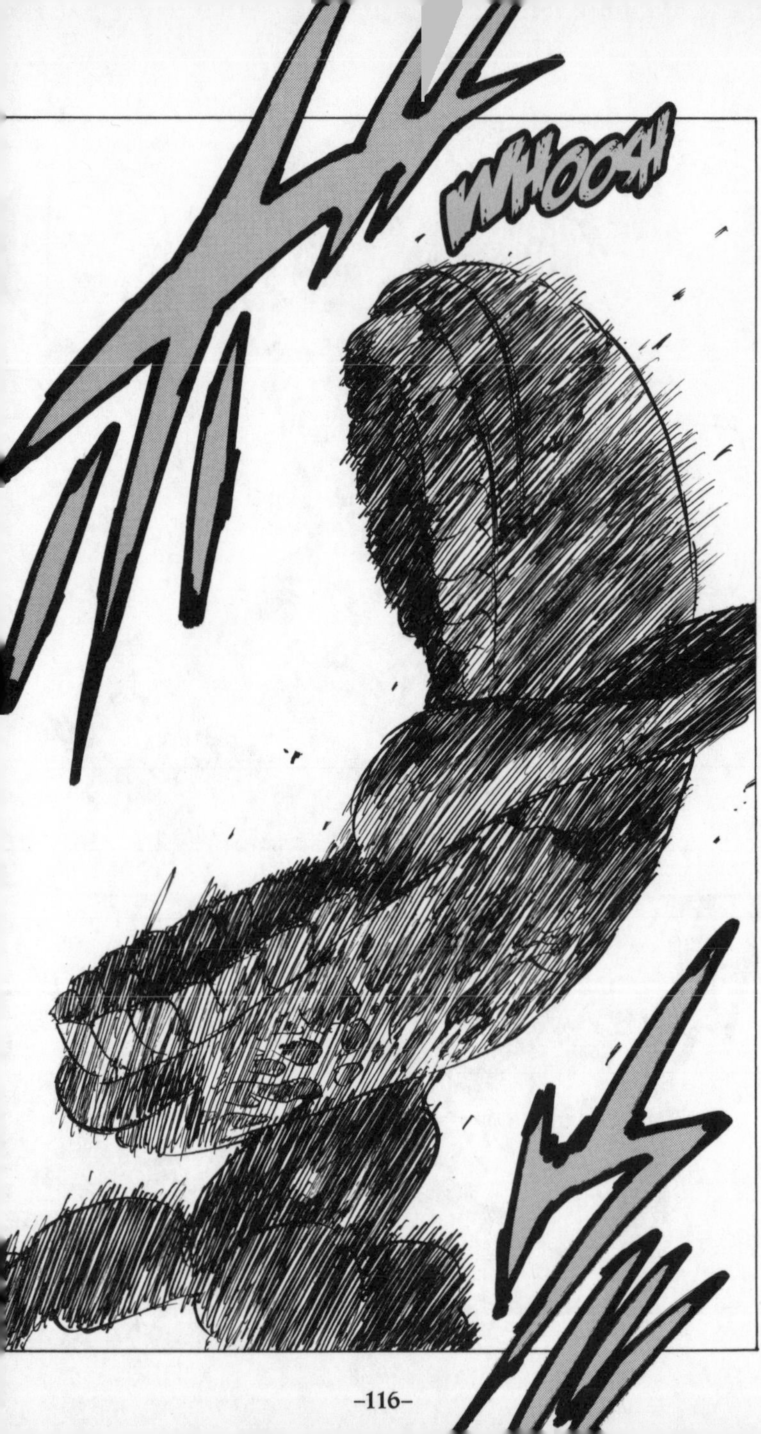
WHOOSH

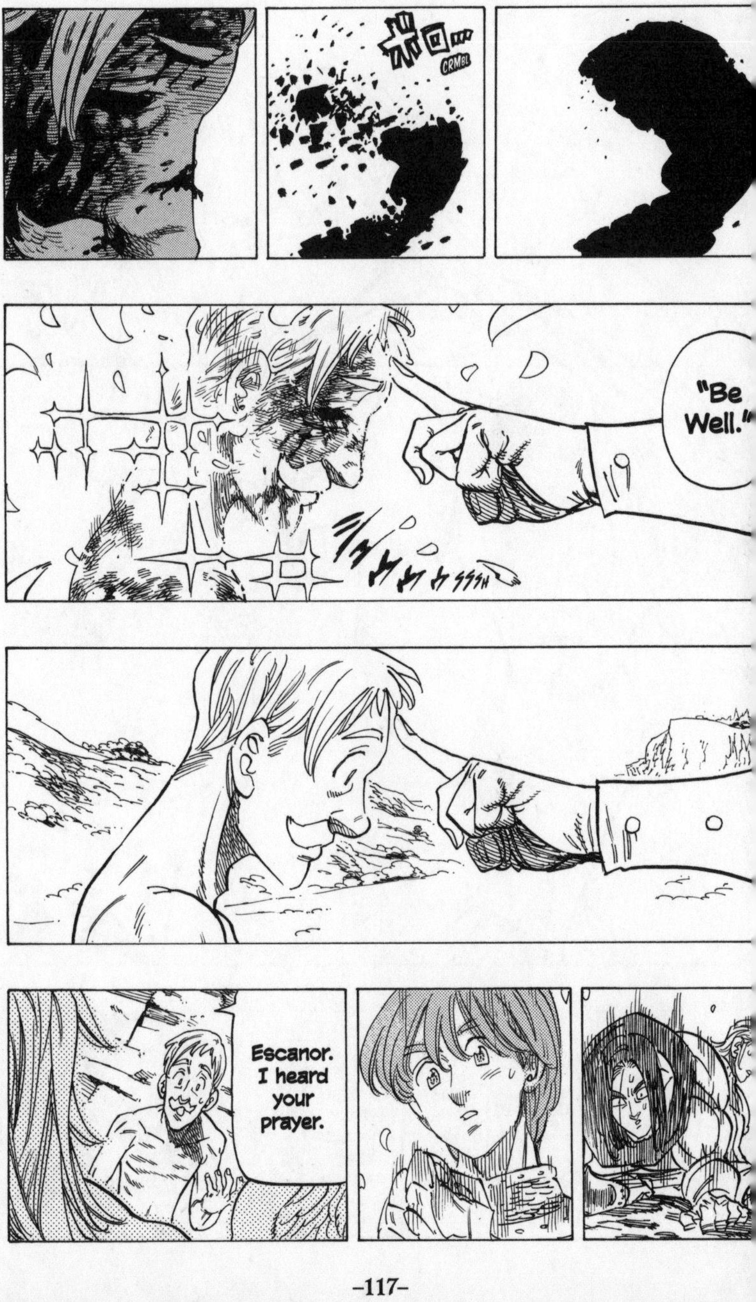
CRMBL
"Be Well."
HSSS
Escanor. I heard your prayer.

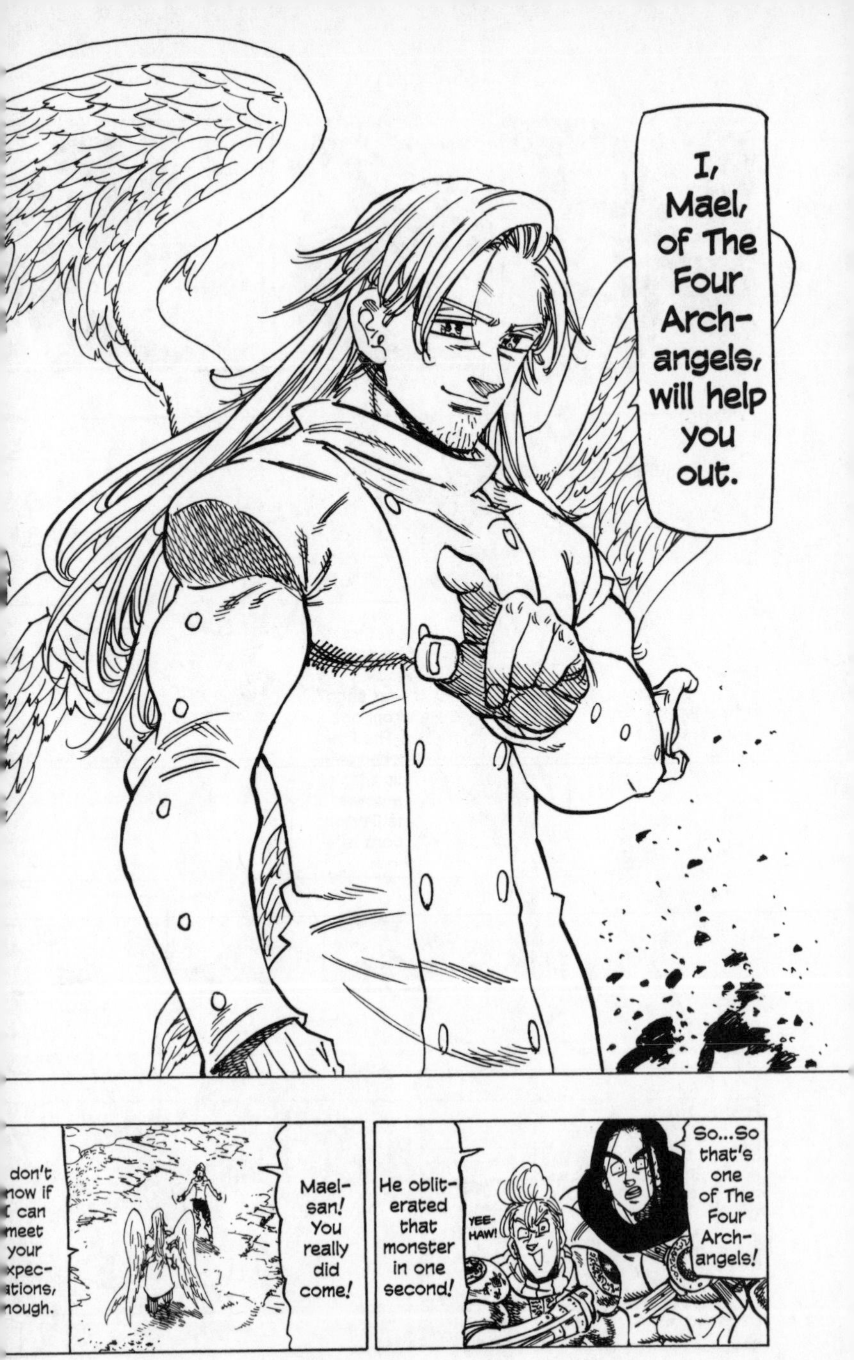
I, Mael, of The Four Arch-angels, will help you out.
So...So that's one of The Four Arch-angels!
YEE-HAW!
He oblit-erated that monster in one second!
Mael-san! You really did come!
don't
now if
can
meet
your
xpec-
ations,
hough.

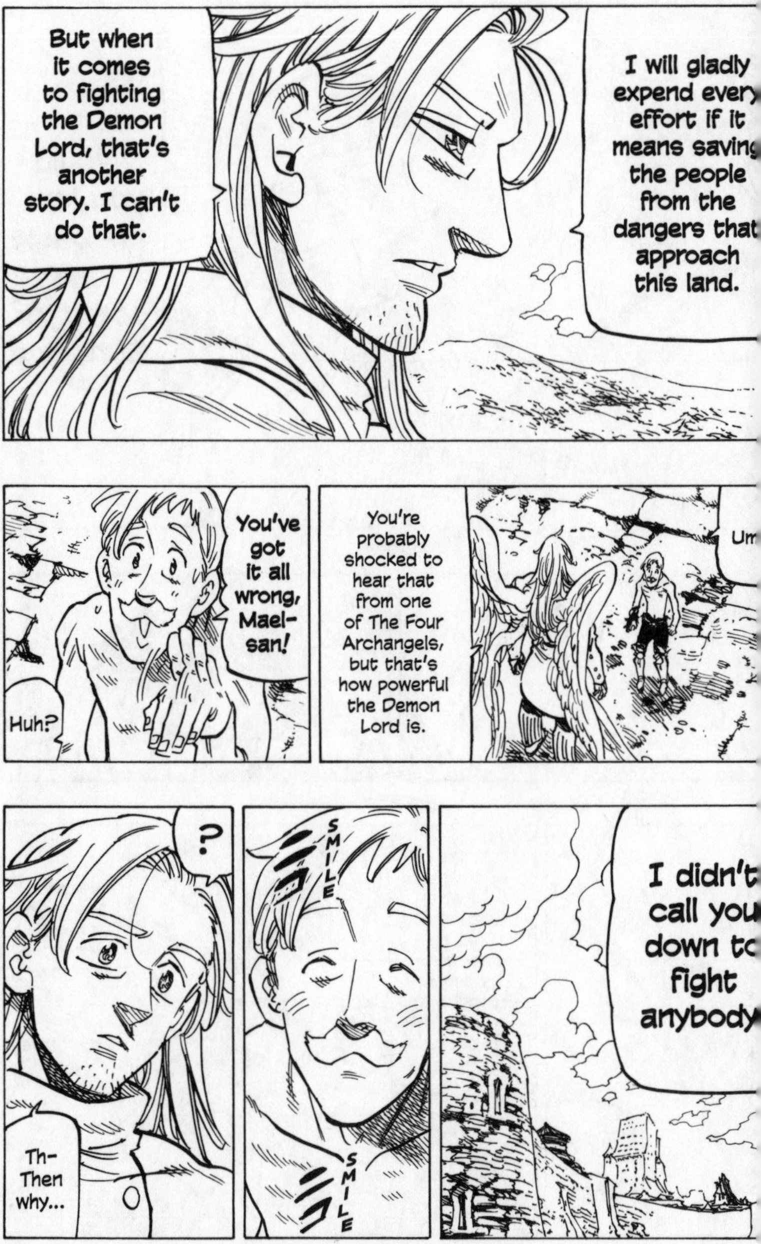

I will gladly expend every effort if it means saving the people from the dangers that approach this land.
But when it comes to fighting the Demon Lord, that's another story. I can't do that.
Um
You're probably shocked to hear that from one of The Four Archangels, but that's how powerful the Demon Lord is.
You've got it all wrong, Mael-san!
Huh?
I didn't call you down to fight anybody
SMILE
SMILE
?
Th- Then why...

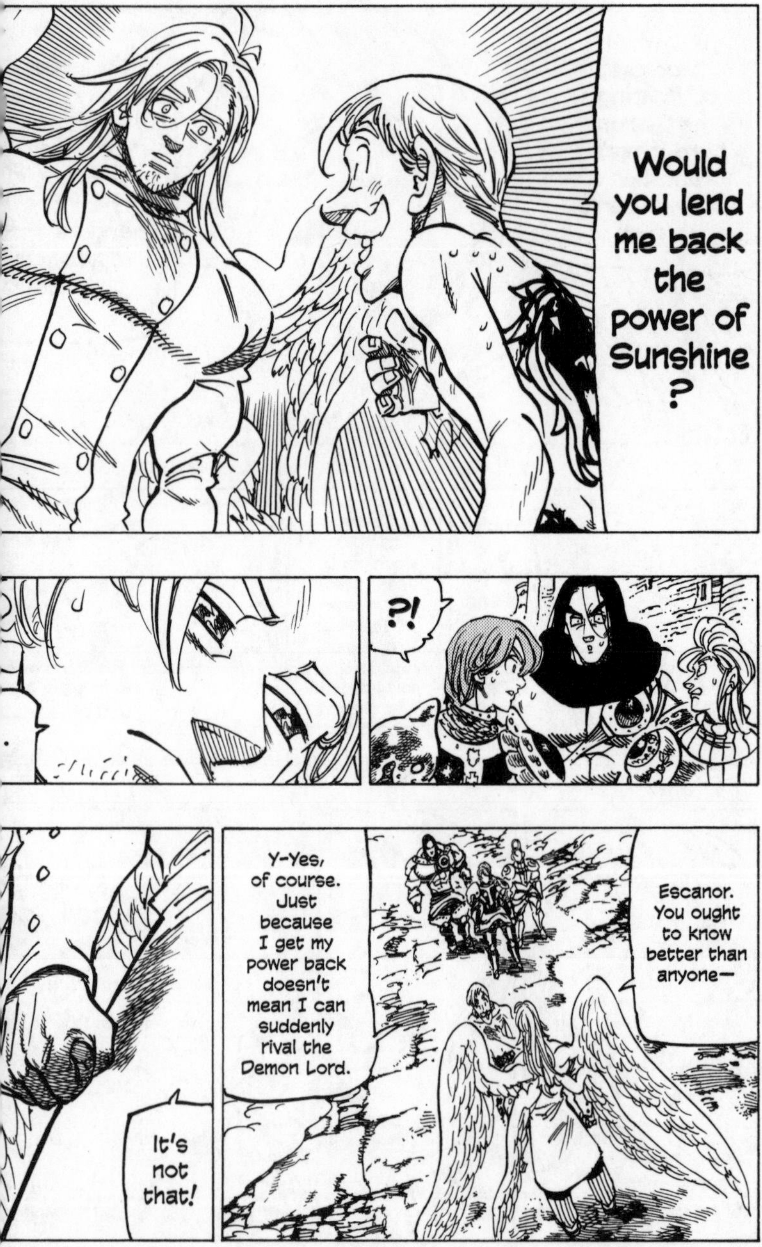
Would you lend me back the power of Sunshine?
?!
Escanor. You ought to know better than anyone—
Y-Yes, of course. Just because I get my power back doesn't mean I can suddenly rival the Demon Lord.
It's not that!

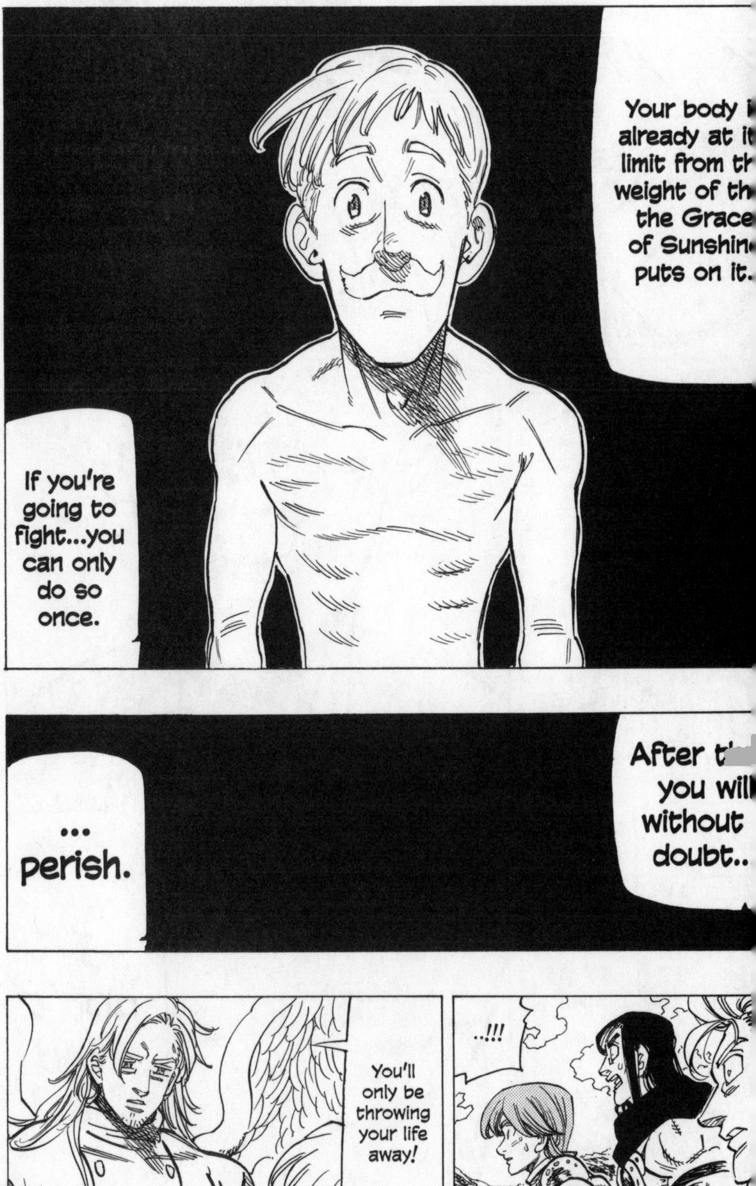
Your body i already at it limit from th weight of th the Grace of Sunshin puts on it.
If you're going to fight...you can only do so once.
After t you wil without doubt..
...perish.
..!!!
You'll only be throwing your life away!

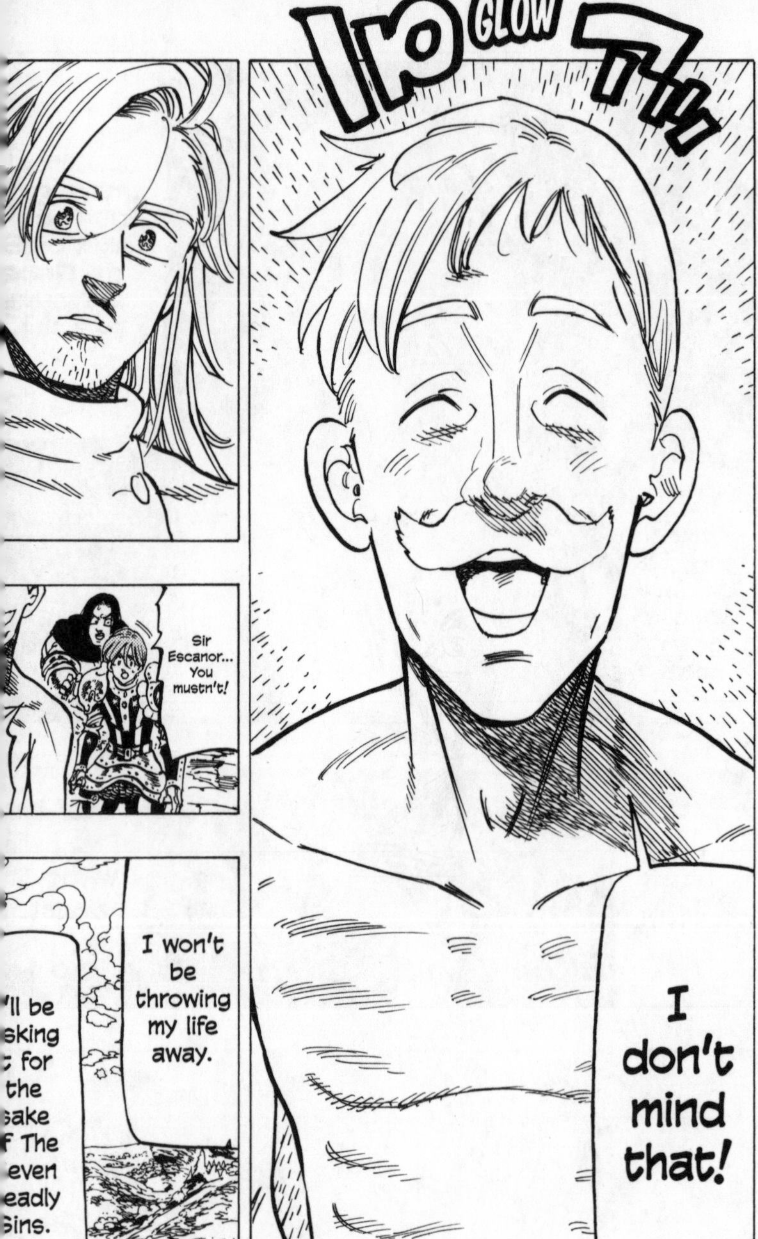
GLOW
I don't mind that!
Sir Escanor... You mustn't!
I won't be throwing my life away.
'll be sking for the sake f The even eadly Sins.

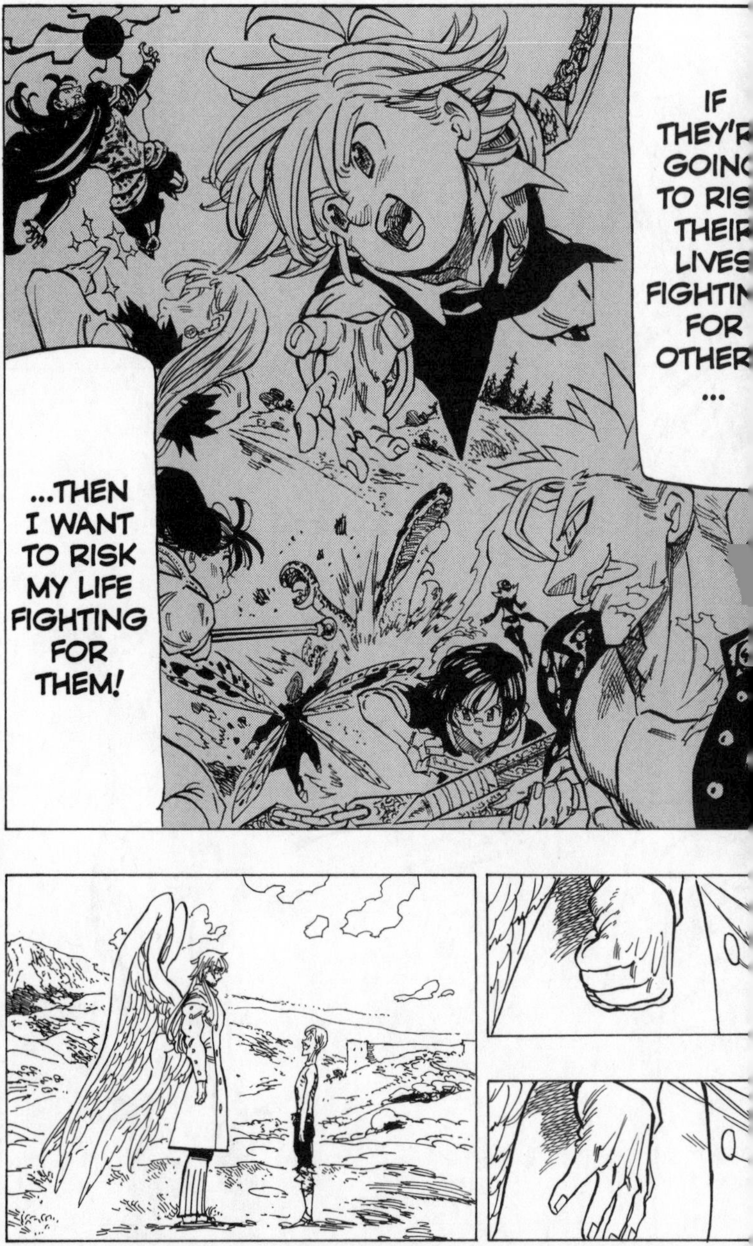
IF THEY'R GOIN TO RIS THEIR LIVES FIGHTIN FOR OTHER ...
...THEN I WANT TO RISK MY LIFE FIGHTING FOR THEM!

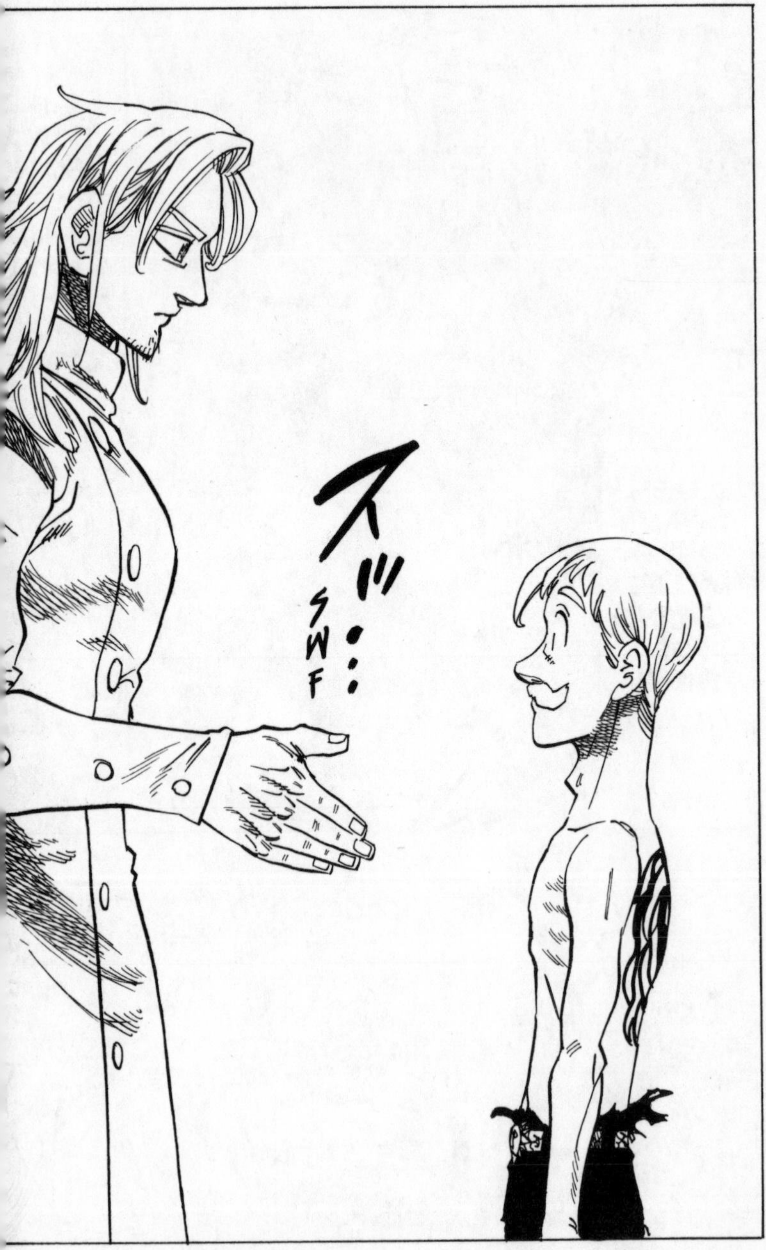
SWF

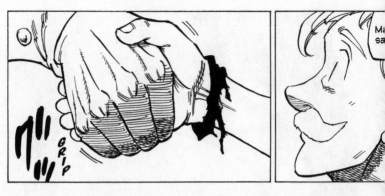

There's still time before noon.

...You right

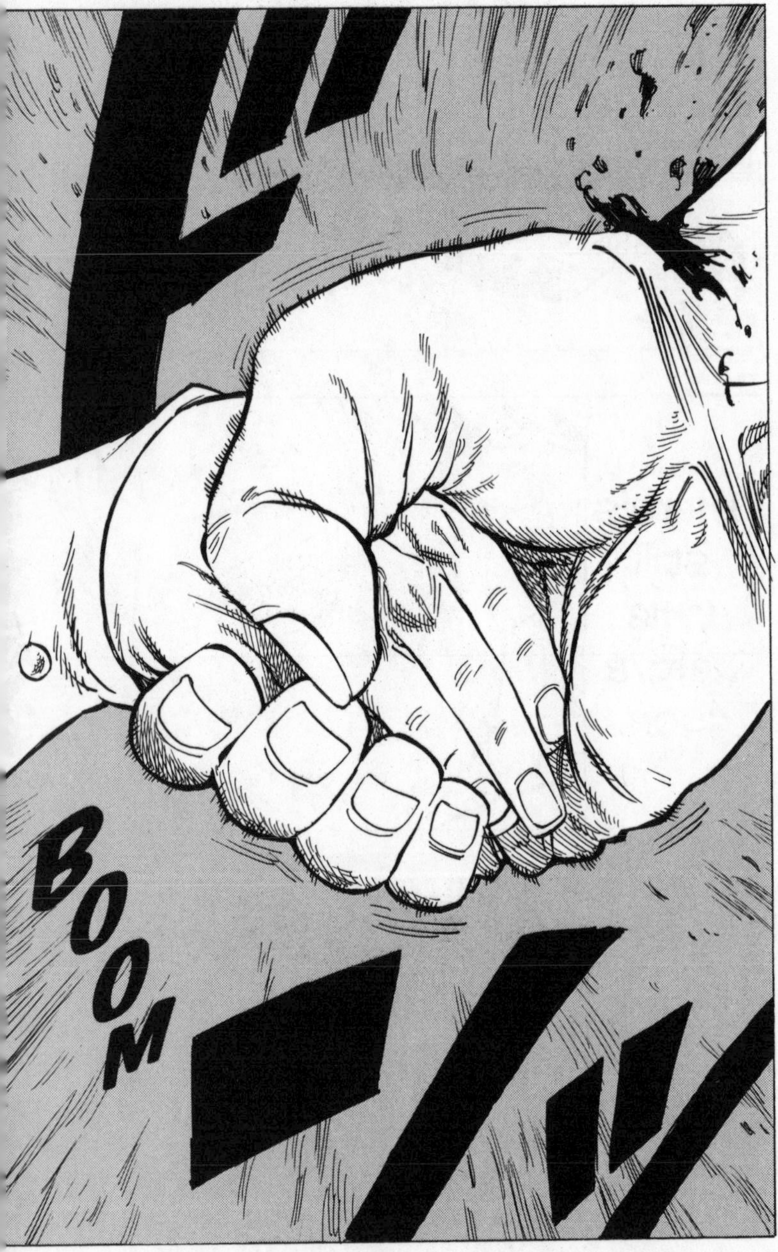
BOOM

THE SEVEN DEADLY SINS

Chapter 318 - Ambiguous Fight

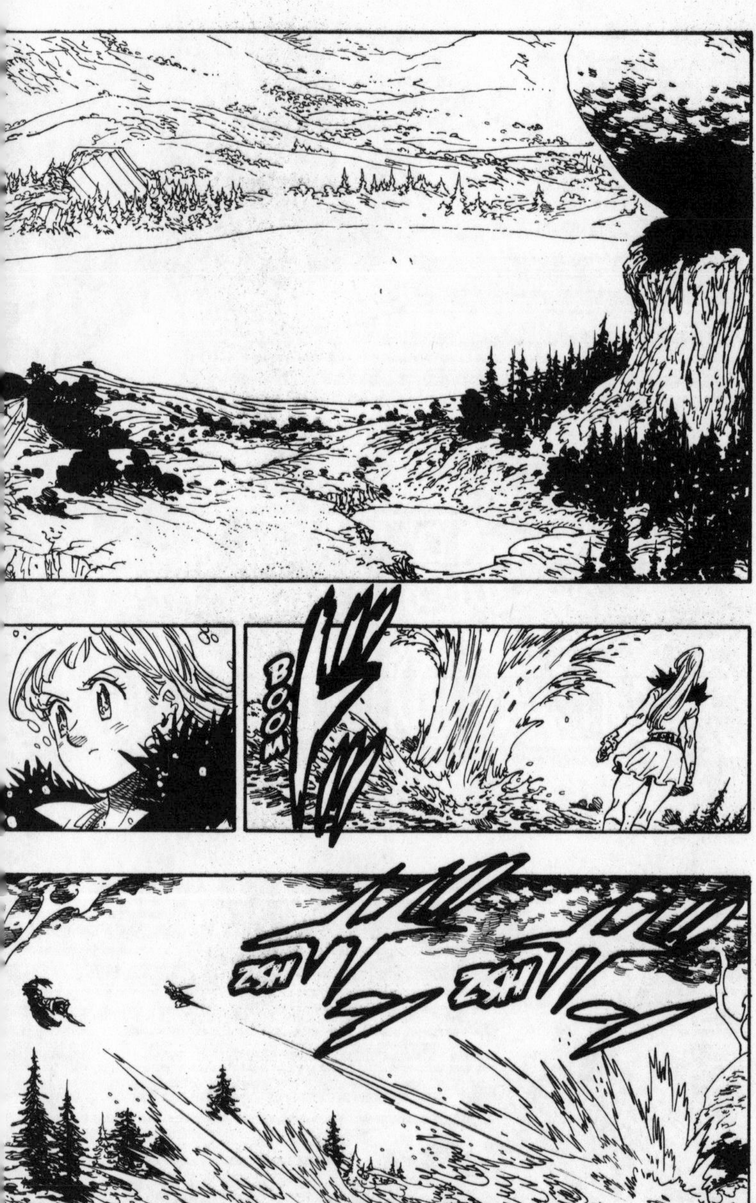
BOOM
ZSH
ZSH

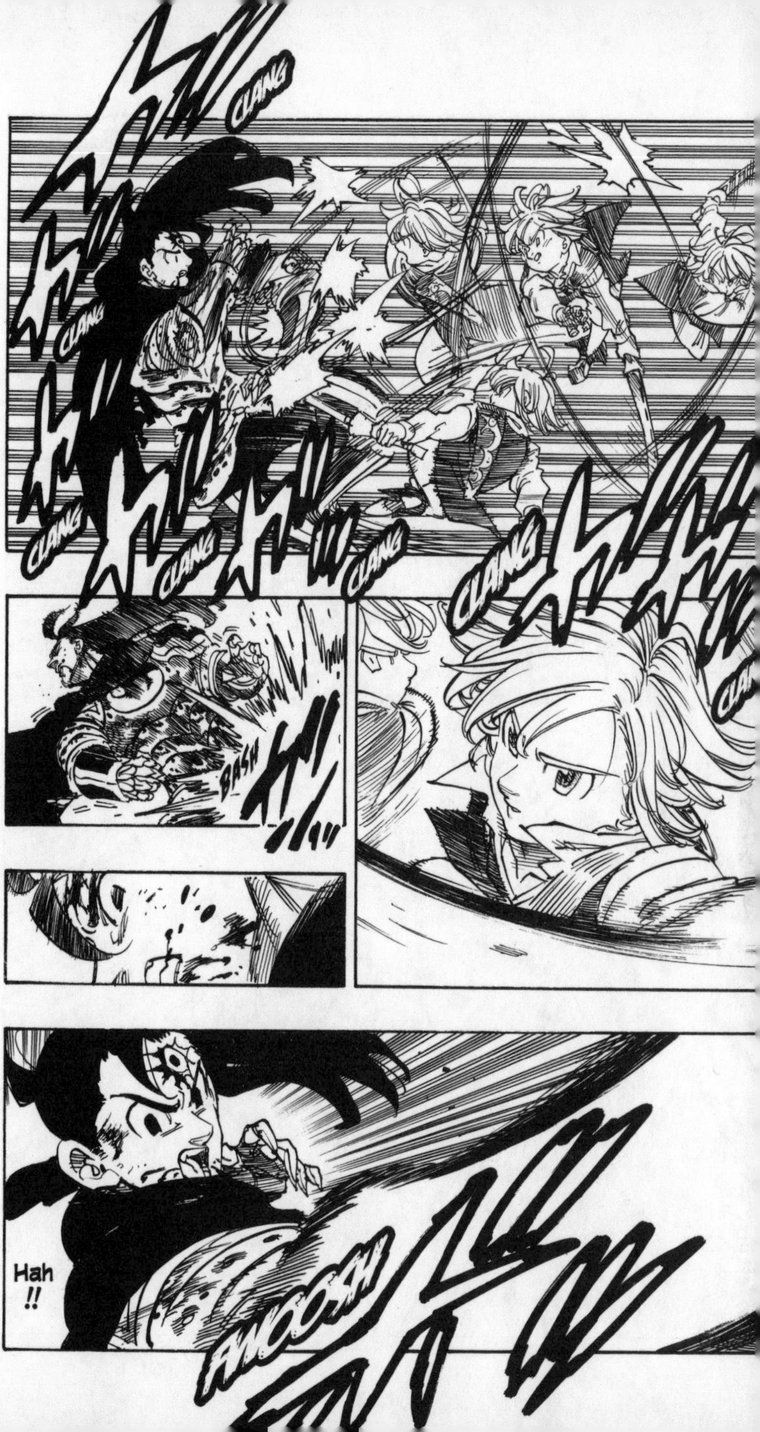
CLANG
CLANG
CLANG
CLANG
CLANG
CLANG
CLANG
BASH
Hah!!
FWOOSH

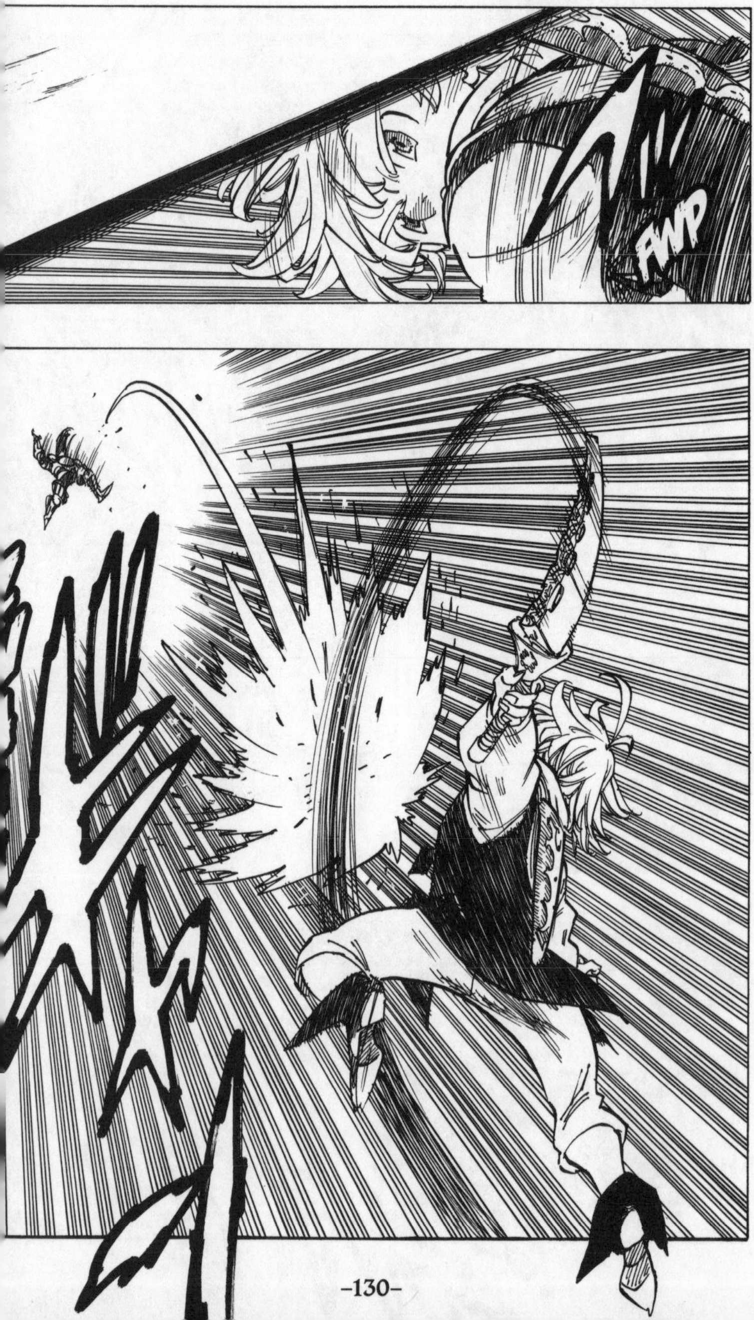
FWP

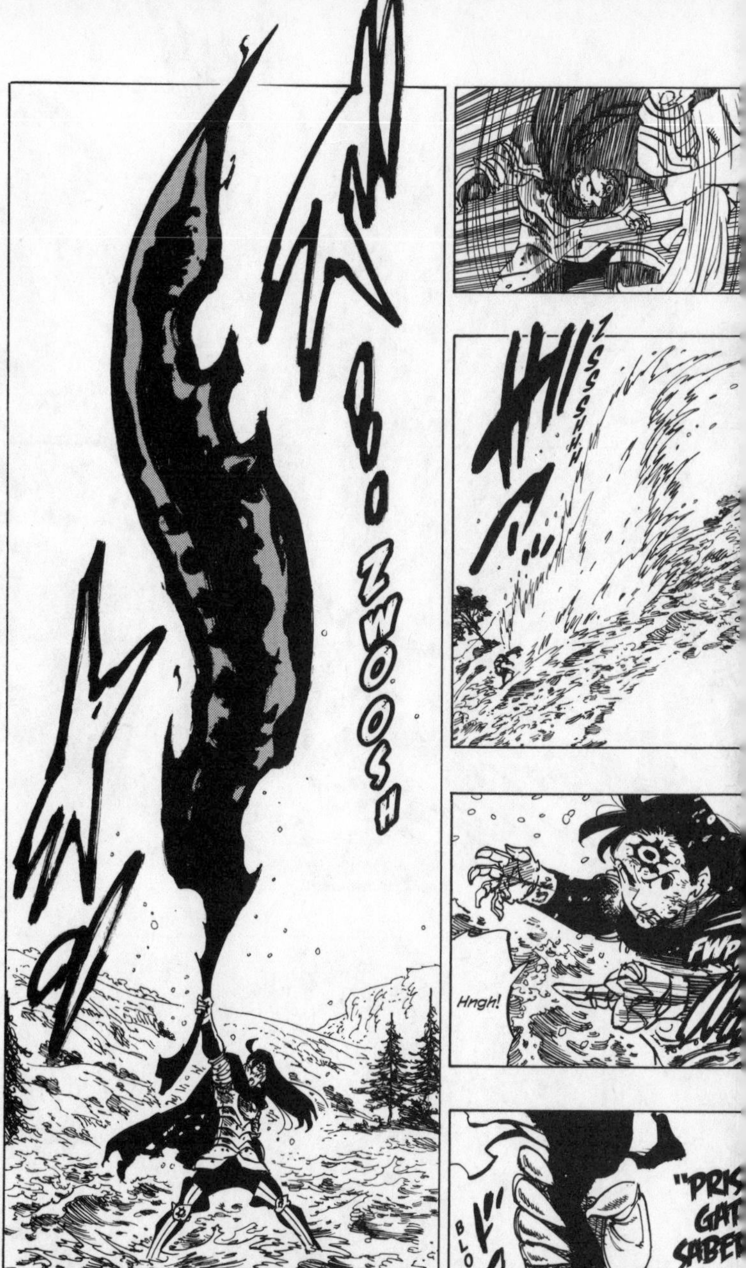
ZSSSHHH
FWP
Hngh!
BLOOP
"PRIS
GAT
SABE
ZWOOOSH

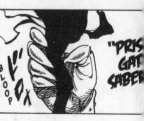

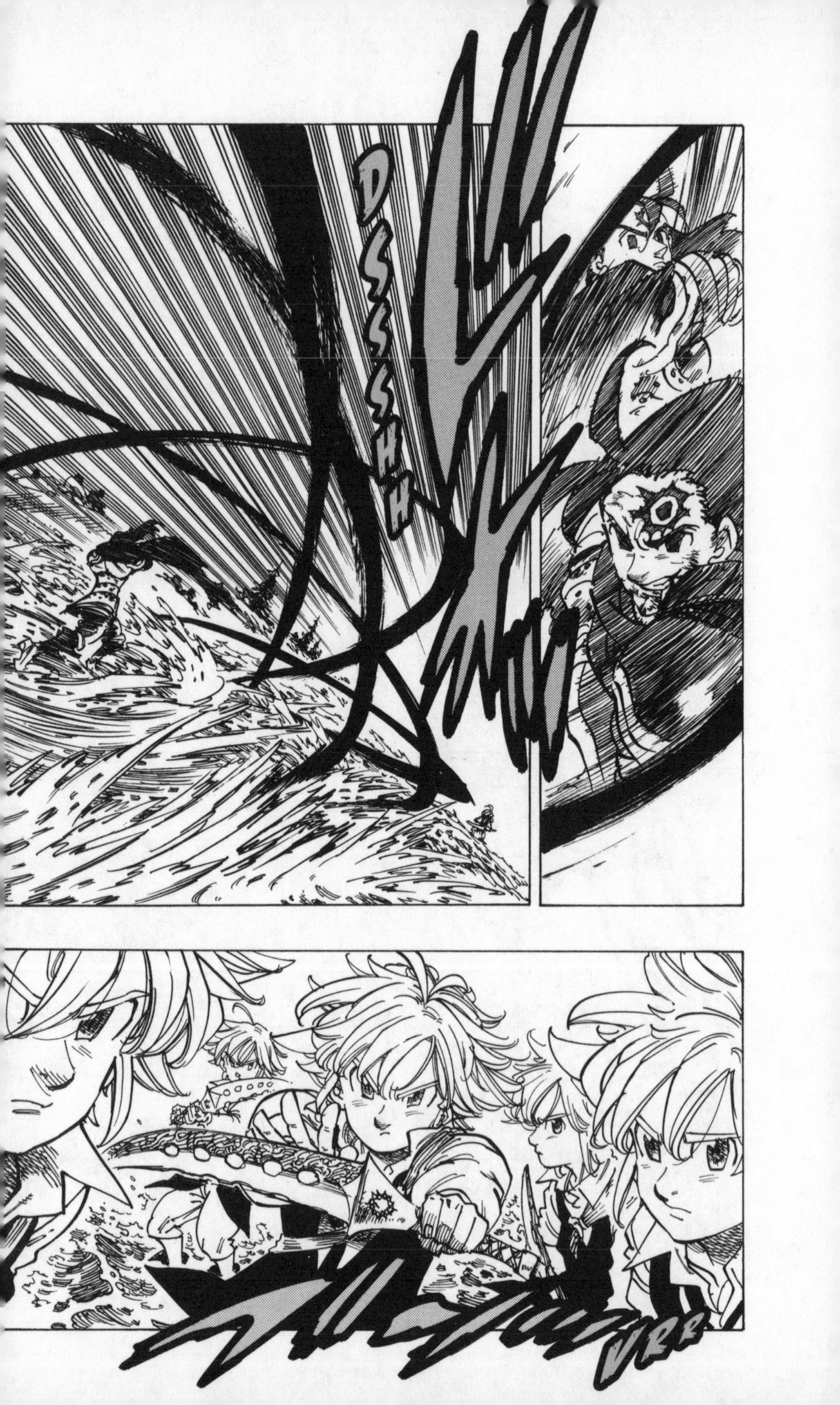
DSSSHH
VRR

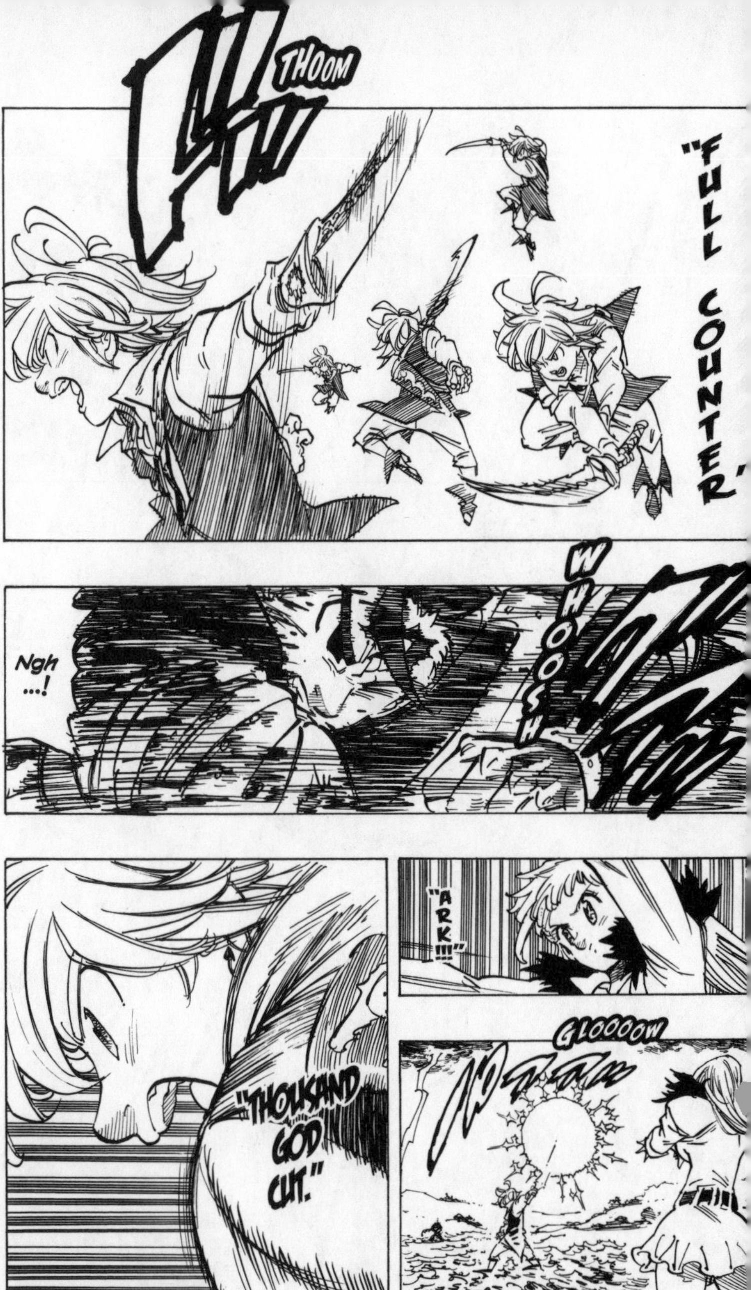
THOOM
"FULL COUNTER,"
WHOOOSH
Ngh ...!
"ARK!!!"
"THOUSAND GOD CUT."
GLOOOOW

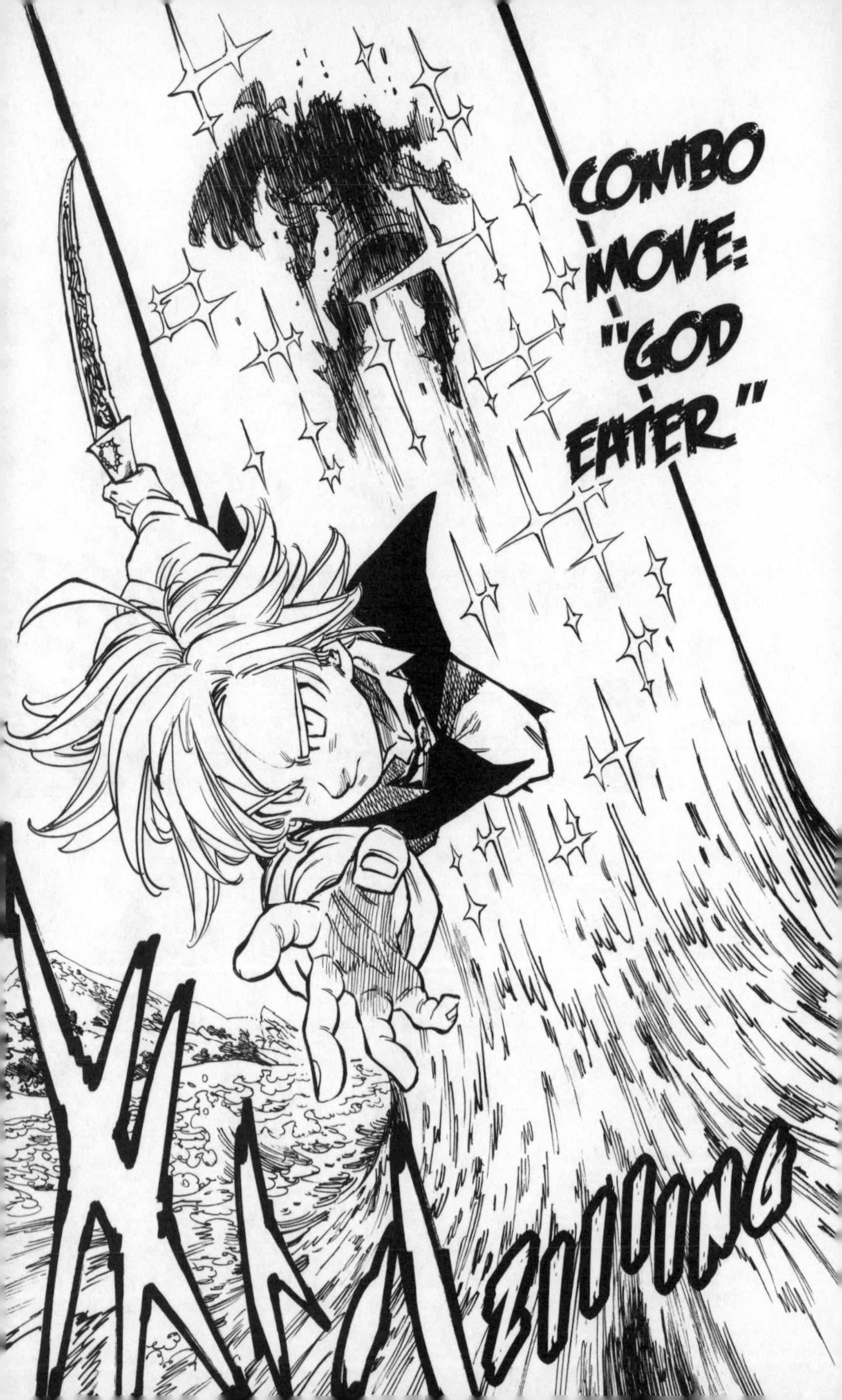
COMBO MOVE: "GOD EATER"
ZOOOONG

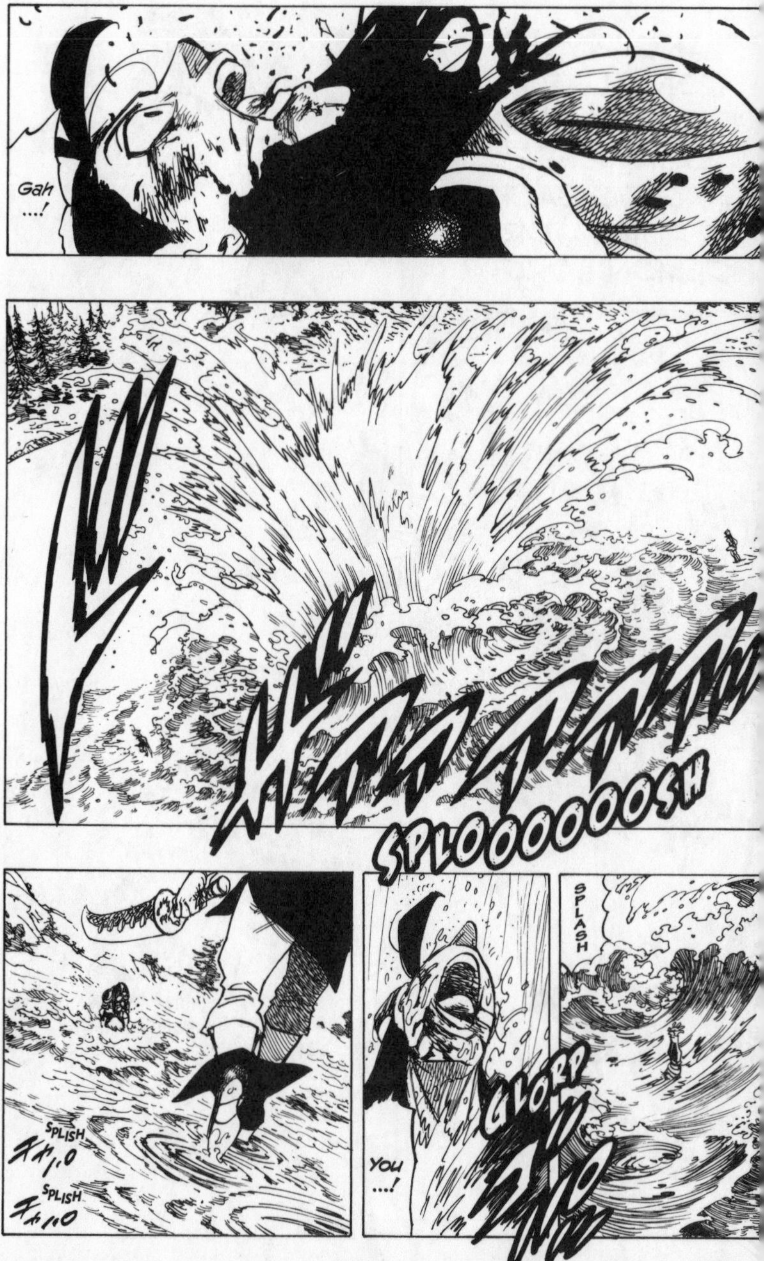
Gah ...!
SPLOOOOOOOSH
SPLASH
GLORP
You ...!
SPLISH
SPLISH

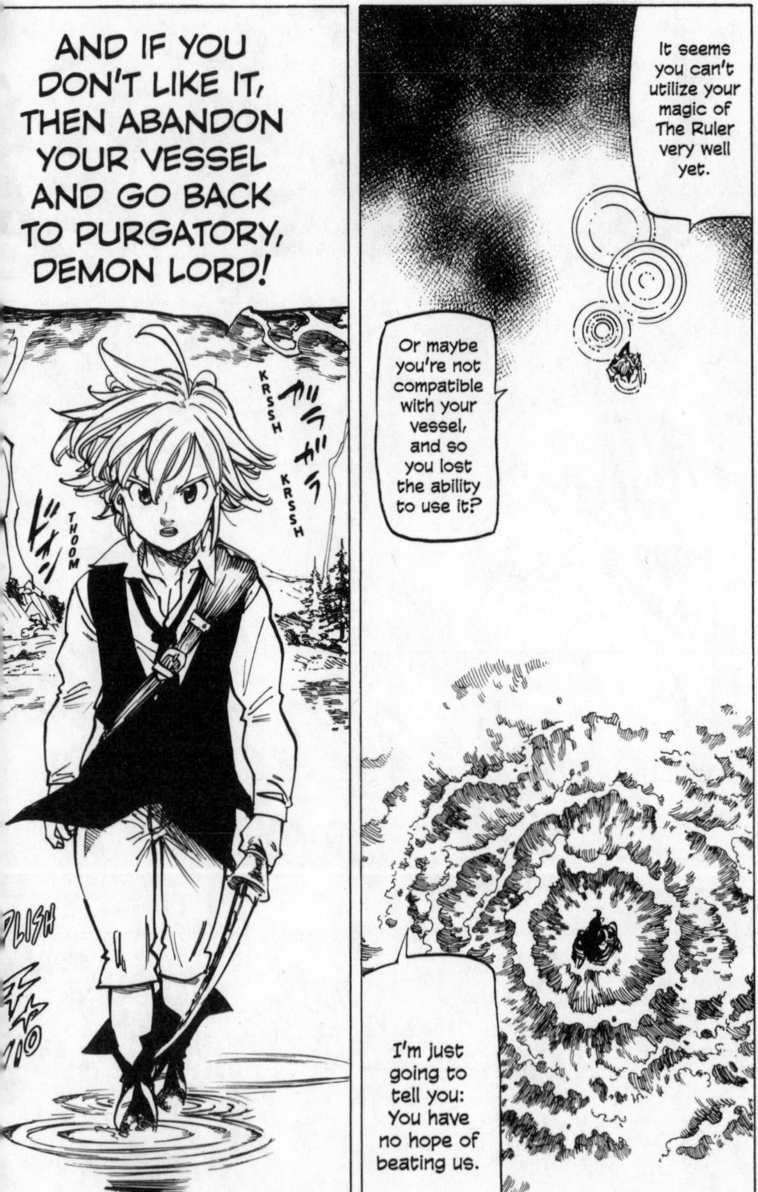
It seems you can't utilize your magic of The Ruler very well yet.
Or maybe you're not compatible with your vessel, and so you lost the ability to use it?
I'm just going to tell you: You have no hope of beating us.
AND IF YOU DON'T LIKE IT, THEN ABANDON YOUR VESSEL AND GO BACK TO PURGATORY, DEMON LORD!
KRSSH
KRSSH
THOOM

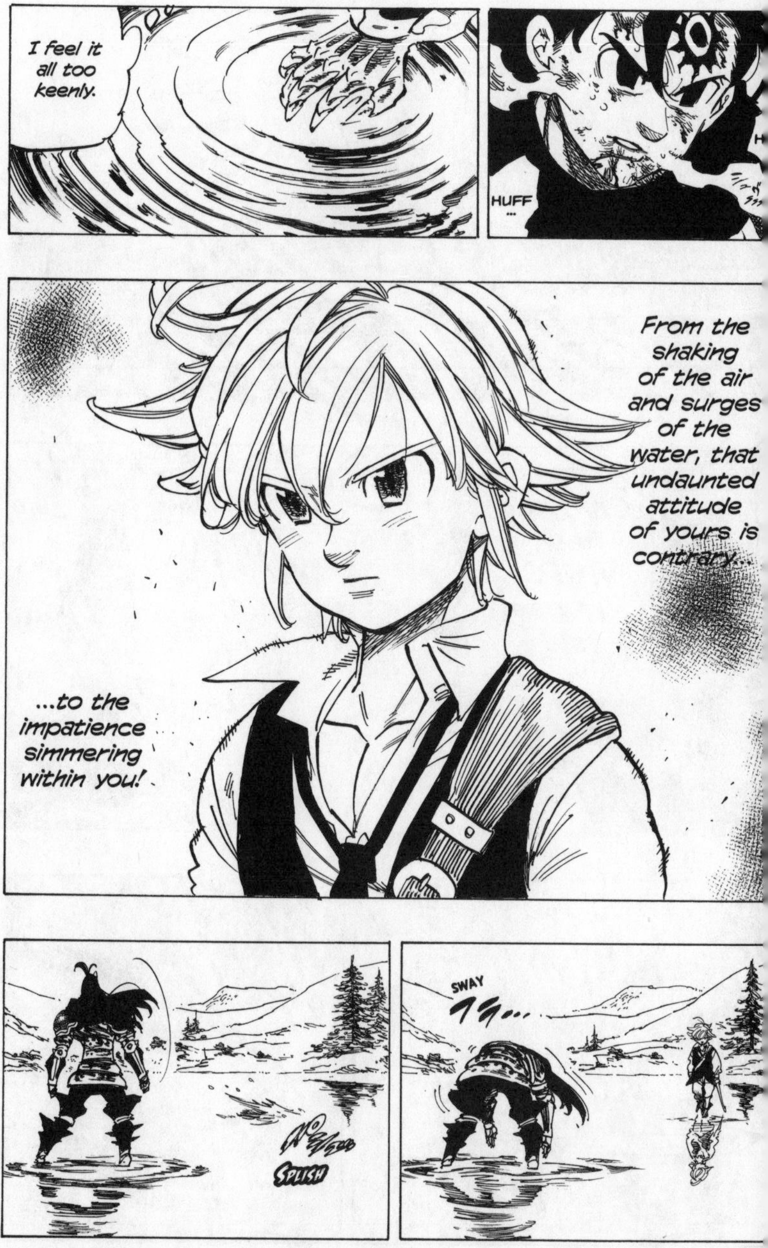
HUFF ...
I feel it all too keenly.
From the shaking of the air and surges of the water, that undaunted attitude of yours is contrary...
...to the impatience simmering within you!
SWAY
SPLISH

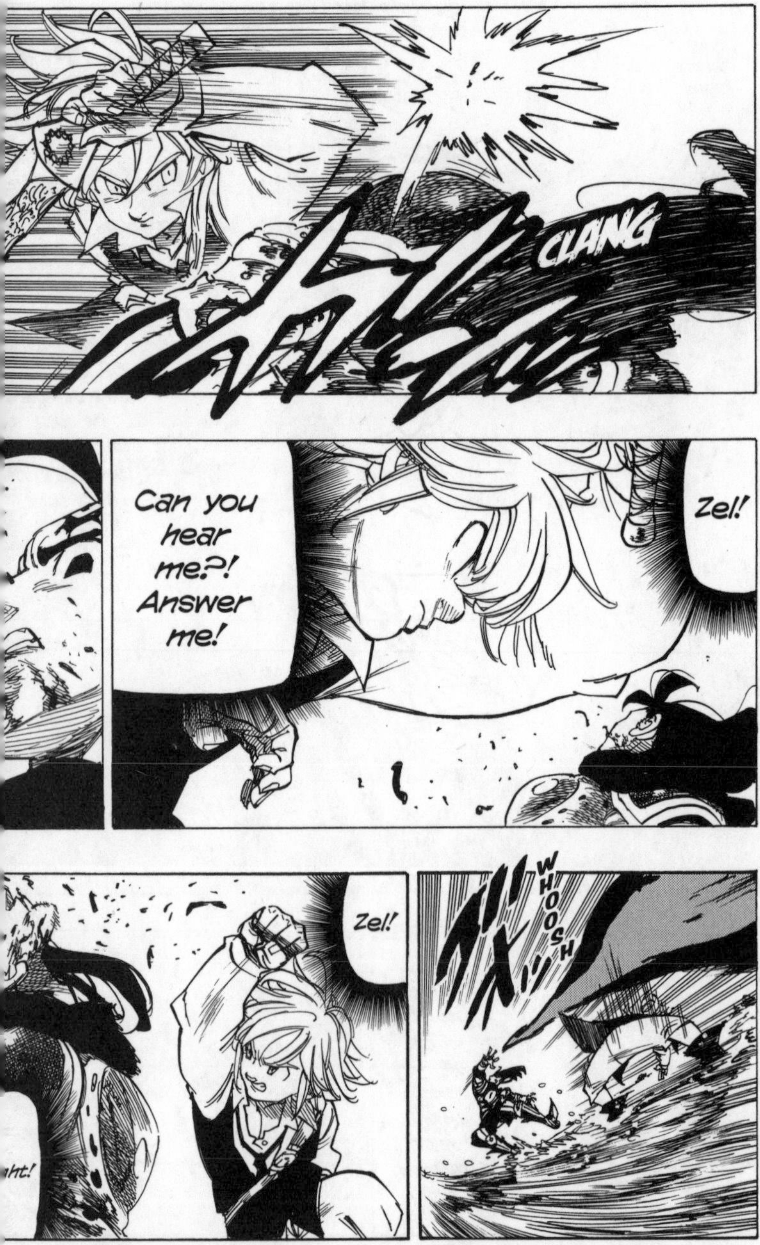
CLANG
Zel!
Can you hear me?! Answer me!
WHOOSH
Zel!

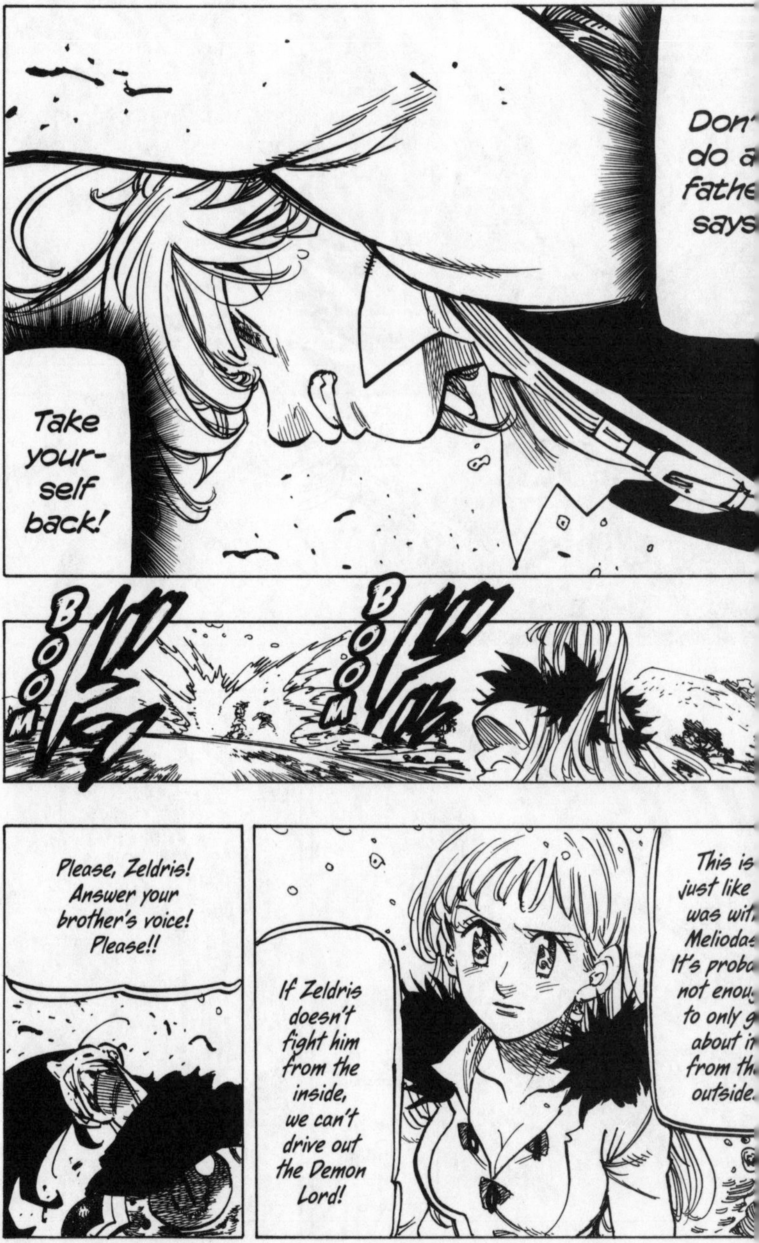
Don' do a fathe says
Take your-self back!
BOOOM
BOOOM
This is just like was wit Meliodas It's proba not enou to only g about i from th outside.
If Zeldris doesn't fight him from the inside, we can't drive out the Demon Lord!
Please, Zeldris! Answer your brother's voice! Please!!

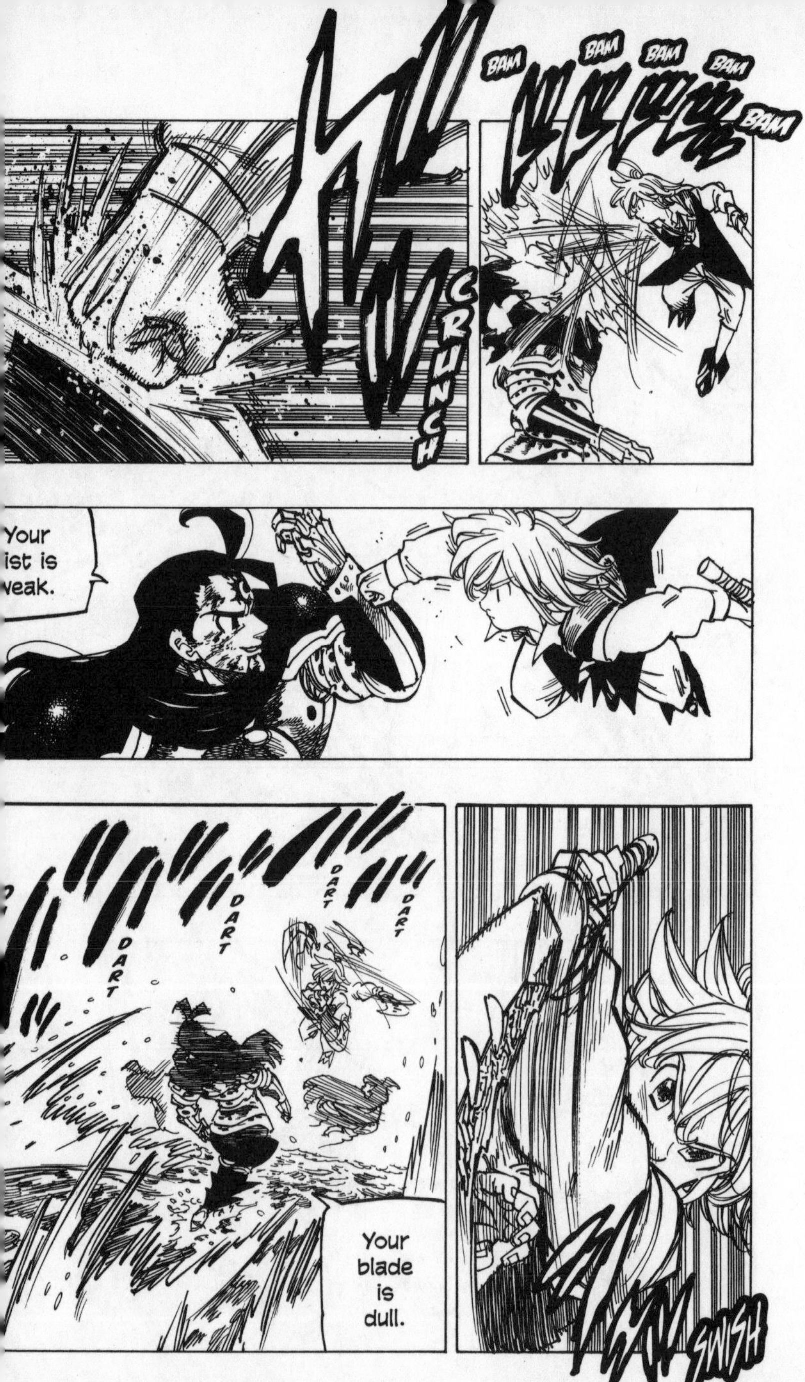
BAM BAM BAM BAM BAM
CRUNCH
Your ist is weak.
Your blade is dull.
SWISH
DART
DART
DART
DART

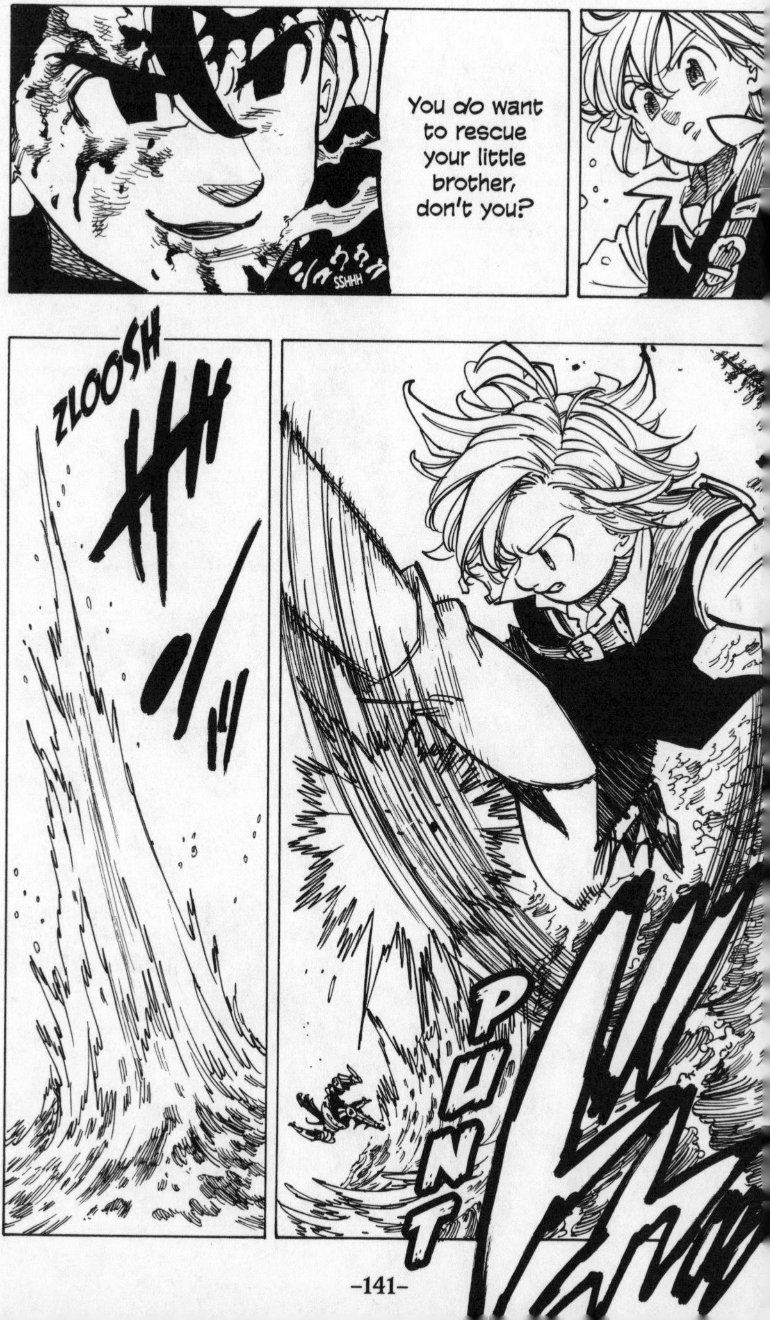
You do want to rescue your little brother, don't you?
SSHHH
PUNT
ZLOOSH

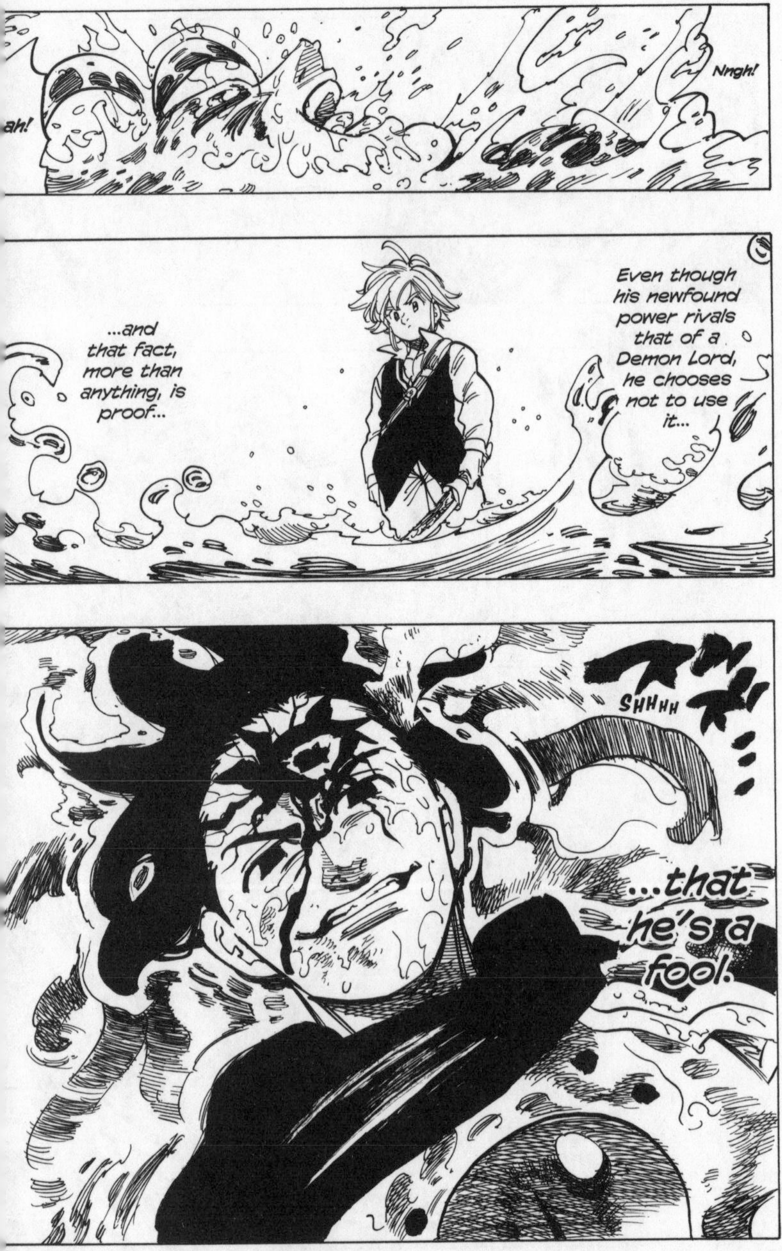
Nngh!
ah!
Even though his newfound power rivals that of a Demon Lord, he chooses not to use it...
...and that fact, more than anything, is proof...
SHHHH
...that he's a fool.

Chapter 319 - Unforgivable Deadlock

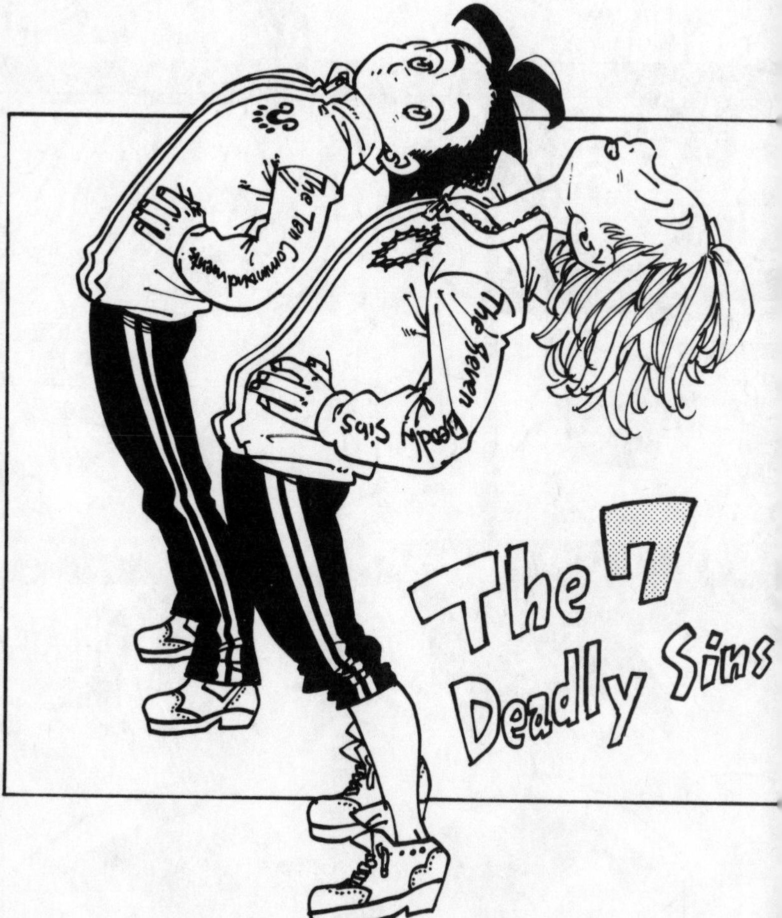
The Ten Commandments
The Seven Deadly Sins
The 7 Deadly Sins

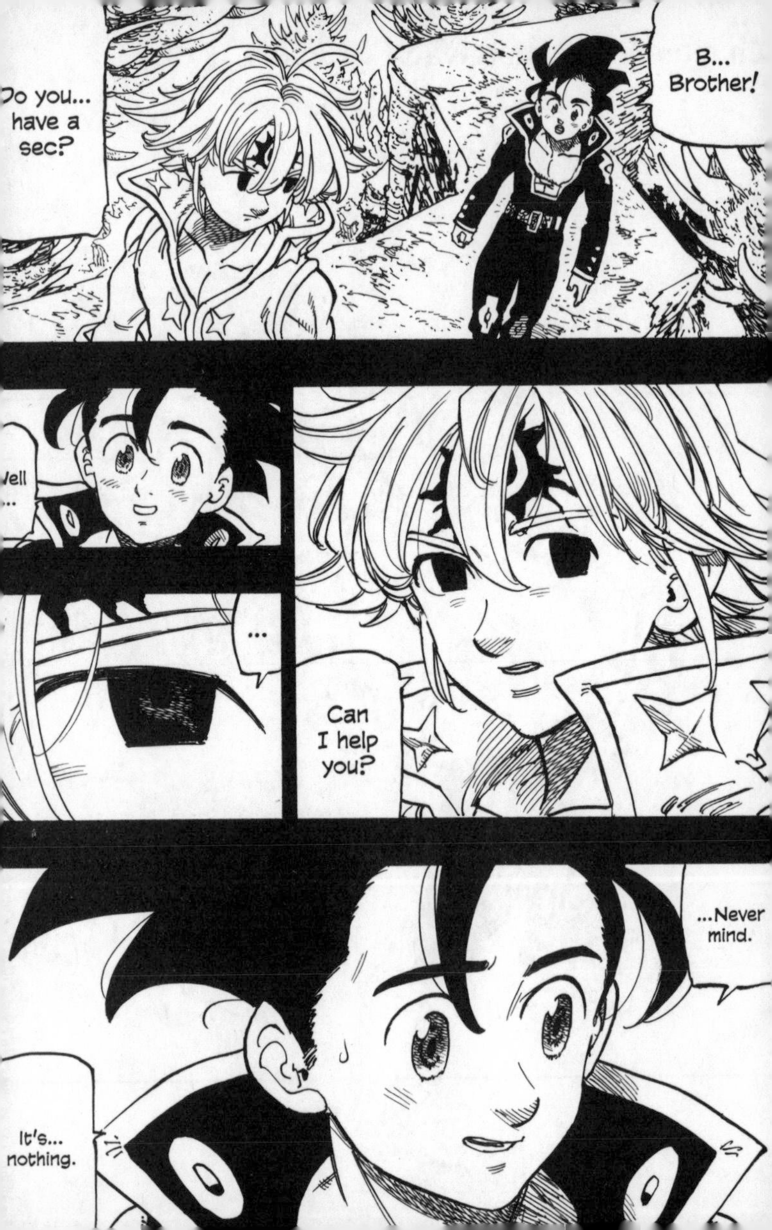
B... Brother!
Do you... have a sec?
Can I help you?
Well...
...
...Never mind.
It's... nothing.

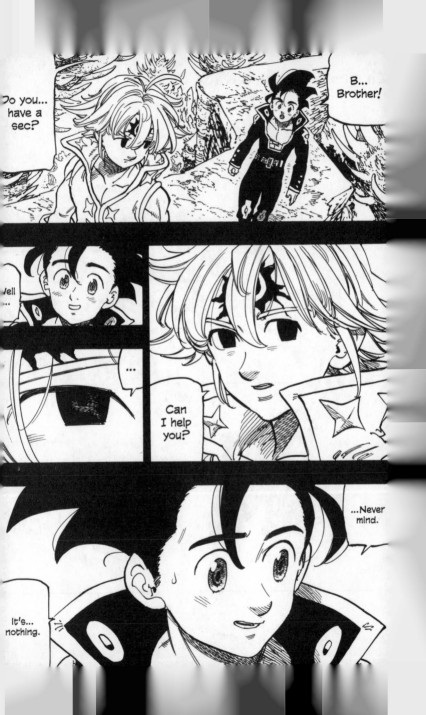

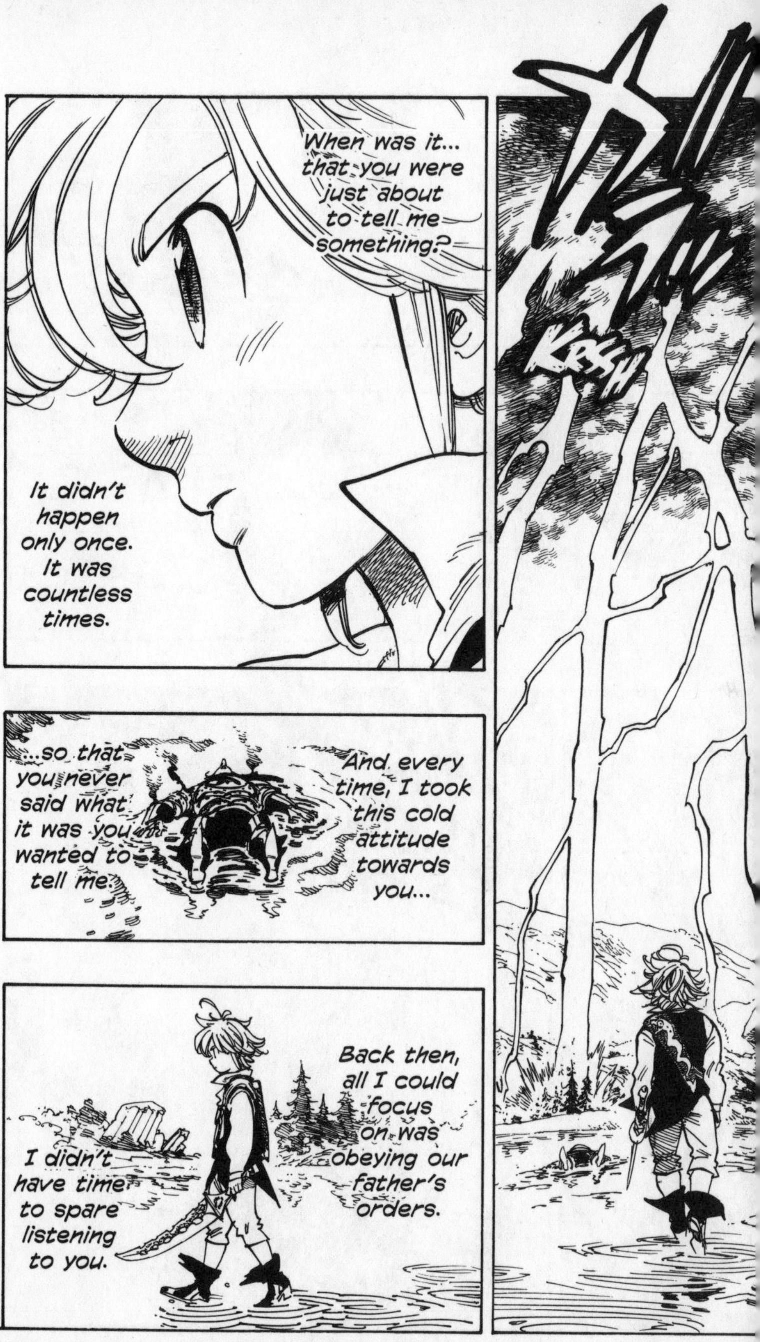
KRSH
When was it... that you were just about to tell me something?
It didn't happen only once. It was countless times.
And every time, I took this cold attitude towards you...
...so that you never said what it was you wanted to tell me.
Back then, all I could focus on was obeying our father's orders.
I didn't have time to spare listening to you.

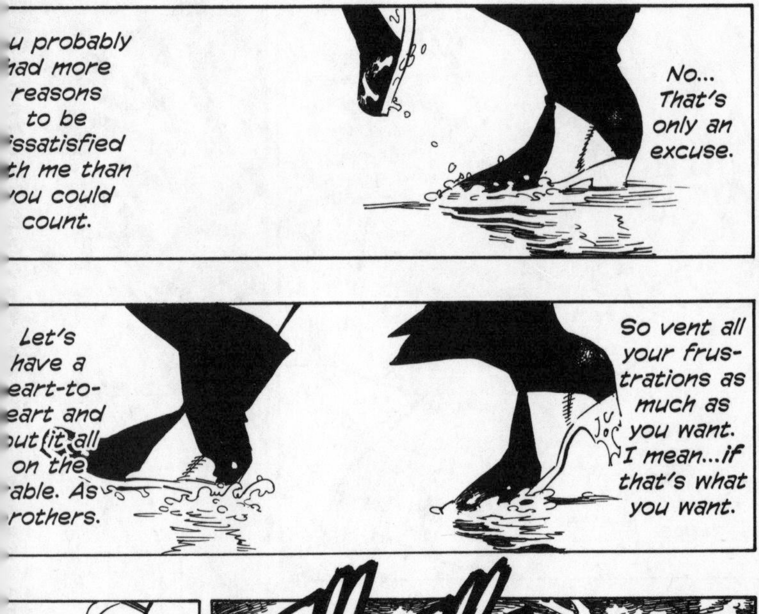

No... That's only an excuse.
u probably had more reasons to be ssatisfied th me than you could count.
So vent all your frus-trations as much as you want. I mean...if that's what you want.
Let's have a eart-to-eart and out it all on the able. As rothers.
RRRUMBLE
ZSH
Ha...
Ha...
...

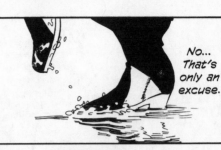

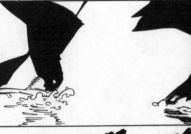

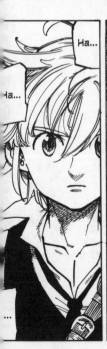

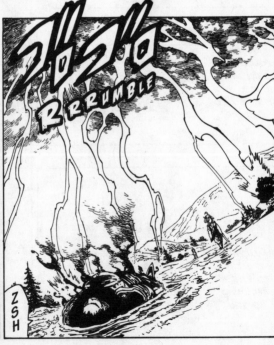

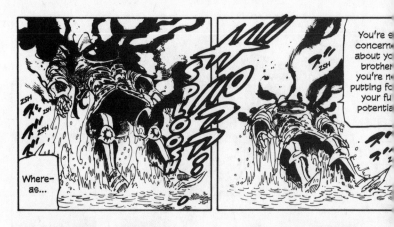

You're s[o] concerne[d] about yo[ur] brother[s] you're n[ot] putting fo[rth] your fu[ll] potentia[l].

Where-as...

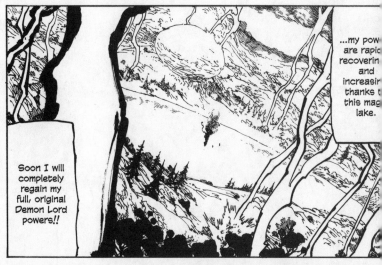

...my pow[ers] are rapid[ly] recoverin[g] and increasin[g] thanks t[o] this mag[ic] lake.

Soon I will completely regain my full, original Demon Lord powers!!

There is only one likely conclusion.

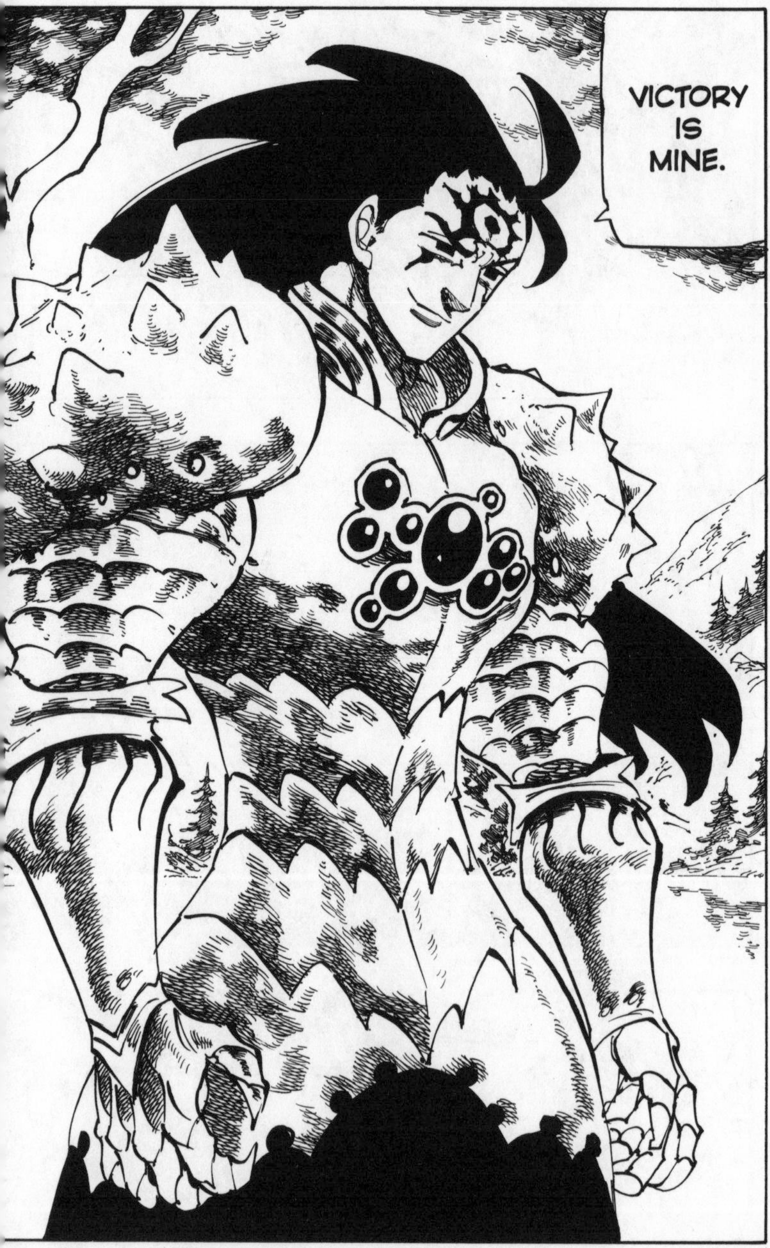
VICTORY IS MINE.

ZELDRIS
DON'T
LET HIM
TAKE
OVER!

KPOW

It'
no
use

Zeldris's
conscious-
ness is lost
in the sweet
illusions he
so desired.
He will
eventually
vanish.

WHOOSH

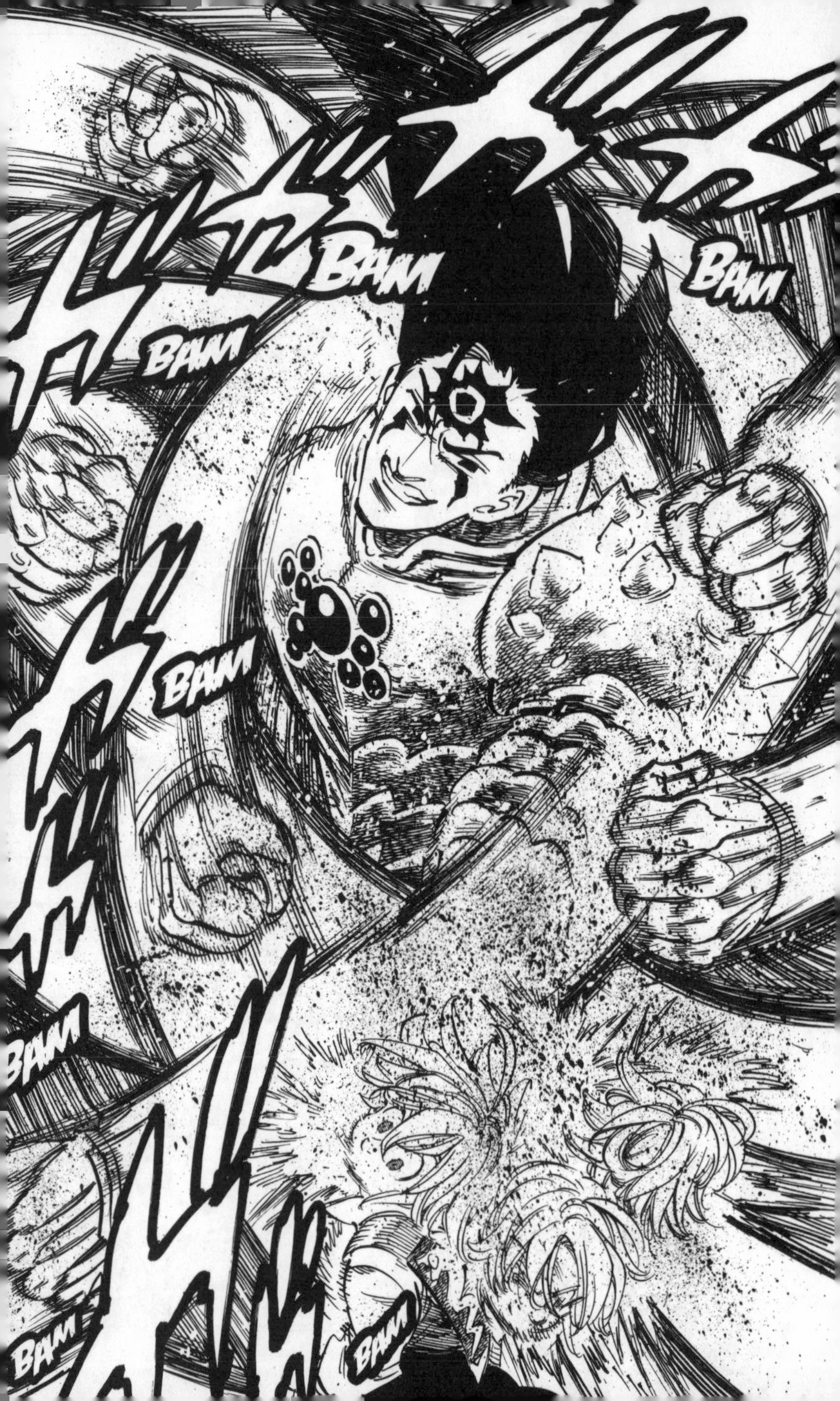
BAM
BAM
BAM
BAM
BAM
BAM
BAM

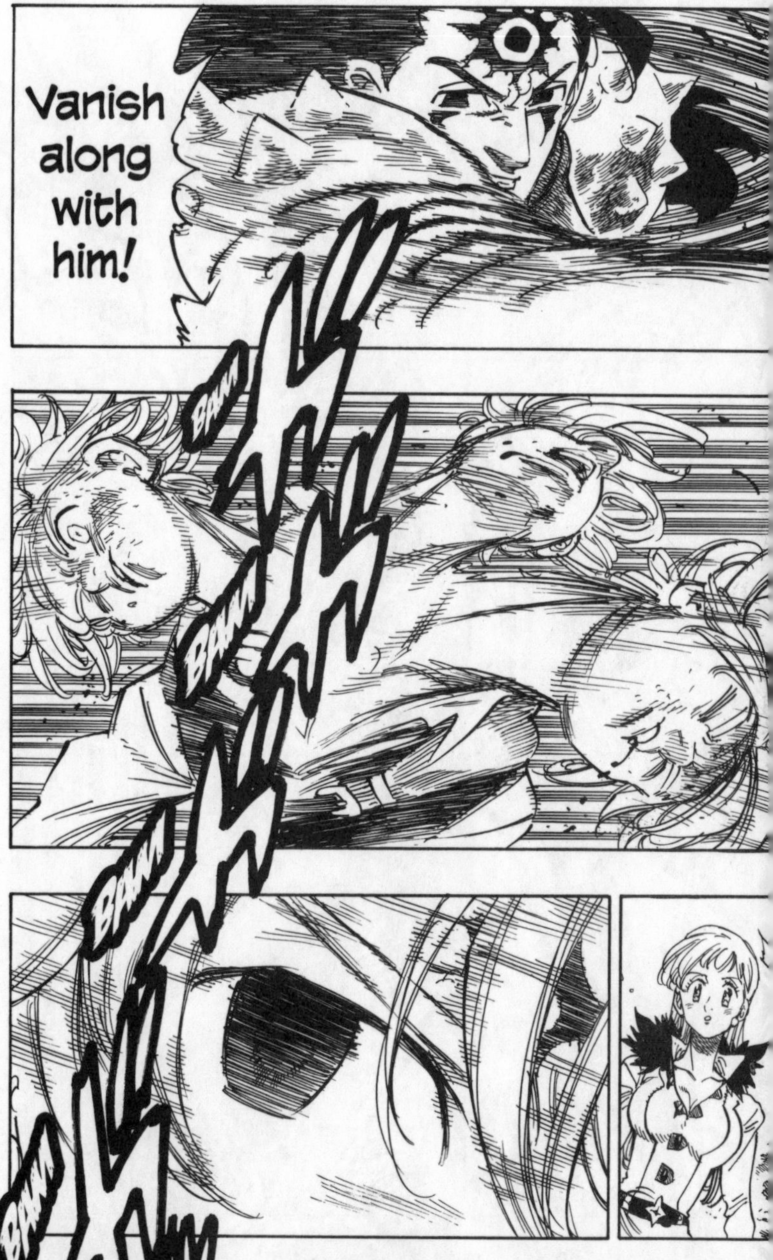
Vanish along with him!
BAM
BAM
BAM
BAM

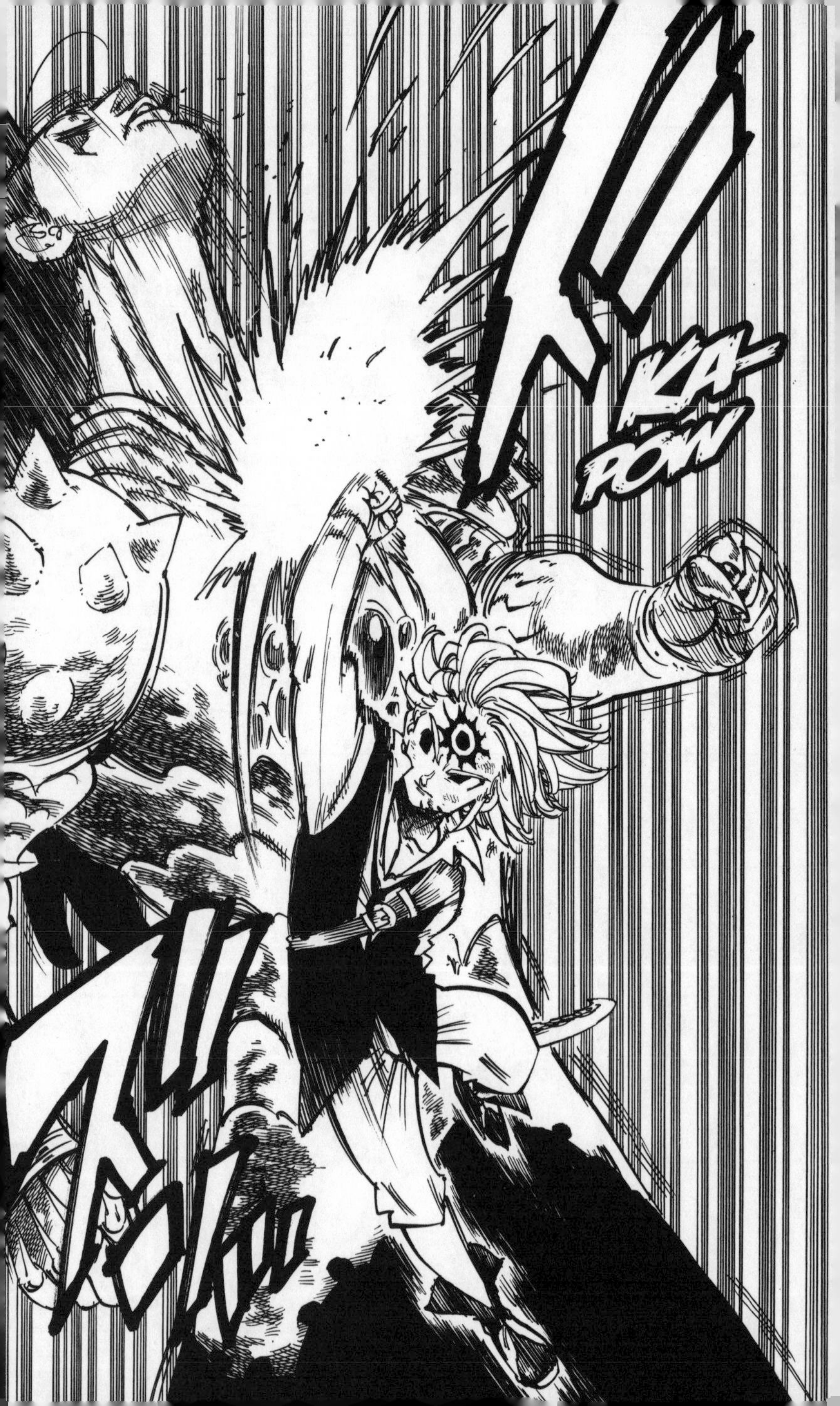
KA-POW

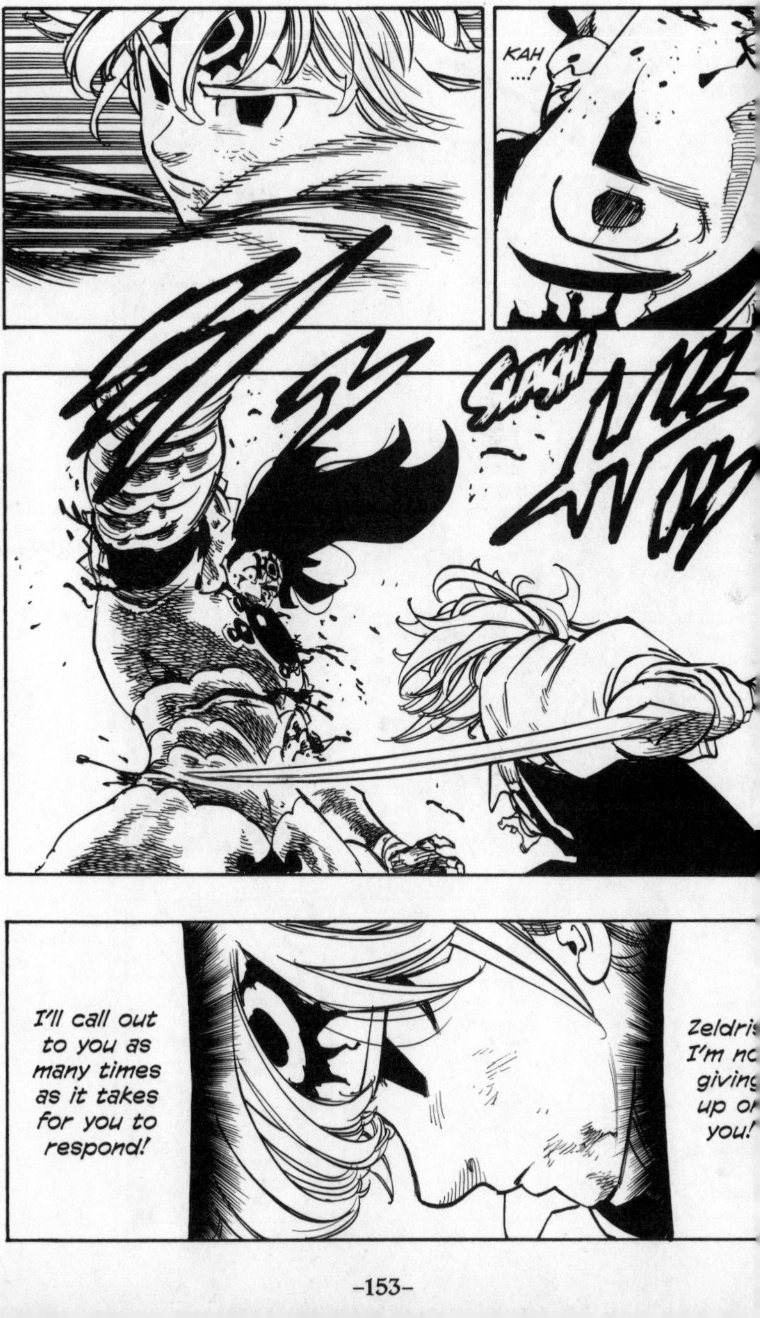
KAH ...!
SLASH
Zeldris I'm no giving up o you!
I'll call out to you as many times as it takes for you to respond!

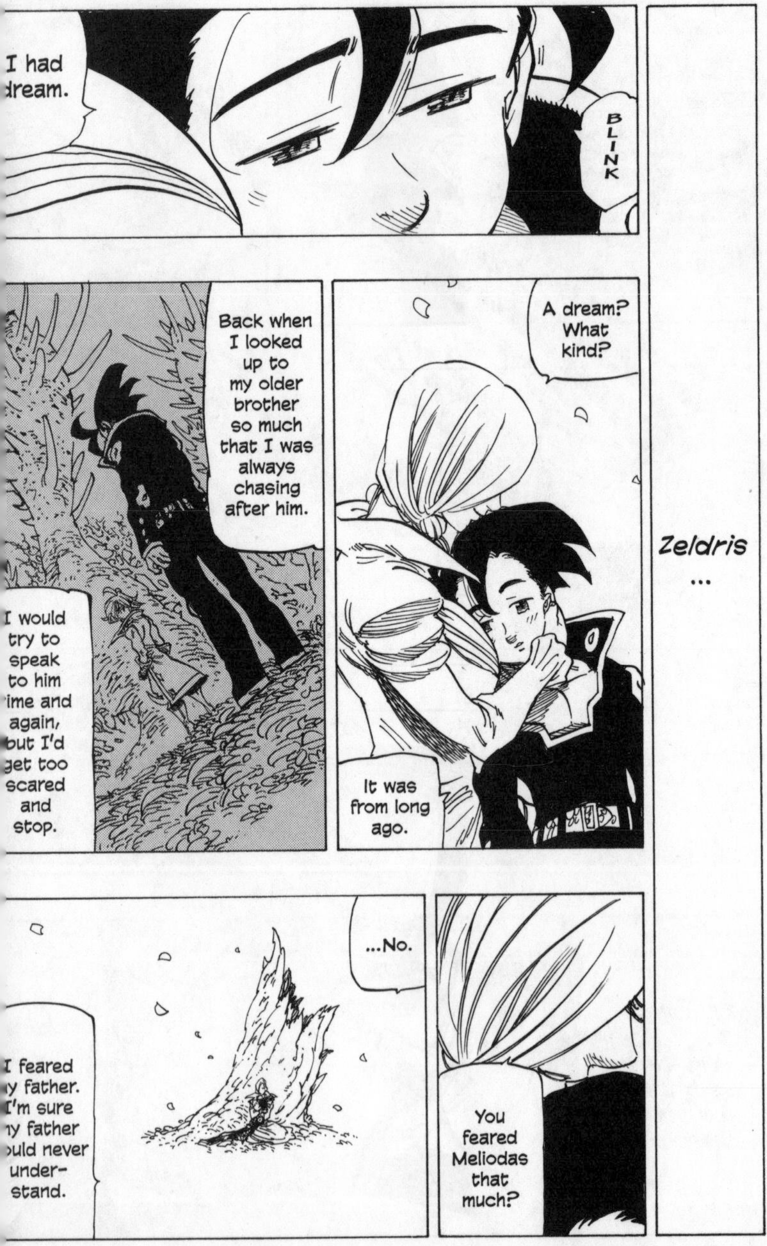
Zeldris ...
BLINK
I had dream.
A dream? What kind?
It was from long ago.
Back when I looked up to my older brother so much that I was always chasing after him.
I would try to speak to him ime and again, but I'd et too scared and stop.
You feared Meliodas that much?
...No.
I feared y father. I'm sure y father ould never under-stand.

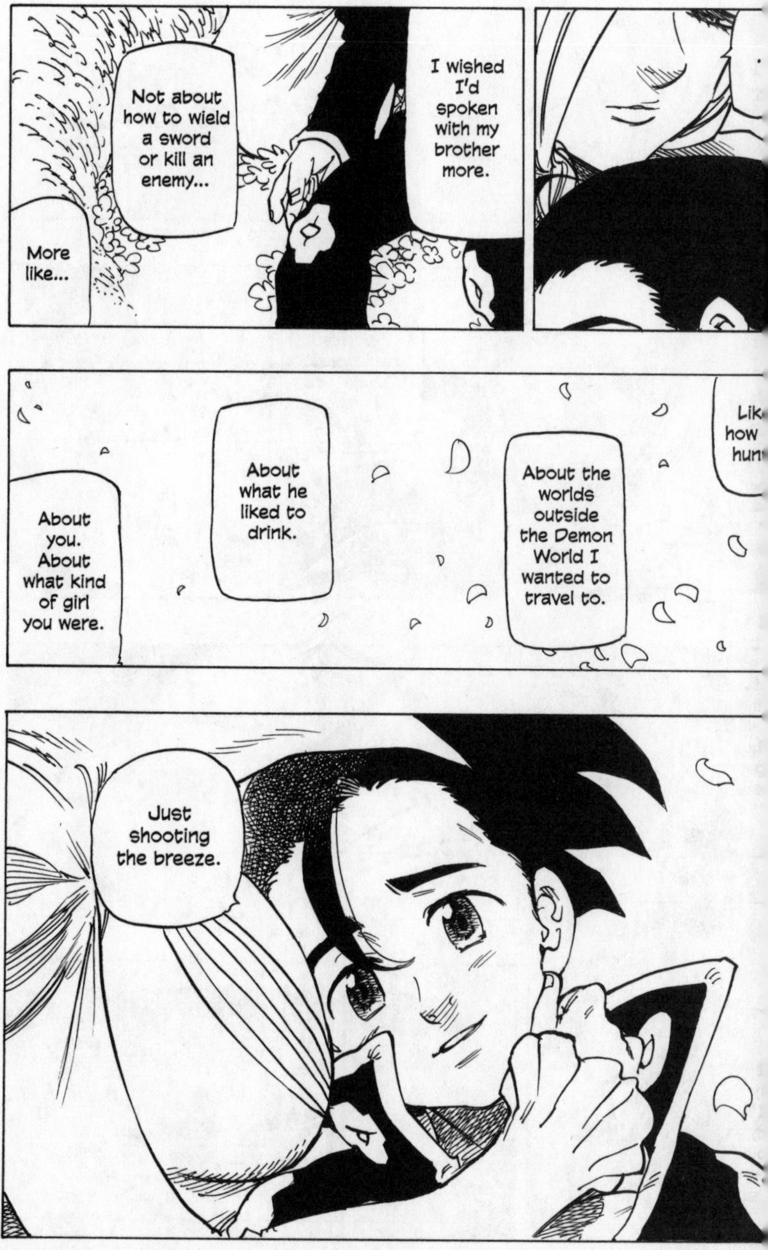
I wished I'd spoken with my brother more.
Not about how to wield a sword or kill an enemy...
More like...
About the worlds outside the Demon World I wanted to travel to.
About what he liked to drink.
About you. About what kind of girl you were.
Just shooting the breeze.

THAT'S RIDICU-LOUS.

Who cares about any of that anymore? Come, you must be tired.

ou can eep n my ap.

Gel... da?

It's all done and gone now...

Oh... yeah.

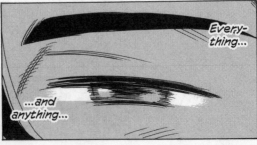

Every-thing...

...and anything...

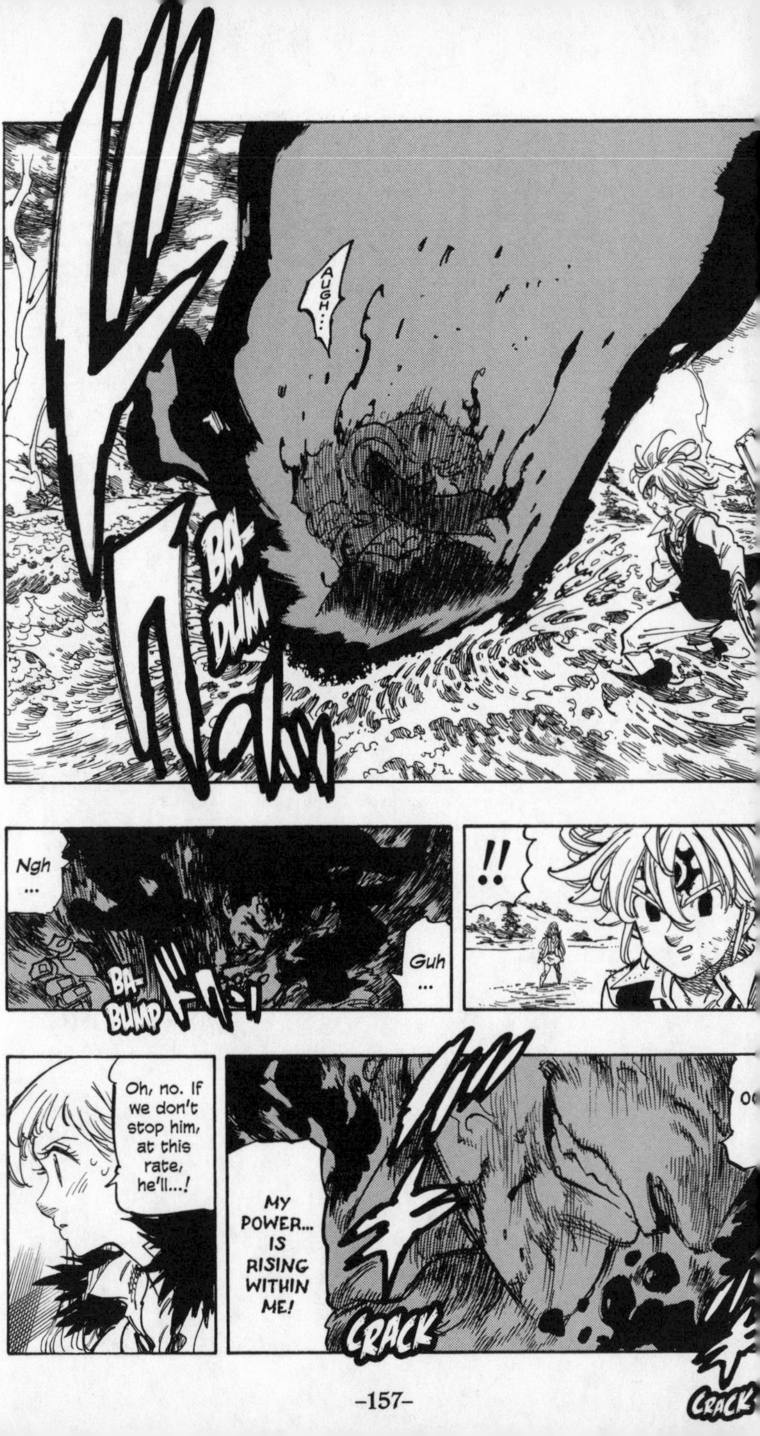
AUGH...
BA-DUM
!!
Ngh...
Guh...
BA-BUMP
MY POWER... IS RISING WITHIN ME!
CRACK
CRACK
Oh, no. If we don't stop him, at this rate, he'll...!

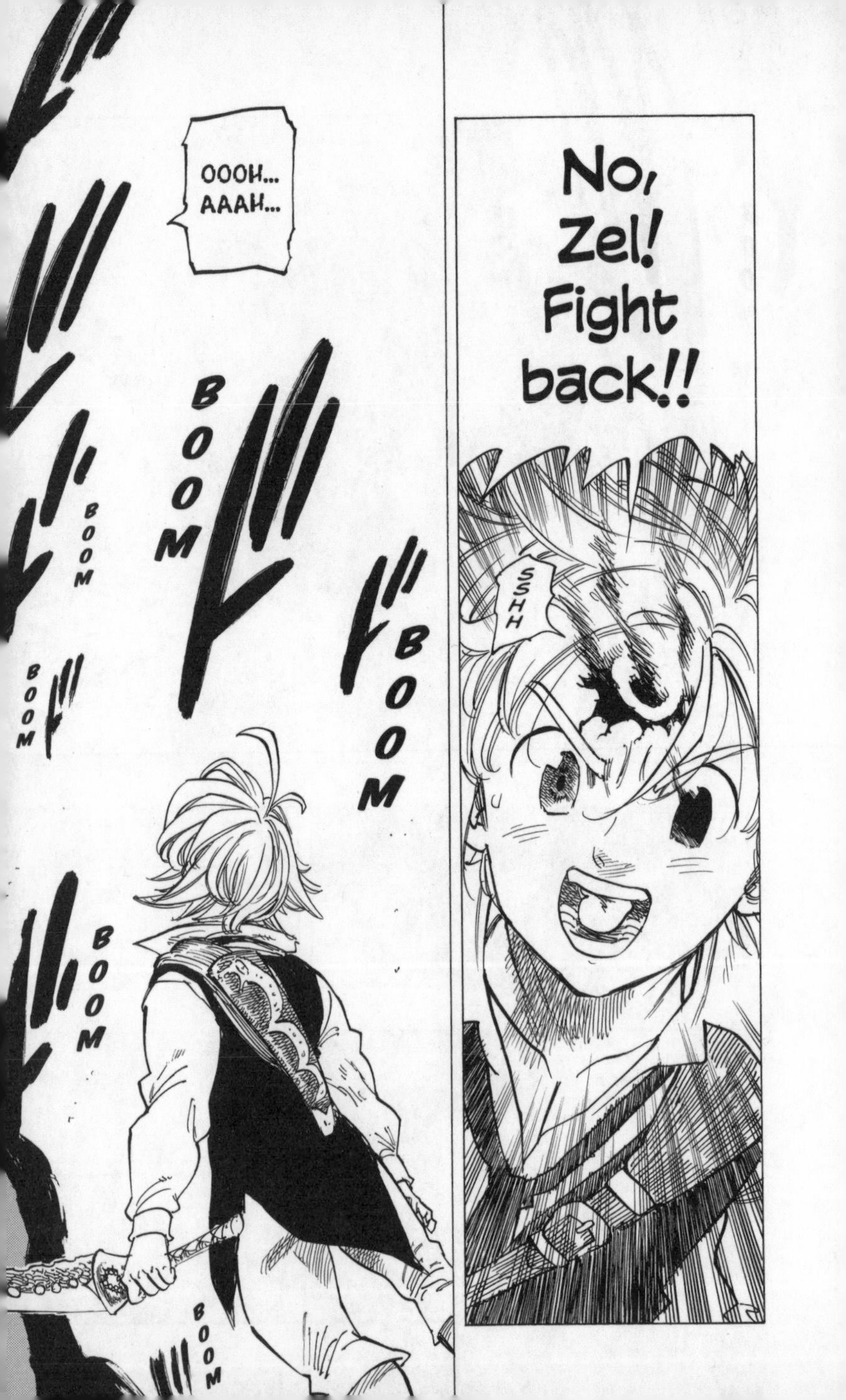
No, Zel! Fight back!!
SSHH
OOOH... AAAH...
BOOM
BOOM
BOOM
BOOM
BOOM
BOOM

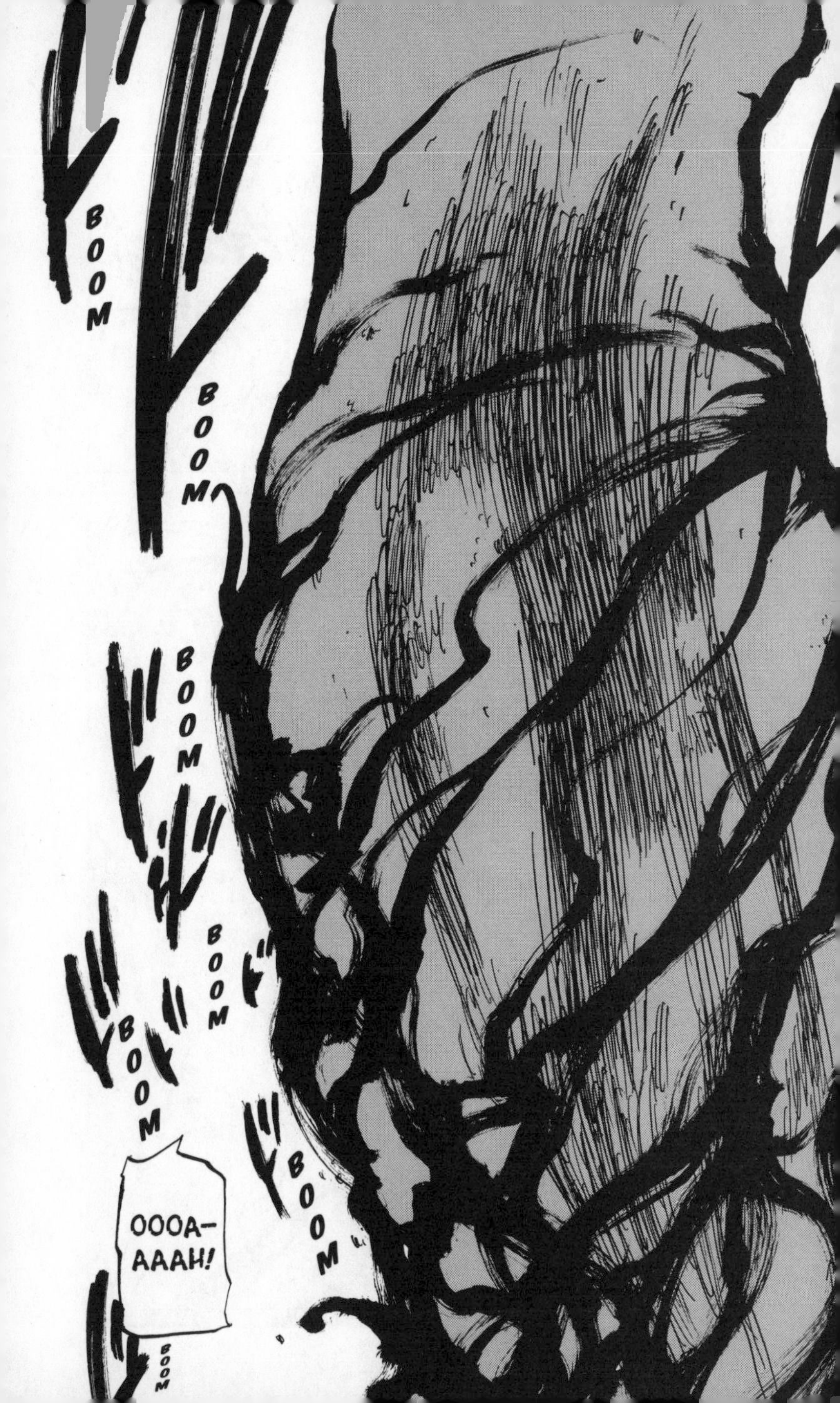
BOOM
BOOM
BOOM
BOOM
BOOM
BOOM
OOOA-AAAH!
BOOM

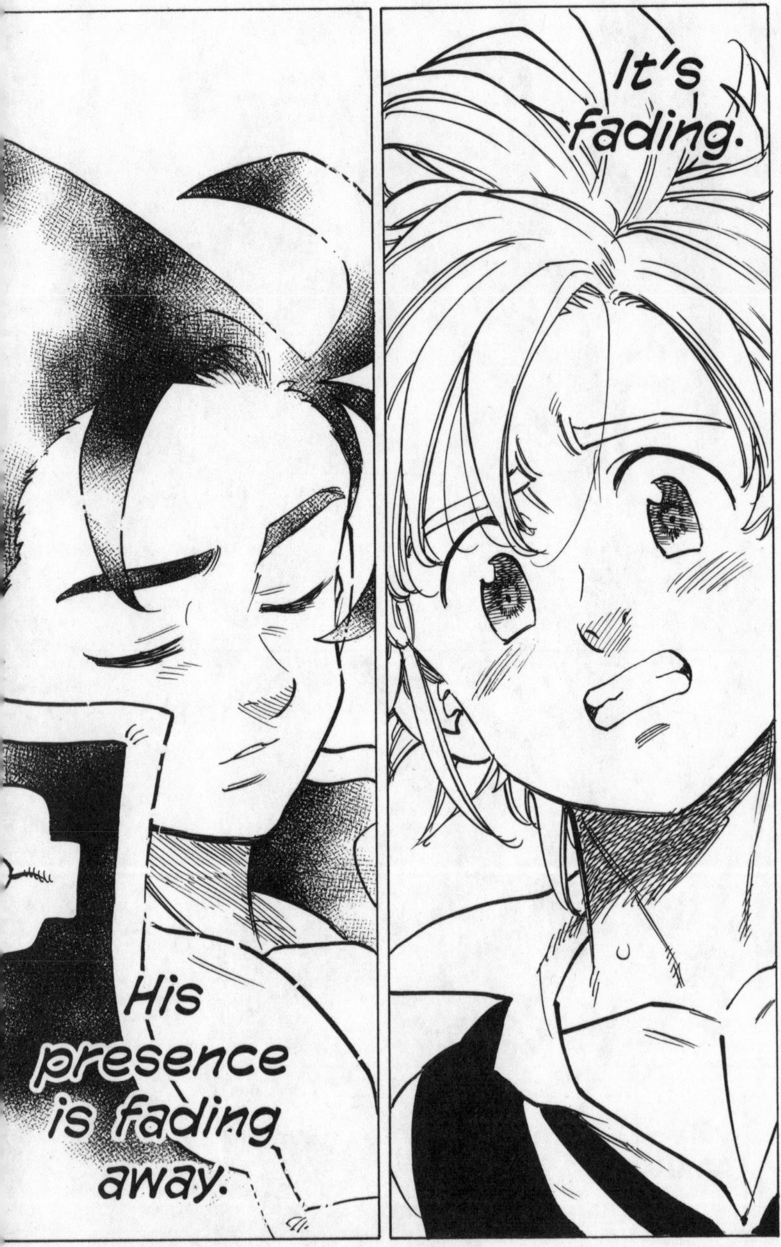
It's fading.
His presence is fading away.

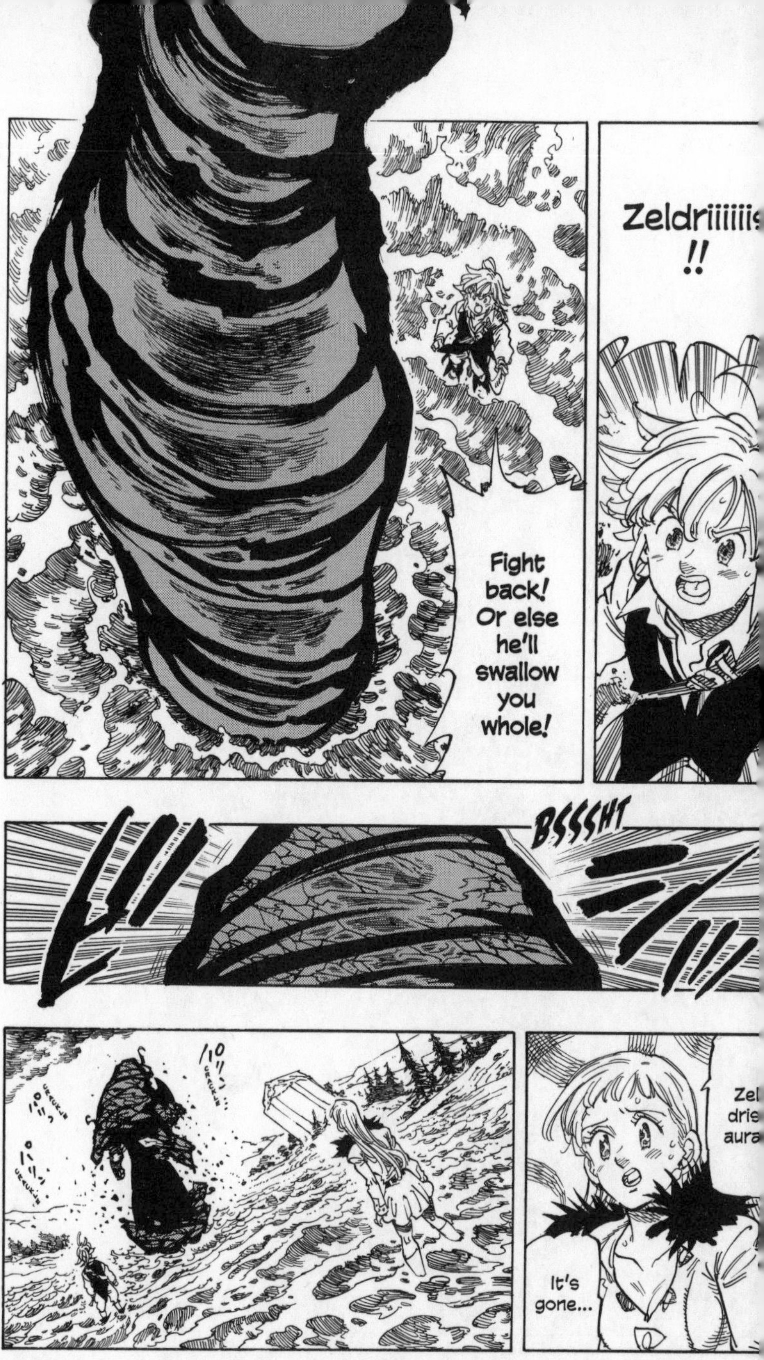
Zeldriiiiiis !!
Fight back! Or else he'll swallow you whole!
BSSSHT
Zel
dris
aura
It's gone...
CRACKLE
CRACKLE
CRACKLE

Chapter 320 - Brothers of Despair

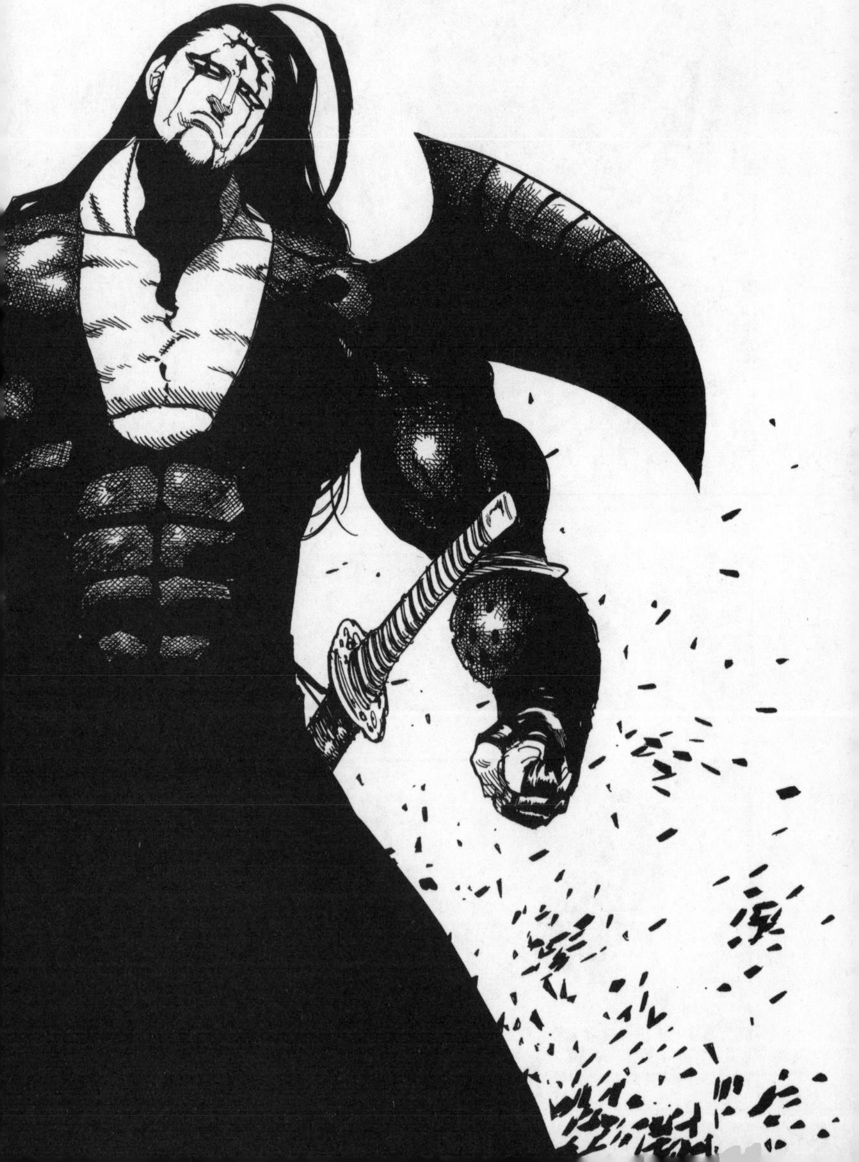

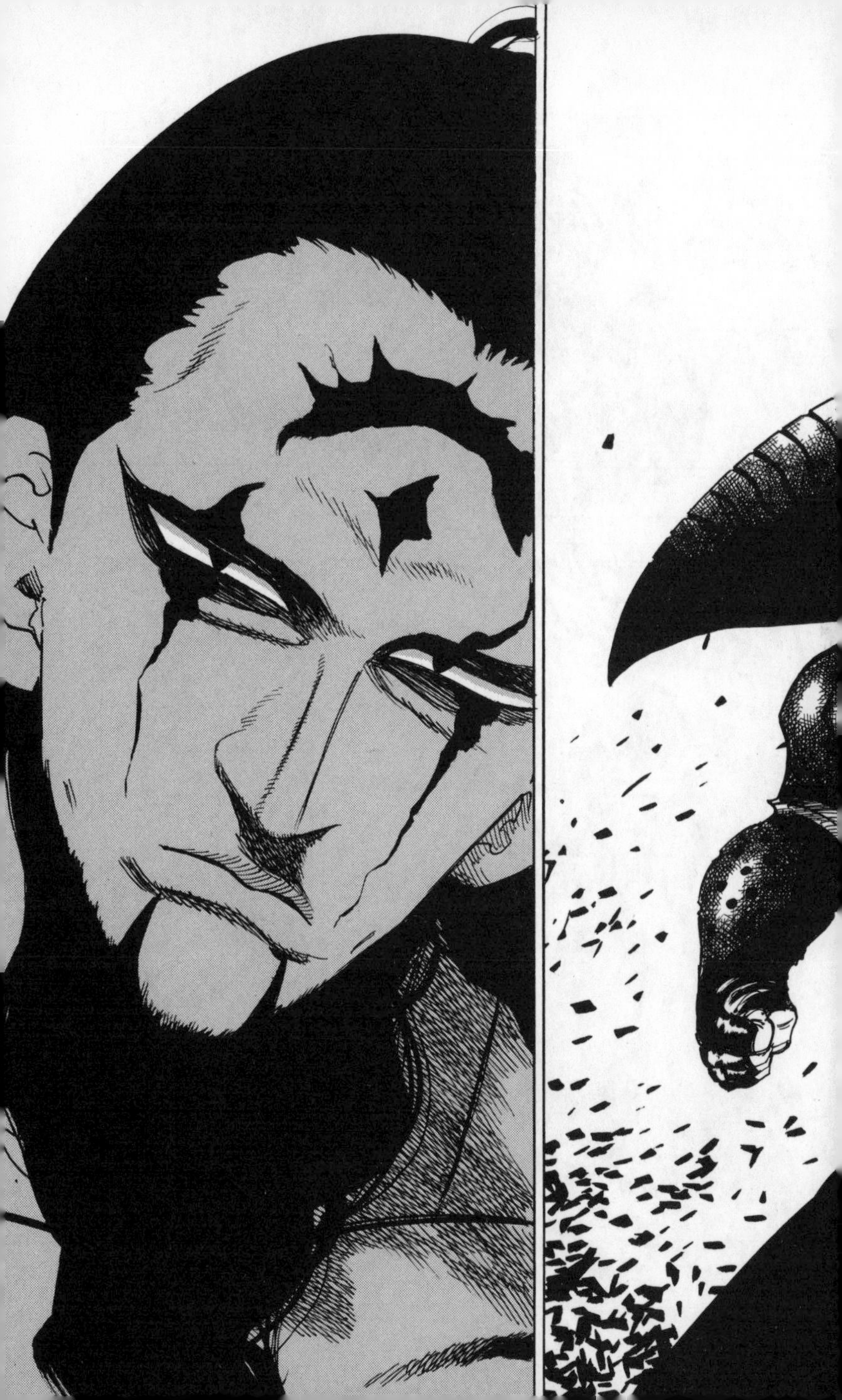

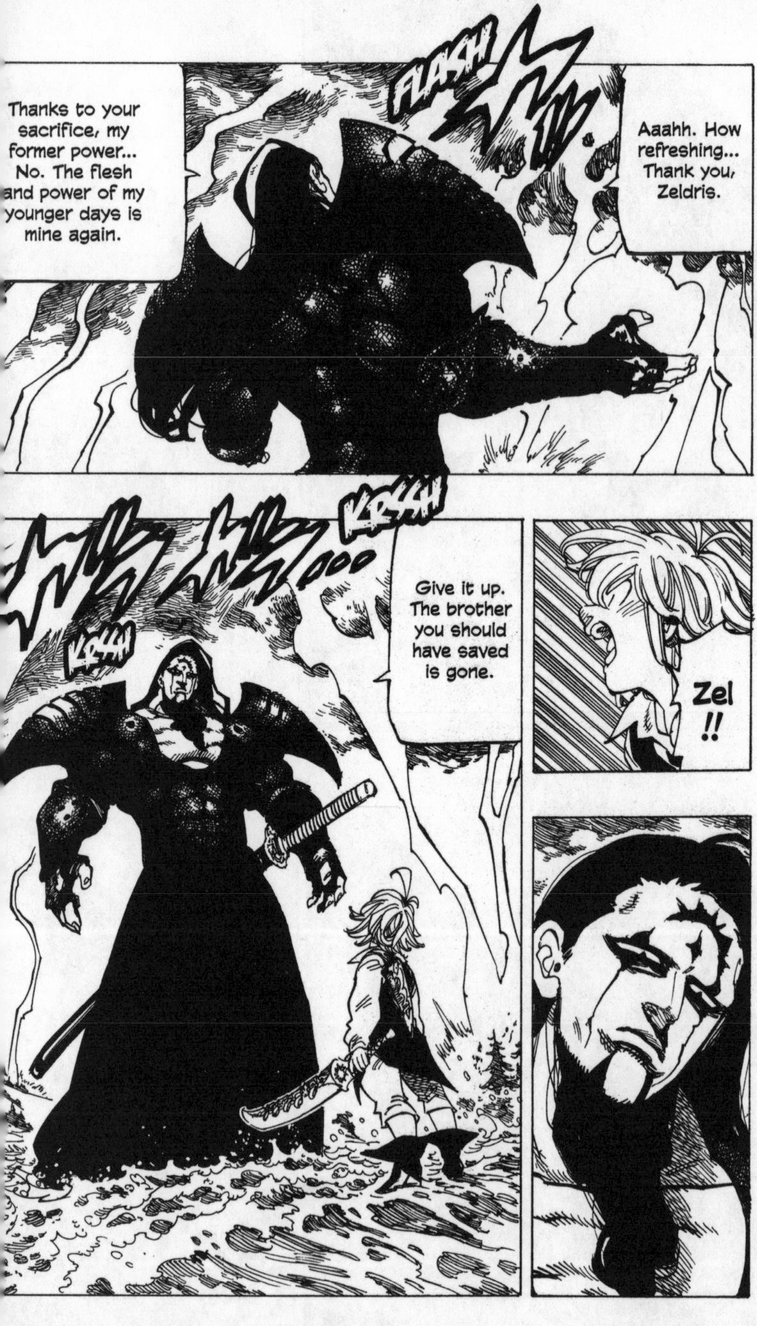
FLASH
Aaahh. How refreshing... Thank you, Zeldris.
Thanks to your sacrifice, my former power... No. The flesh and power of my younger days is mine again.
Zel !!
KRSSH
Give it up. The brother you should have saved is gone.
KRSSH

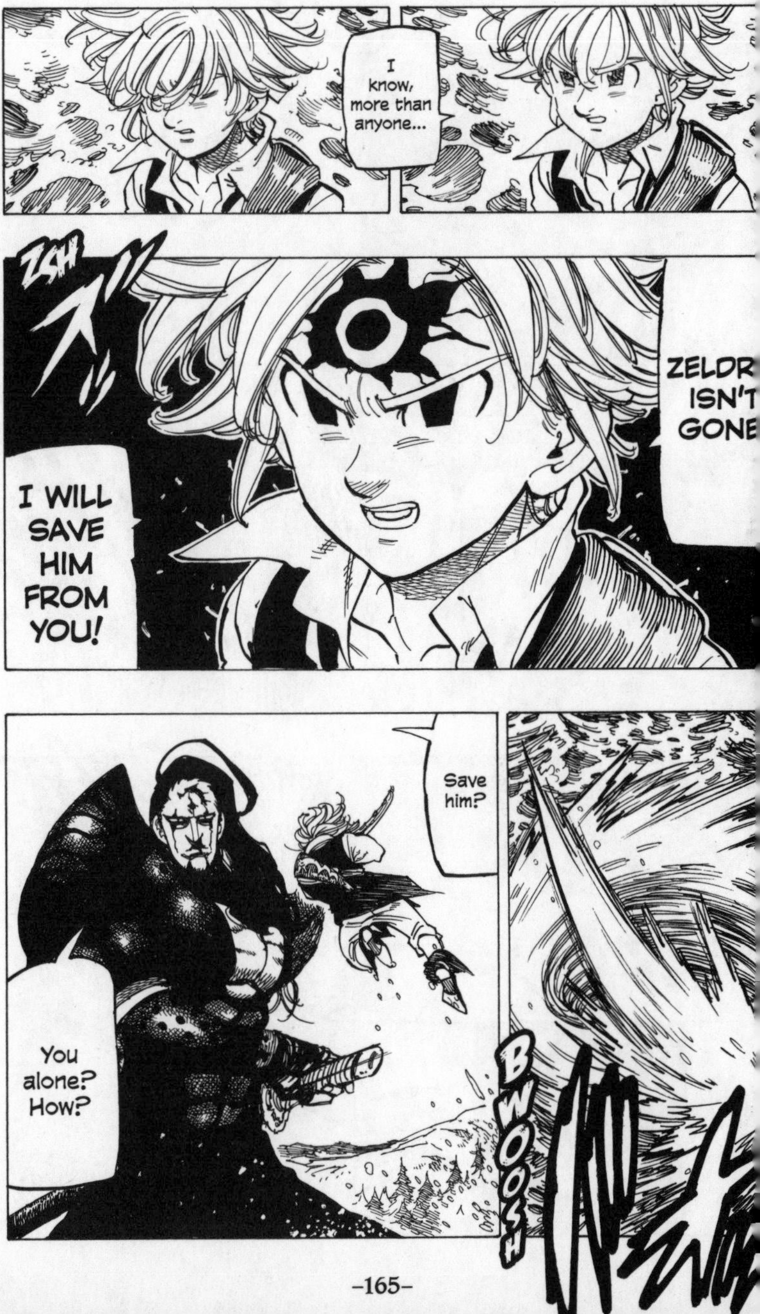
I know, more than anyone...
ZELDR ISN'T GONE
ZSH
I WILL SAVE HIM FROM YOU!
BWOOSH
Save him?
You alone? How?

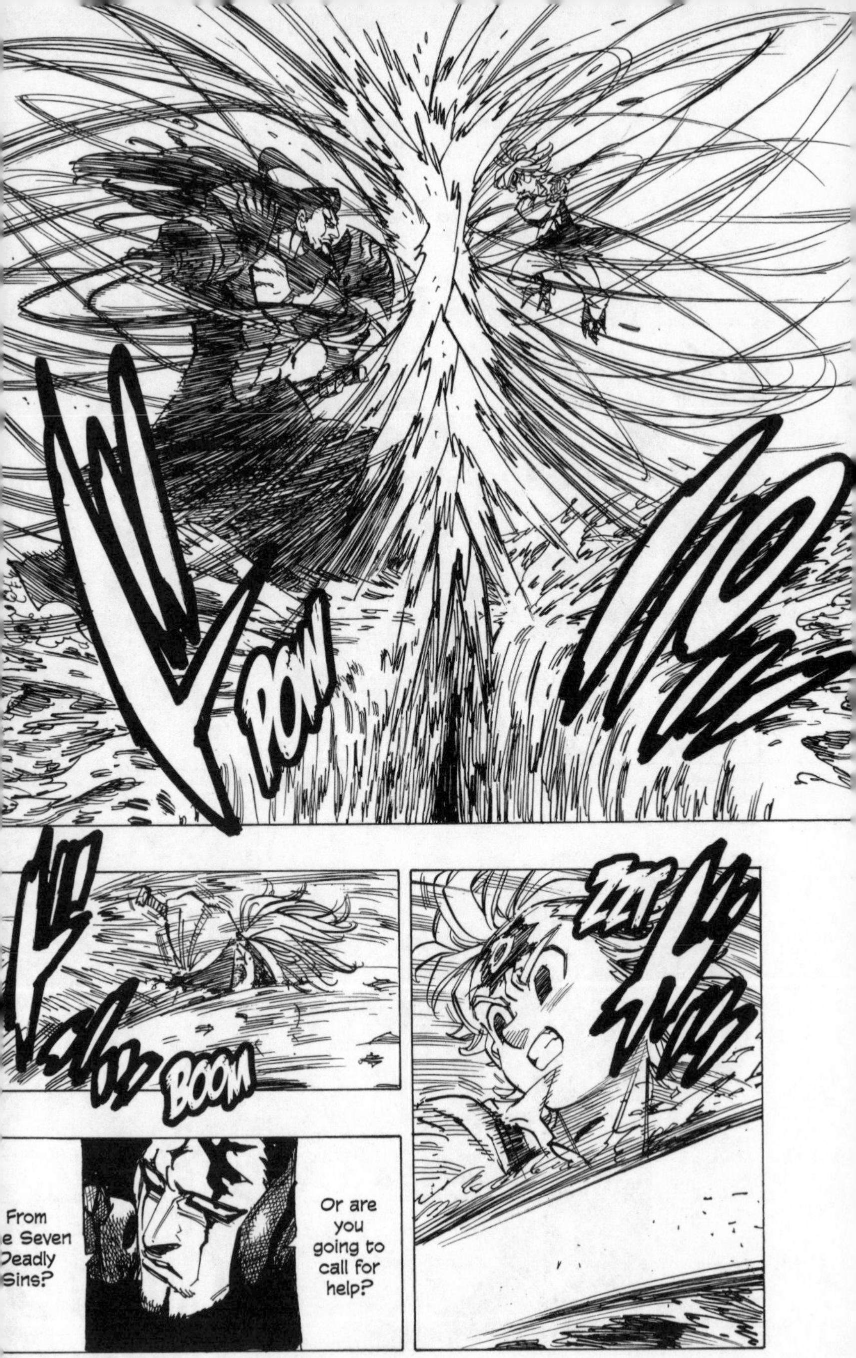
POW
BOOM
Or are you going to call for help?
From e Seven Deadly Sins?

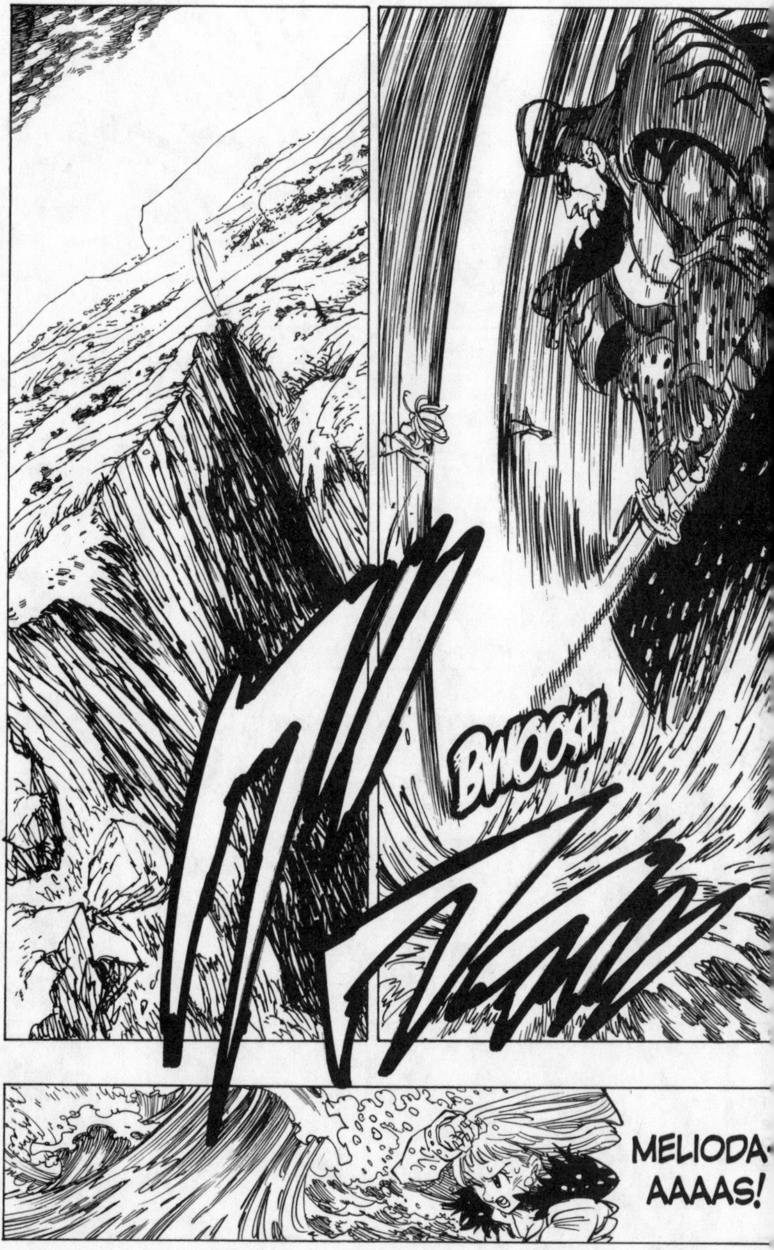
BWOOSH
MELIODA-
AAAAS!

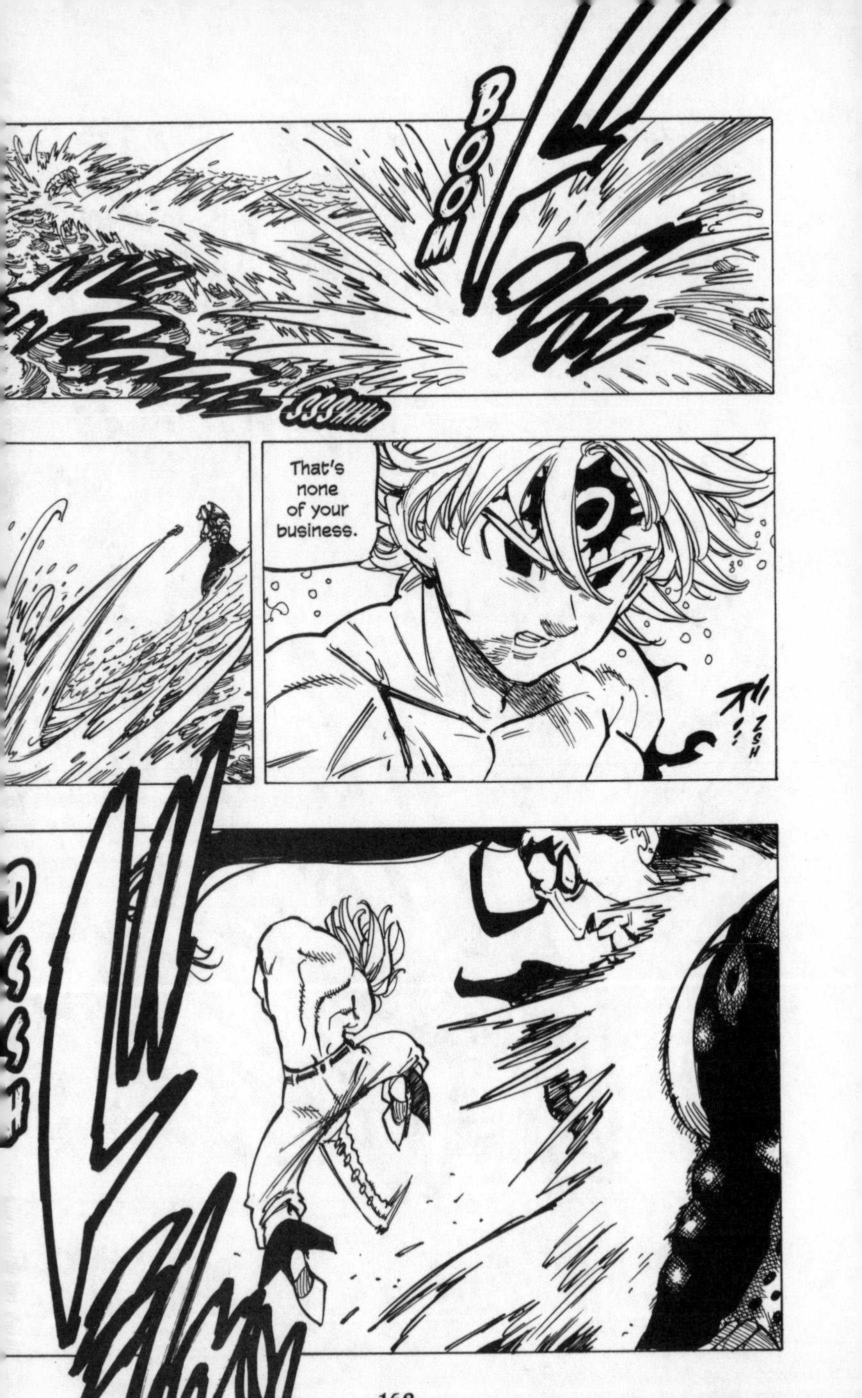
BOOM
SSSHHH
That's none of your business.
ZSH
DSSSH

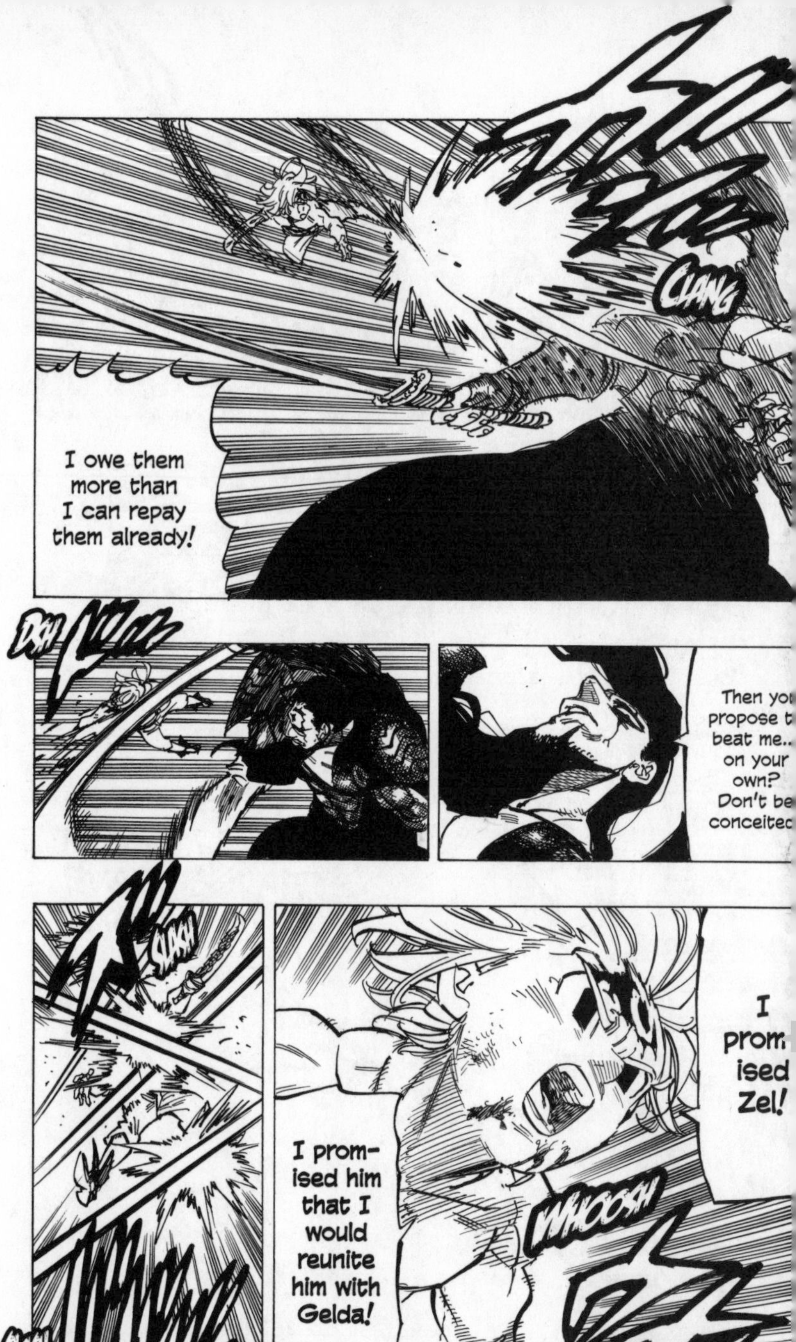
CLANG
I owe them more than I can repay them already!
Then yo propose t beat me.. on your own? Don't be conceitec
DSH
I prom ised Zel!
I prom-ised him that I would reunite him with Gelda!
WHOOSH
SLASH
SLASH
SLASH

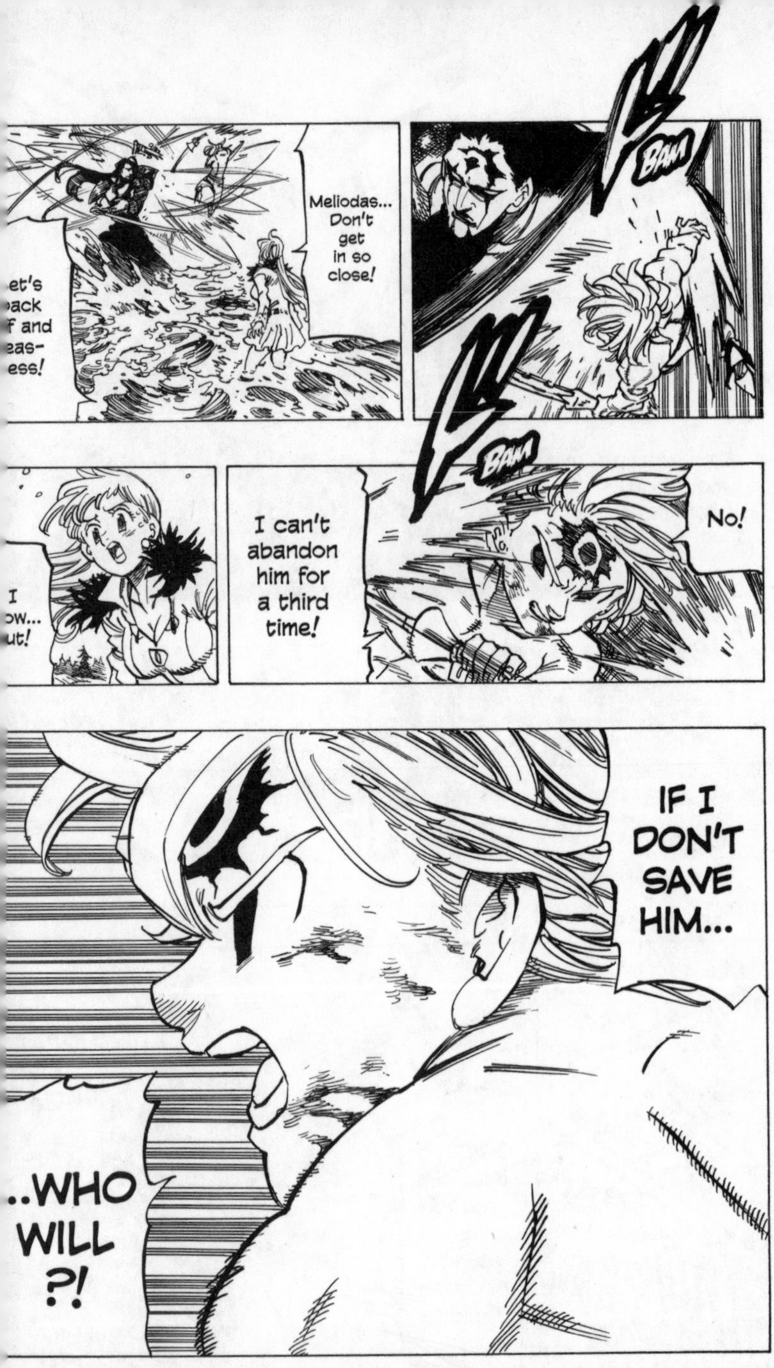
BAM
Meliodas... Don't get in so close!
BAM
No!
I can't abandon him for a third time!
IF I DON'T SAVE HIM...
..WHO WILL ?!

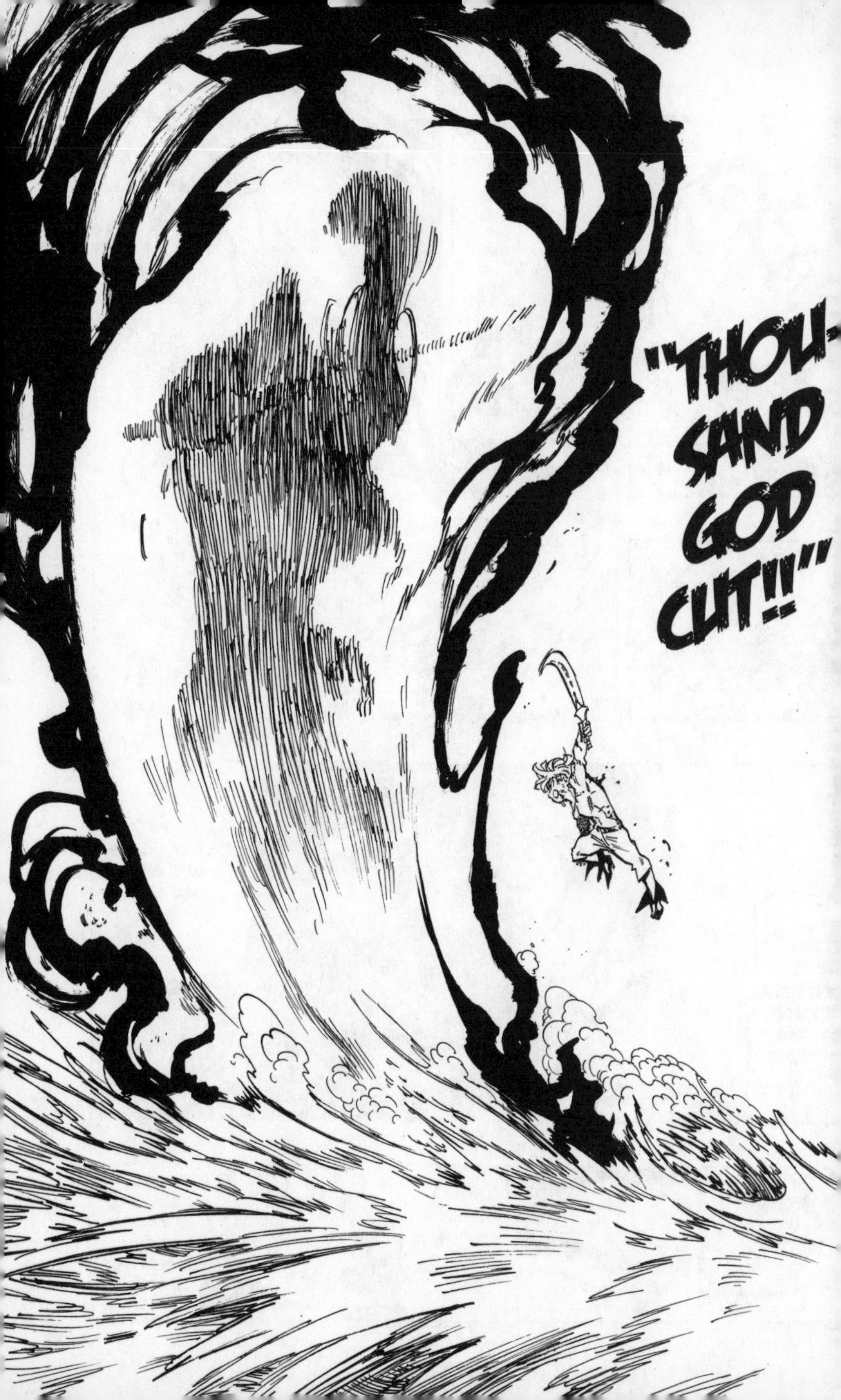
"THOU-SAND GOD CUT!!"

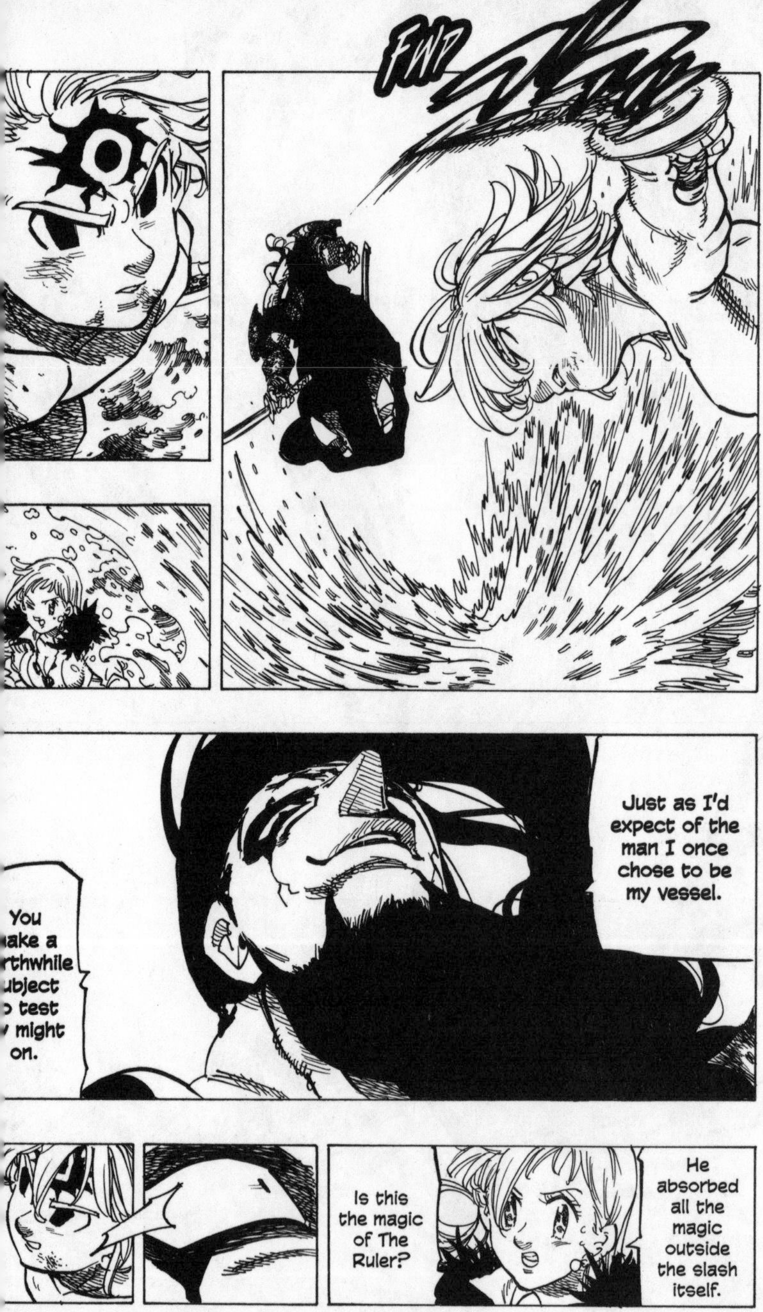
FWP
Just as I'd expect of the man I once chose to be my vessel.
You ake a rthwhile ubject o test might on.
He absorbed all the magic outside the slash itself.
Is this the magic of The Ruler?

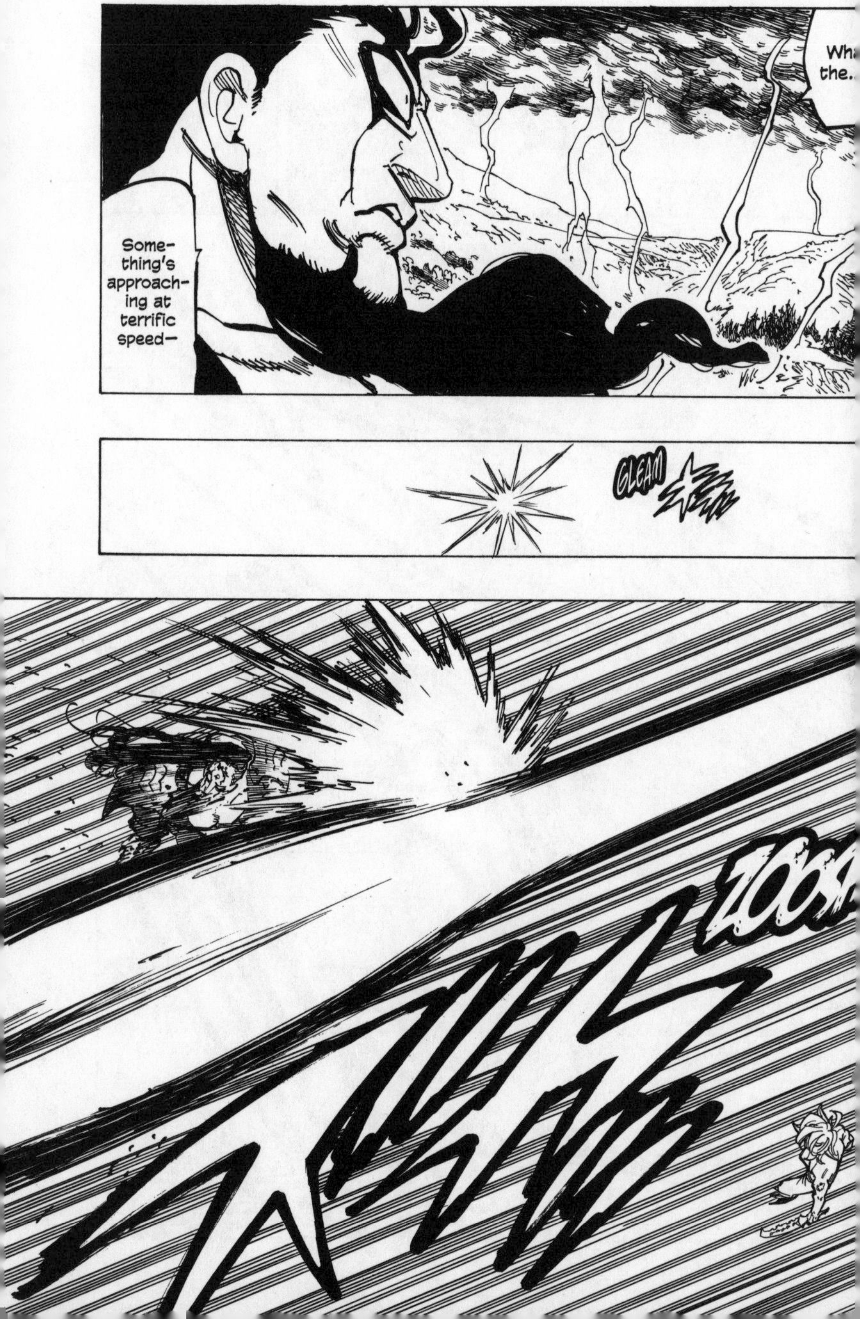
Wha
the..
Something's approaching at terrific speed—
GLEAM

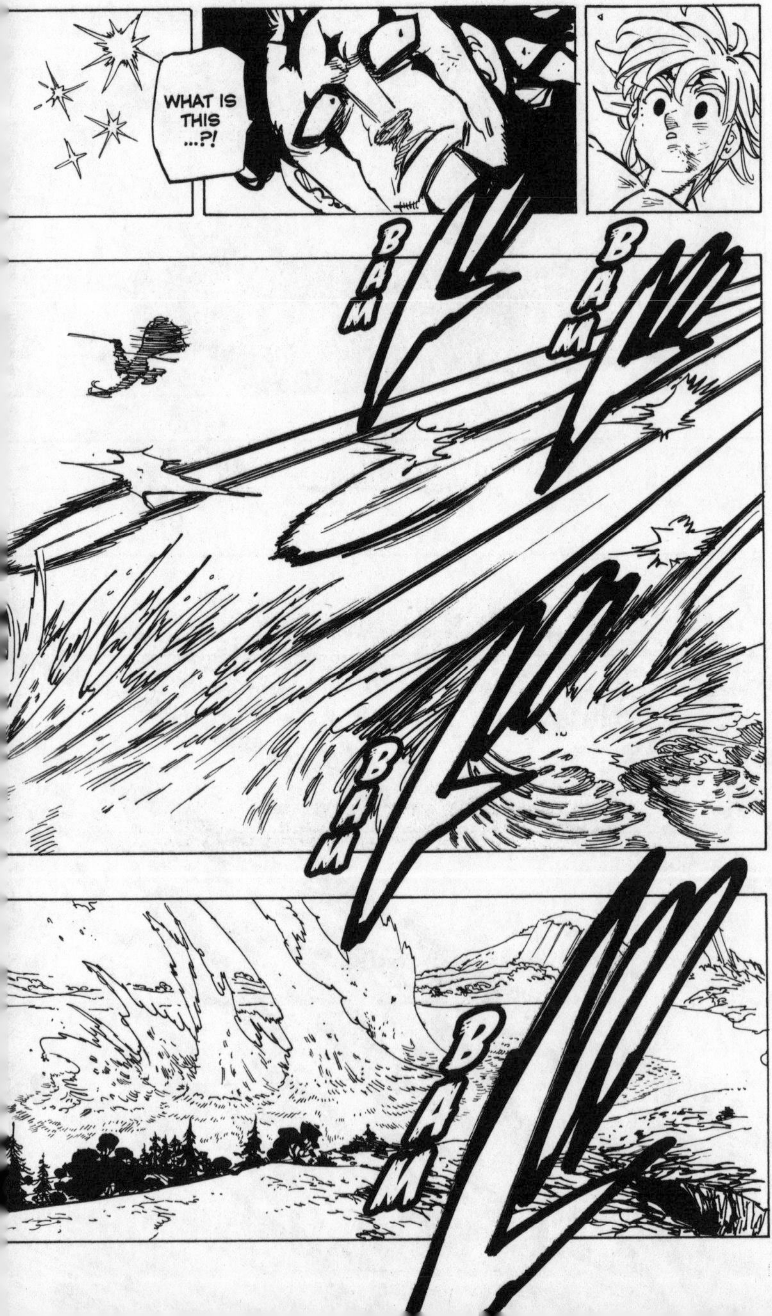
WHAT IS THIS ...?!
BAM
BAM
BAM
BAM

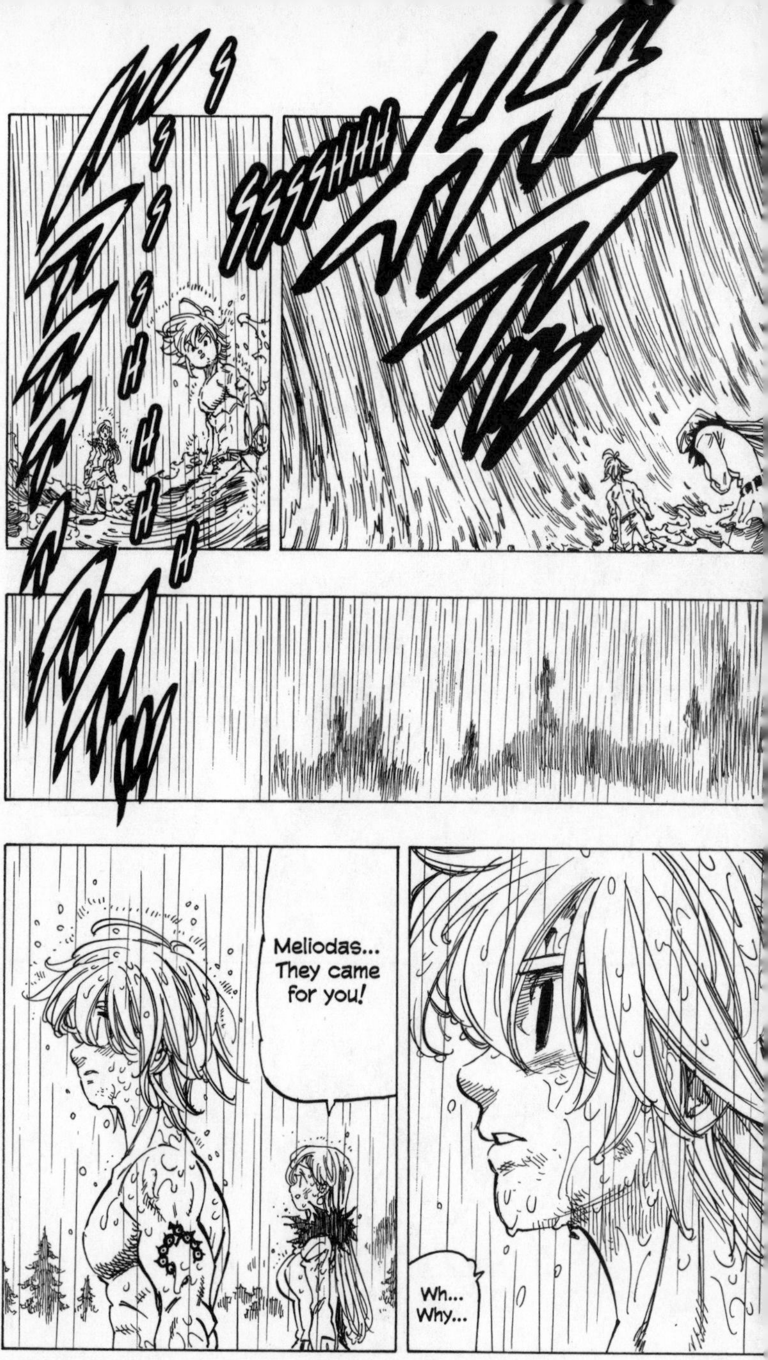
SSSSHHHH
Wh... Why...
Meliodas... They came for you!

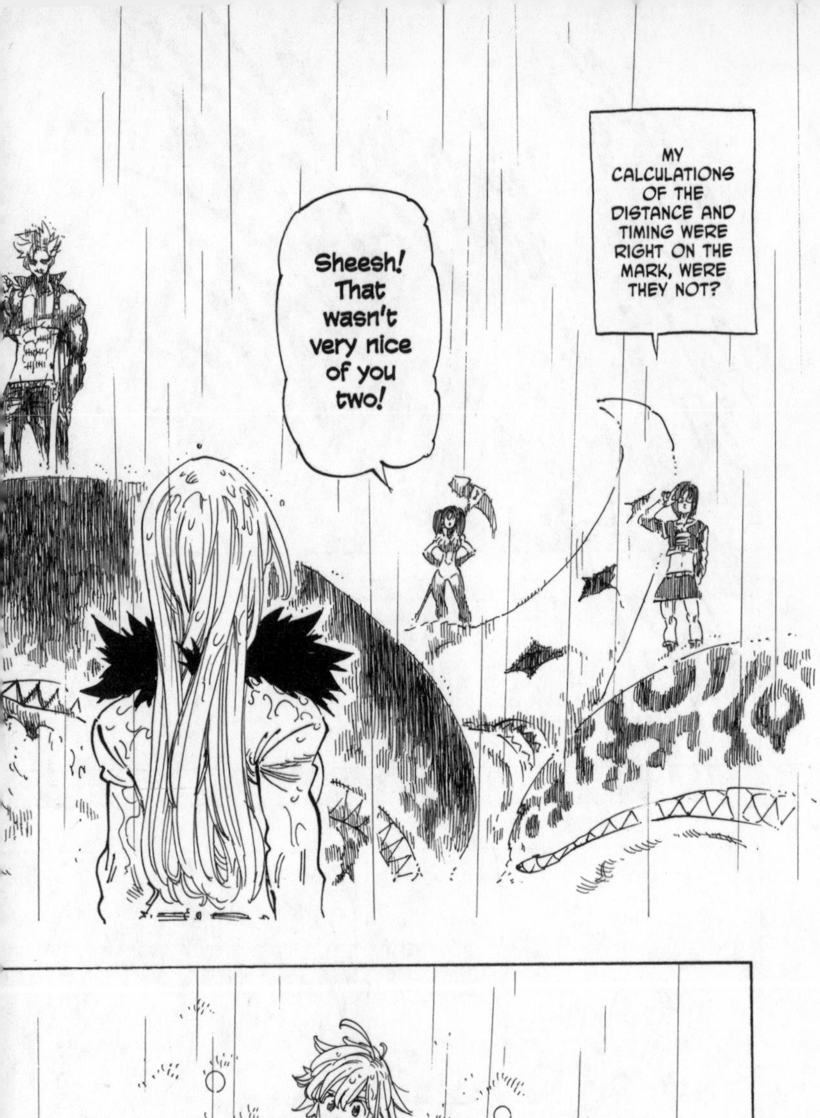
MY CALCULATIONS OF THE DISTANCE AND TIMING WERE RIGHT ON THE MARK, WERE THEY NOT?
Sheesh! That wasn't very nice of you two!

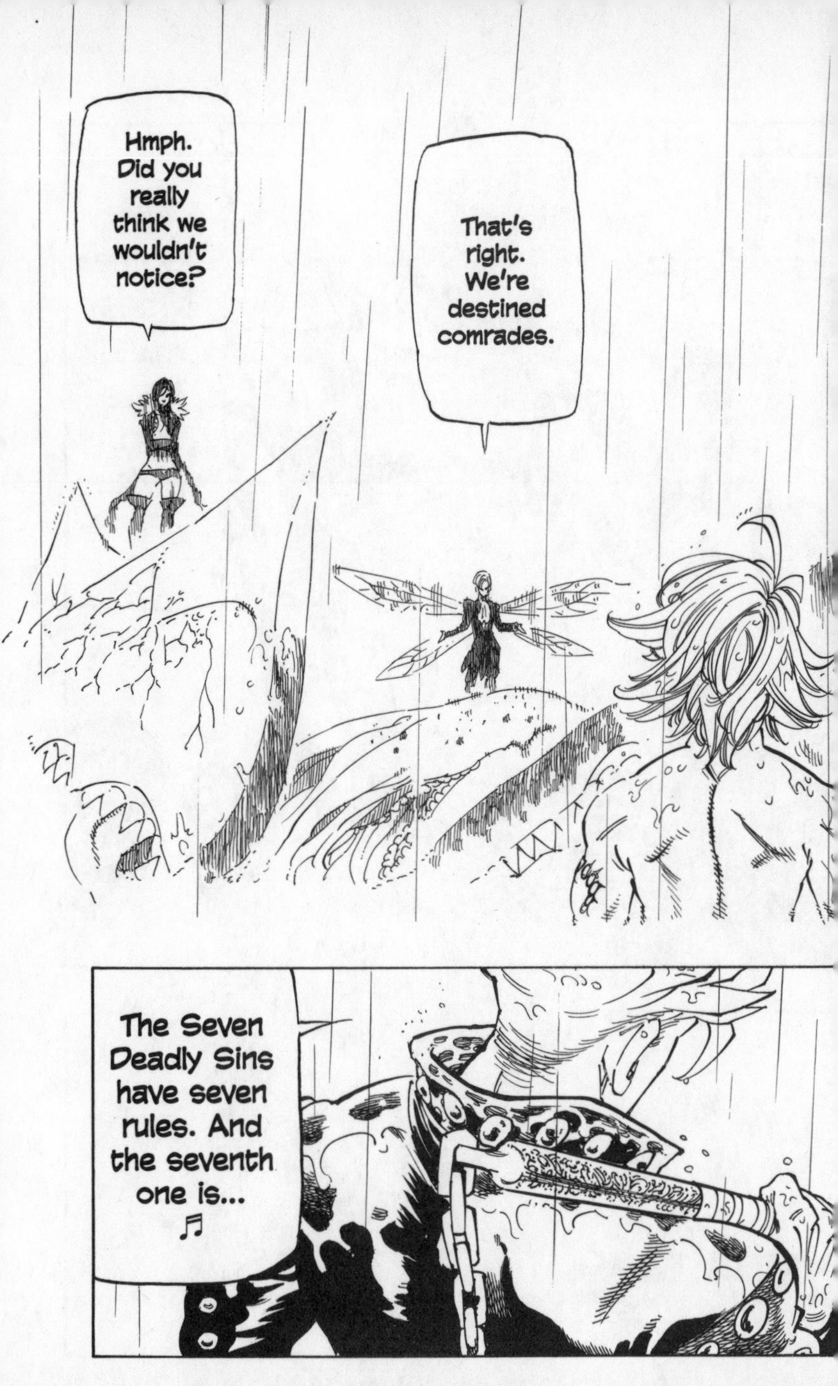
That's right. We're destined comrades.
Hmph. Did you really think we wouldn't notice?
The Seven Deadly Sins have seven rules. And the seventh one is... ♬

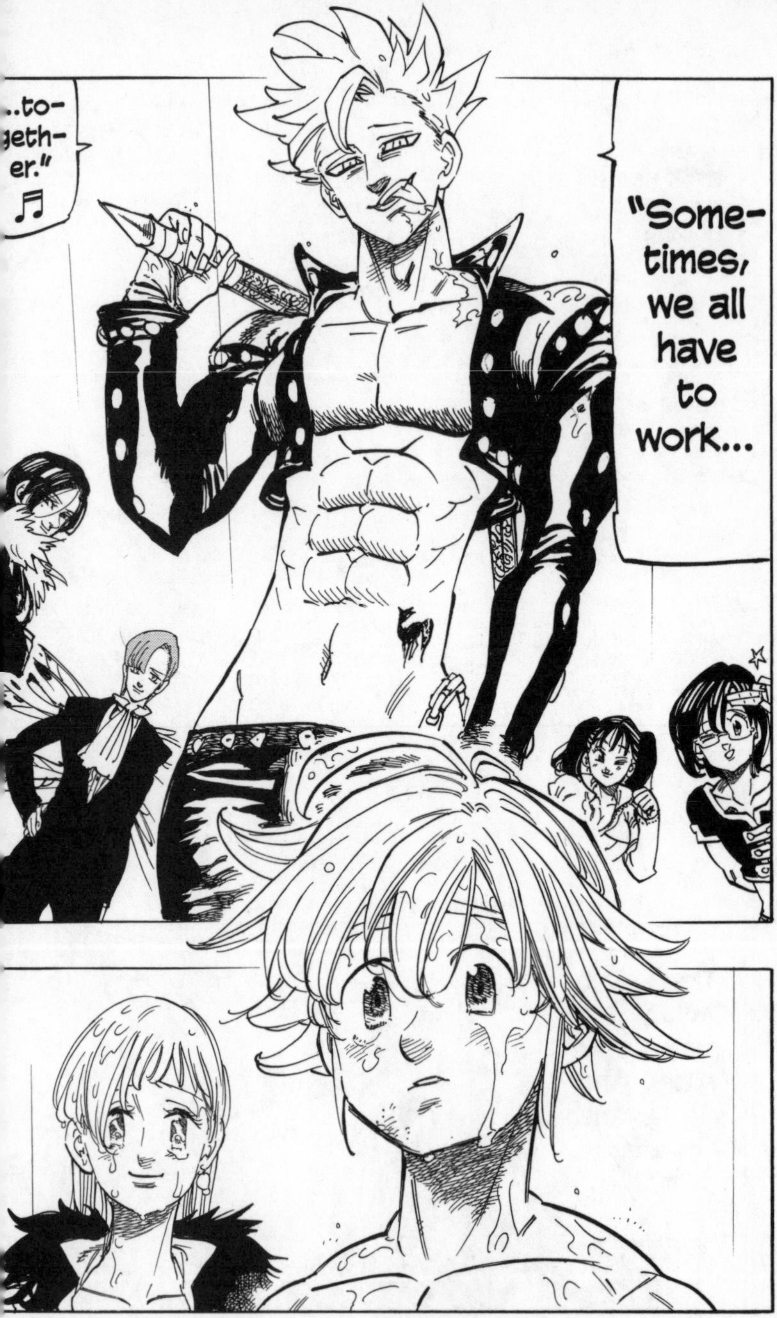
"Some-times, we all have to work...
..to-gether." ♫

To Be Continued in Volume 39...

"THE SEVEN DEADLY SINS" ILLUSTRATION CORNER

"THE DRAWING KNIGHTHOOD" SPACE

In The World

This time we've assembled members from abroad!

M = H = E = D = B = K = G = Mer = Esc = El = J =

SPECIAL PRIZE

RUSSIA / MARIA LARIKOVA-SAN

"Gyaaah! There's a bug on my cake!"

"I'll protect you!" (splat)

"The cake's been reduced to food scraps..."

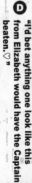

VIETNAM / LE ANH TUAN-SAN

D "I'd bet anything one look like this from Elizabeth would have the Captain beaten.♡"

K "Haha! That's rare. The Captain's actually blushing."

USA / ASIA LEE-SAN

Z "Sheesh. I can't believe I...mistoc a member of the Goddesses for m own brother."

M "It'll all be over soon. It's time to settle this thing!"

E "You can do it, Meliodas!"

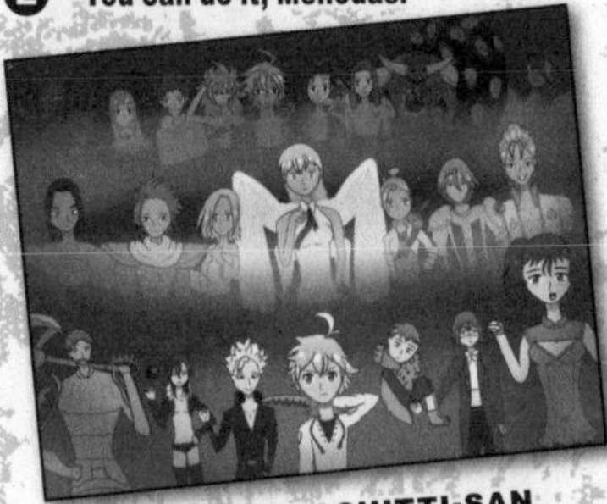

USA / KATIE SCACHITTI-SAN

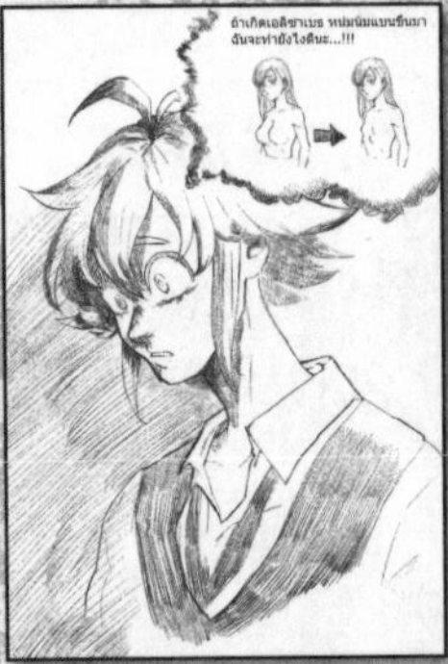

THAI / CHOCOLATE IN MY HEART-SAN

H "He's worrying about what he'd do if Elizabeth-can's bust went away? What kind of worry is that?! You pervert of a captain!"

Mer "Now...where will I find another guinea pig to satisfy my hunger next...?"

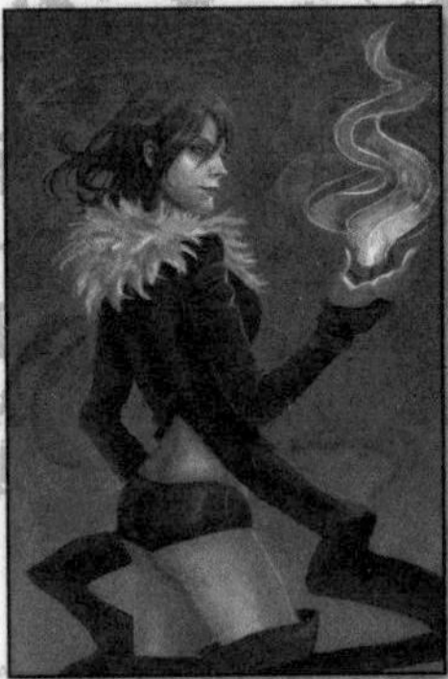

RUSSIA / YANA MUTYANOVA-SAN

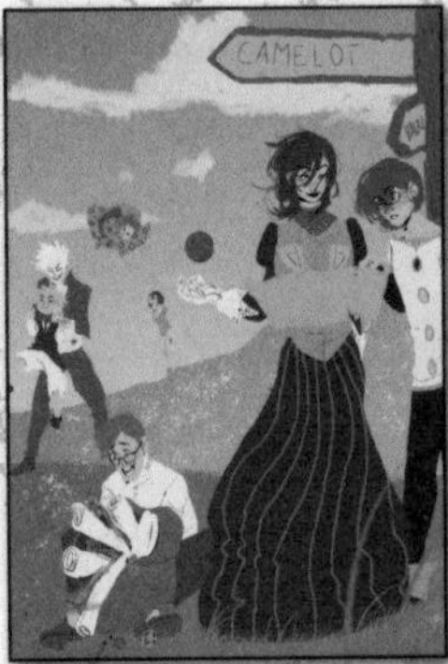
CAMELOT

FRANCE / EMYLOU DUBUIS-SAN

H "Snoink. This shot does a great job of showing the lack of unity in this group!"

E "But everyone still gets along well."

SPAIN / ARNAU PÉREZ MALUENDA-SAN

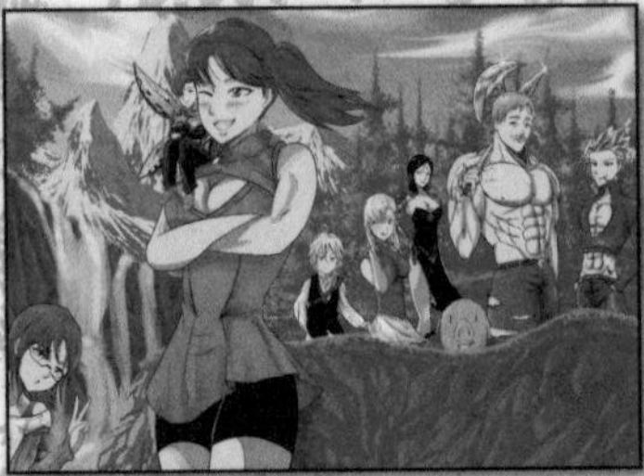

D "That reminds me, King. Since you've awoken, where has your Spirit Spear gone?"

K "Oh, it's just been rendered invisible."

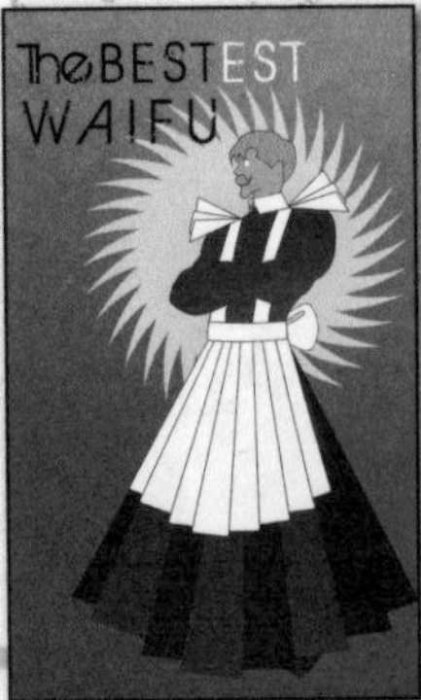
The BESTEST WAIFU

POLAND / BAK MAGDALENA-SAN

Es "Who do you think I am? I am the strongest maid. Anyone who dare thinks he's my master is an arrogant fool!"

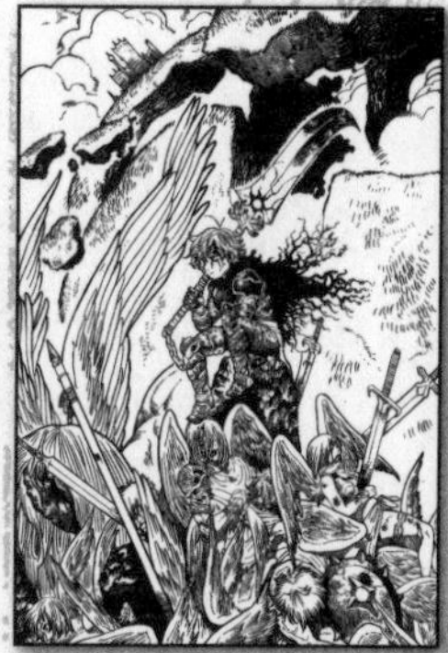

CHINA / KUMODE-SAN

M "I wonder what would've become of me had I never met you back then."

E "I wonder that for myself, too."

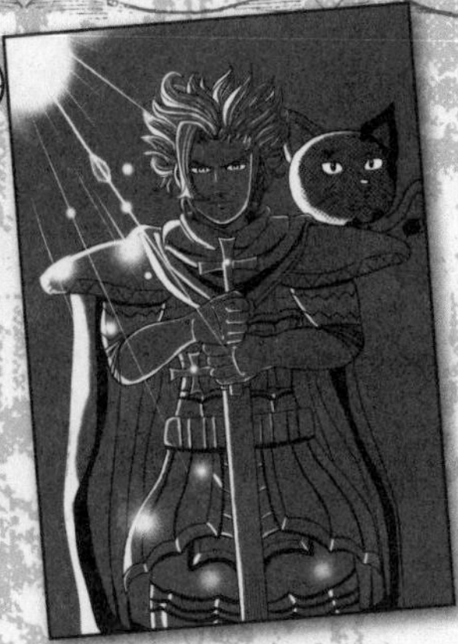

BRAZIL / KENNY MEDEIROS-SAN

"I like this unusually gallant figure of Arthur, too..."

"The intensity of Cath's eyes is amazing."

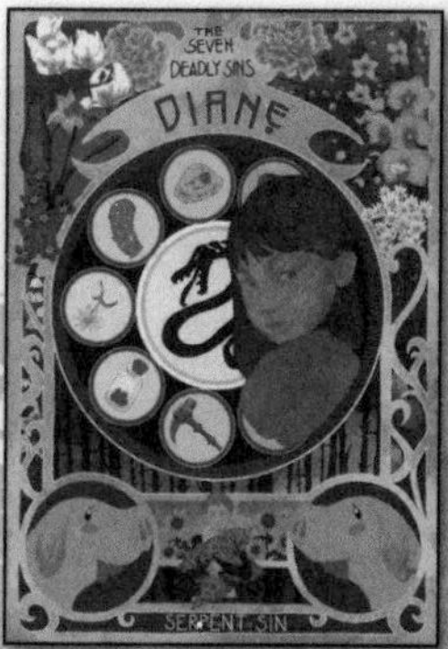
THE SEVEN DEADLY SINS
DIANE
SERPENT SIN

GERMANY / KIRA RANNACHER-SAN

E "Diane looks cute as a prim and proper young lady, too. This looks just like the cover to a picture book."

D "Heheheh! King looks cute down at the bottom there too, doesn't he?"

H "This reminds me that you had a lot of versions, too, Hendrickson!"

Hen "Which me do you like best?"

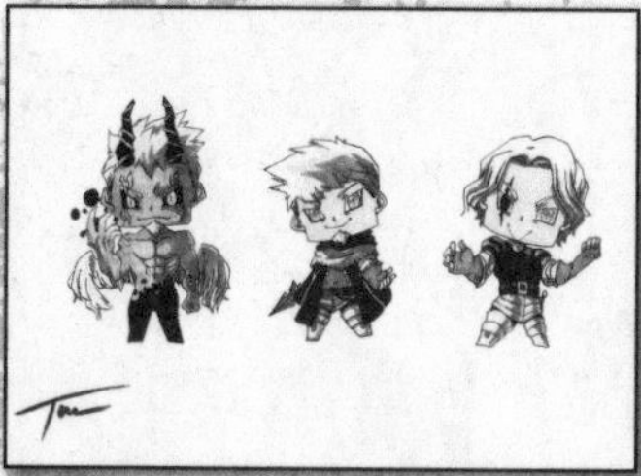

VIETNAM / NGUYEN VAN TRUONG-SAN

USA / LARAYIA HUNTER-SAN

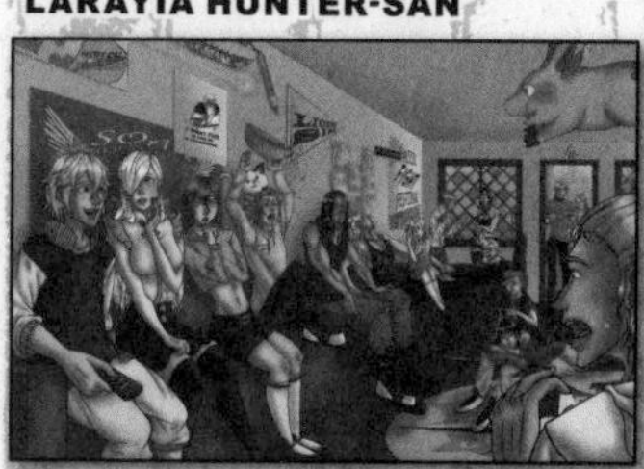

M "Let's all sing and dance and party today!"

H "Wooot! ♡ Leftoveeeers!"

D "Elizabeth has such a feminine feel to her! I wish I could take after her a little, too..."

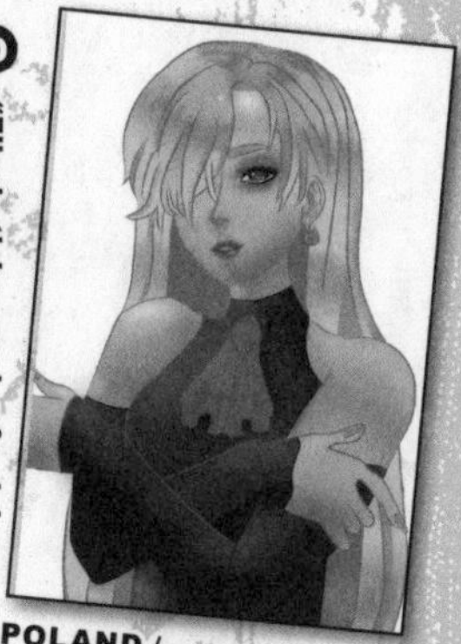

POLAND / KINGA ROZWA-SAN

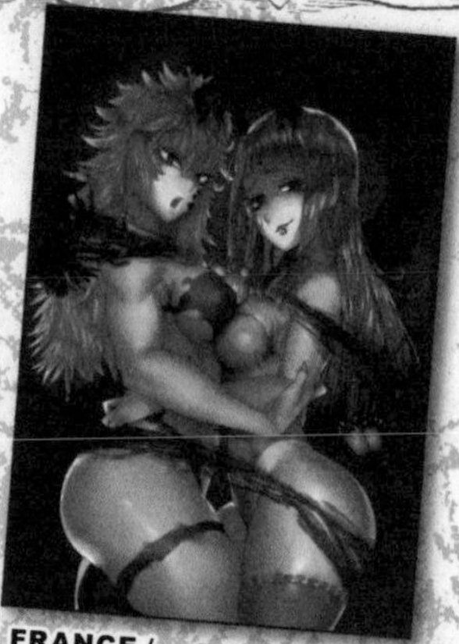

FRANCE / SACHA DELON-SAN

M "It's rare to see the brawns and the brains come together like this, but they'd be insanely strong if they did join forces."

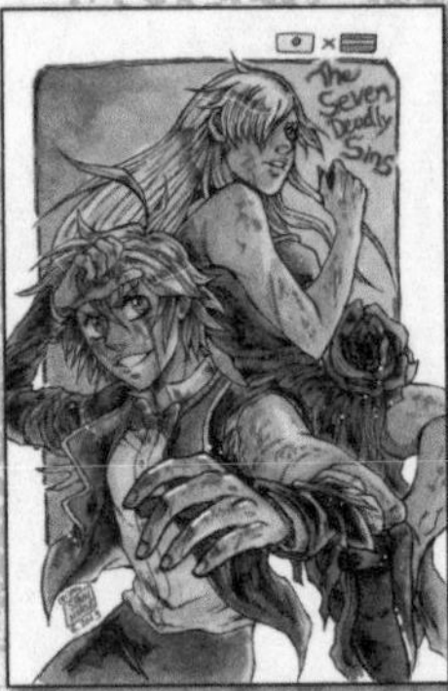
The Seven Deadly Sins

SPAIN / CRISTINA ROPERO VIDAL-SAN

Es "Hmm! Those two are such a passionate pair. How I envy them... I, too, hope to someday be like that with Merlin-san..."

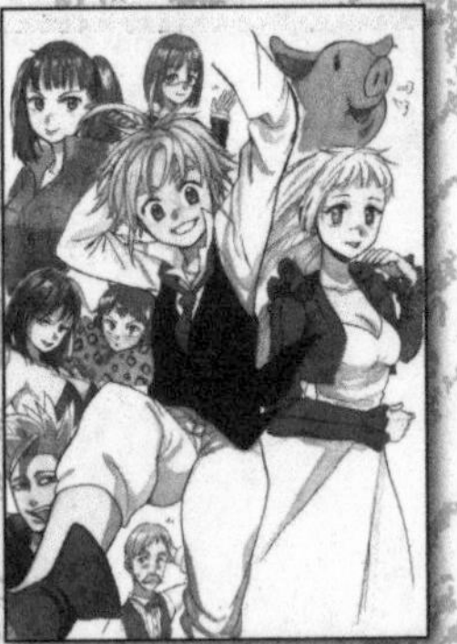

TAIWAN / HIRO-SAN

H "I knew it. Between the great Hawk-sama and The Seven Deadly Sins, the Holy War was a walk through the park!"

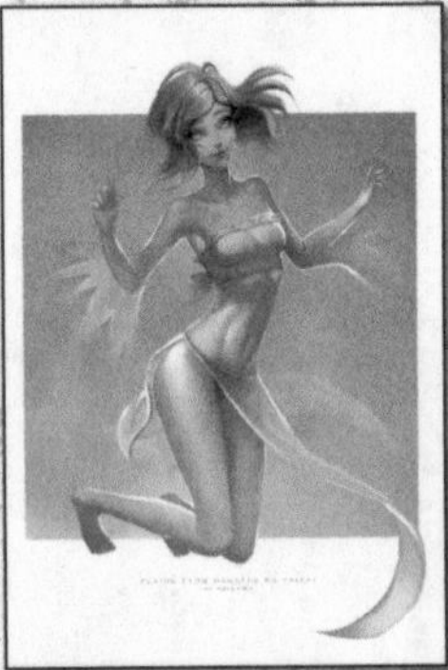

RUSSIA / ANN DZIKAWA-SAN

C "Looking at you with fresh eyes, you really are a fairy, aren't you, Elaine?"

E "Don't stare at me so. It's embarrassing..."

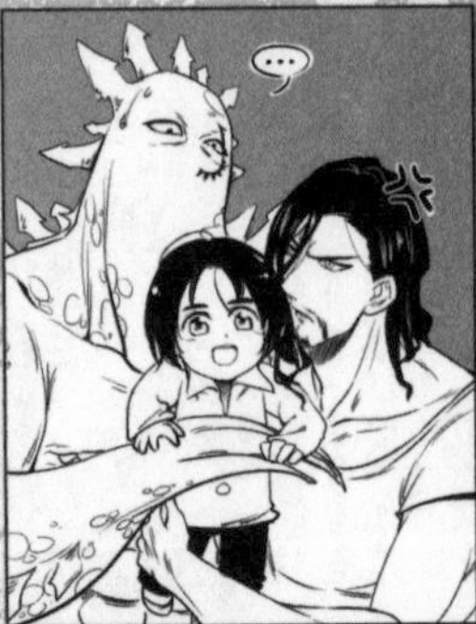
...

CHINA / HEI YE AI MEOW-SAN

Dreyfus "Fraudrin! You're not holding him right! Like this!"

Fraudrin "S...Sorry. Is this better?"

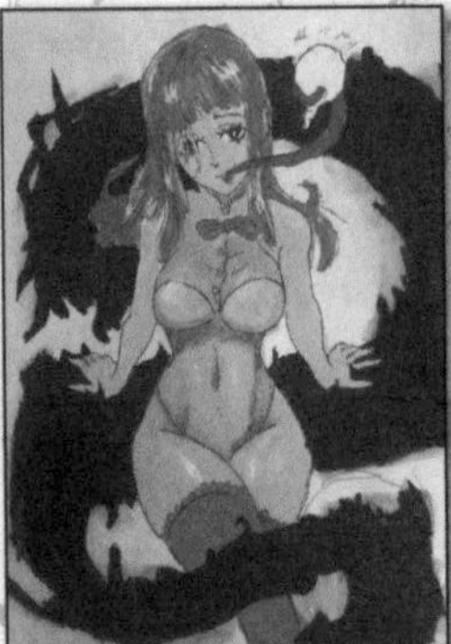

USA / EMILY KIRBY-SAN

H "Oh, yeah. Whatever happened to this girl, anyway?"

M "Apparently, she fled in the middle of the fight in Camelot."

"The Captain looks good no matter what picture he's in. Wouldn't you agree?"

"Hmph. Y...You think so?"

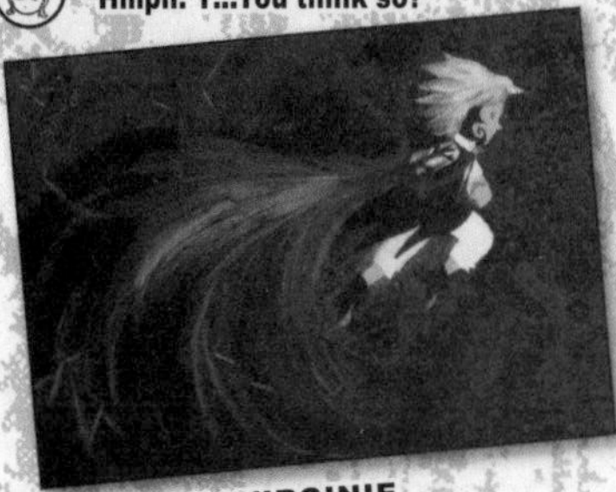

FRANCE / VIRGINIE LETONNELIER-SAN

H "Back when we were fighting against The Ten Commandments, I'd have never dreamed things would turn out like this. Especially with *him*."

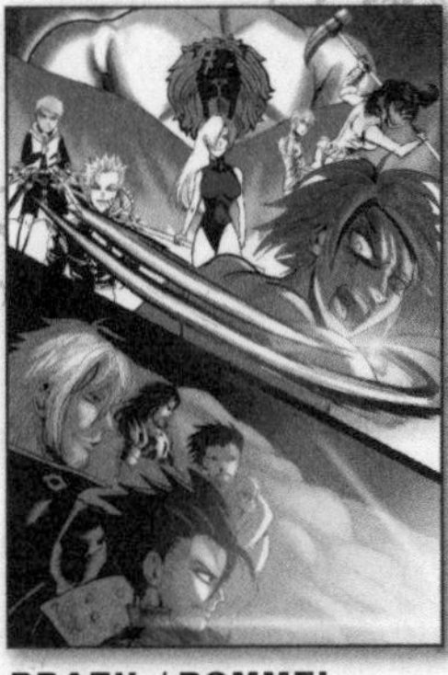

BRAZIL / ROMMEL RODRIGUES SILVA-SAN

K "Ban, I really do admire you for what you've done."

B "Yeah? ♫ Then get down on your knees before me. ♫"

K "Not on your life!"

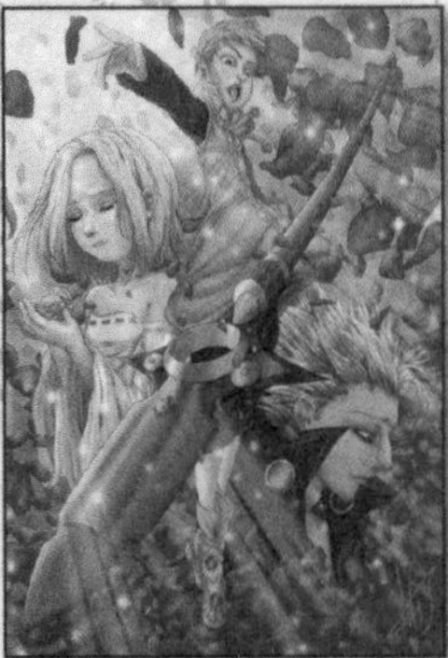

GERMANY / AITOR DE MIGUEL-SAN

E "Good luck, Meliodas! You must save Zeldris from the Demon Lord!"

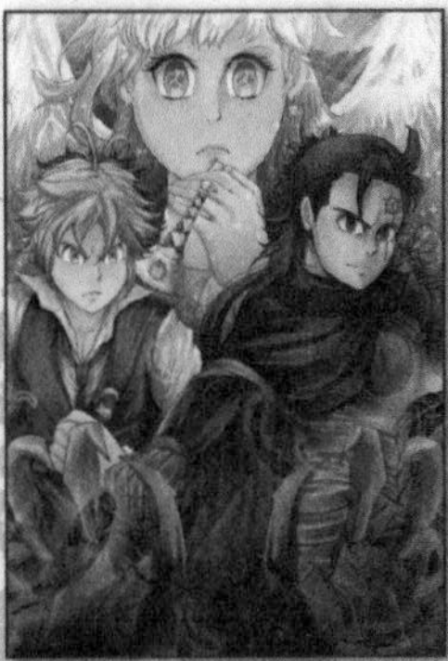

SPAIN / IRVING VALDES-SAN

El "Ban! Look, look at this outfit! Isn't it cute?"

J "Darn it, that's no fair!"

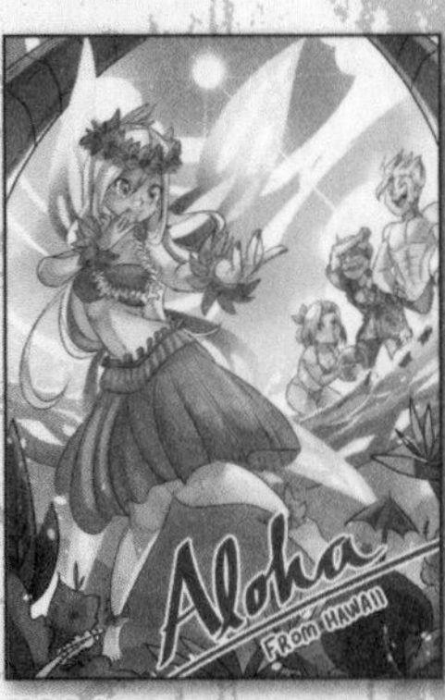
Aloha
FROM HAWAII

USA / MELISSA HAHN-SAN

H "Don't lose, Meliodaaaaaas!!"

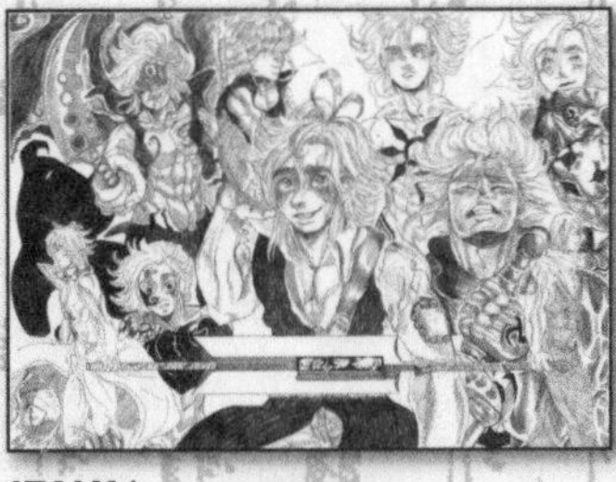

ITALY / MIRIAM CANGEMI-SAN

E "I love the idea of a soft and fluffy Hawk-chan, too!"

Mer "These two are so soothing to behold."

Grüß Gott aus Bad Urach

GERMANY / ISABELLE BRANDENBURG-SAN

E "I'm certain the only reason I've been able to overcome all these hardships so far is thanks to Hawk-chan and everyone in The Seven Deadly Sins."

BRAZIL / CAMILA MADALENA-SAN

H "Everyone's...*yaaawn*...wishing for... *yaaawn*...your happiness together."

FRANCE / NHU-VINH NGUYEN-SAN

B "Whether I'm immortal or not, my feelings for you will never change, Elaine..."

ITALY / LIDIA MISURACA-SAN

H "Chinese food is delicious, but it's something else when Meliodas prepares it..."

M "You trying to say something, you

中華
料亭

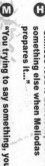

CHINA / ICE CREAM FISH-SAN

K "Elaine's said so herself: the piggy is as comfortable to sleep on as on a big, fat mushroom."

USA / EVELYNN MCGUFFIN-SAN

Es “Captain...and Merlin-san. Meeting you was the miracle of a lifetime.”

The Light That Illuminates My Path

ITALY /
BERTAZSLEEPYHEAD-S

“I really was so happy when you returned home from Purgatory, Meliodas.”

“...Of course!”

BRAZIL /
JORGE FERNANDO-SAN

H “Elizabeth-can, which do you prefer? His Demon version? Or his usual version?”

E “I like them both.”

POLAND / WIKTORIA
DZIEDZIC-SAN

H “Elizabeth-can looks good even as a mermaid. I guess I'd be a blowfish.”

FRANCE / SARAH
LECLERE-SAN

El “Hey, Ban. When this fight is over...”

B “Let's go on a trip together! ♫”

El “Yeah!”

BRAZIL / DITMAR
BOHNAU JUNIOR-SAN

D “This tower's a little crooked. Hup!”

K “No! If you push on it too hard, it'll fall down the other way!”

ITALY /
FABIO VIZIANO-SAN

USA / EVELYNN MCGUFFIN-SAN

M "When I'm in my Demon form, my tolerance for alcohol goes way up!"

H "Seriously?!"

M "No."

USA / SARAH PAN-SAN

G "If it means protecting my friends, I am capable of anything... And that is the truth."

SPAIN / JOSÉ DOCIO DE LERA-SAN

B "This reminds me that King used to spend hours staring at some flower and sighing back in the day."

RUSSIA / KARINA ALISKANTOVA-SAN

K "When the fight's over, will you come live with me in the Fairy King's Forest?"

D "Yes! That sounds delightful!"

BRAZIL / GABRIELE MARQUES-SAN

K "Diane... Your smile belongs only to me now."

M **H** "Cheesy!"

ITALY / DEBORA STANICH-SAN

Z "Come on, guys! Let's go!!"

H "Yes, sir!"

D "All right, brother!"

"That's right! It is I! The Deadly Sins of Leftovers, Piggiodas! Taste the wrath of my "Revenge Meal!"

Hawk-San!!

THAILAND / KAJORNSAK PREECHA BUNLIT-SAN

M "There were so many times when I hung out with these three without a care in the world."

D "I bet you only got into trouble."

FRANCE / NOLWENN BOCRIE-SAN

D "I hope you're able to patch things up between you guys, Captain!"

M "Yeah... Thank you!"

ごめんね…

SPAIN / MÍRIAM ABAD RODRÍGUEZ-SAN

B "Baste Prison would definitely be one of the top three most boring times of my life."

M "Even though you hadn't done anything and let yourself be captured..."

CHINA / YEC NIGHT BUG-SAN

Mer "Now that is one avant-garde Sir Hawk."

H "Yes. I would like to hang it on my wall."

M "Don't hang it in the tavern!"

BRAZIL / RAFAEL DOS SANTOS TOMAS-SAN

H "There's nothing cool about dancing under the moon."

E "Hawk-chan, you should dance too!"

VIETNAM / DOAN HUU LAM HA-SAN

D "We're all dressed up as characters from fairy tales!"

E "Hahaha! Merlin's outfit suits her best!"

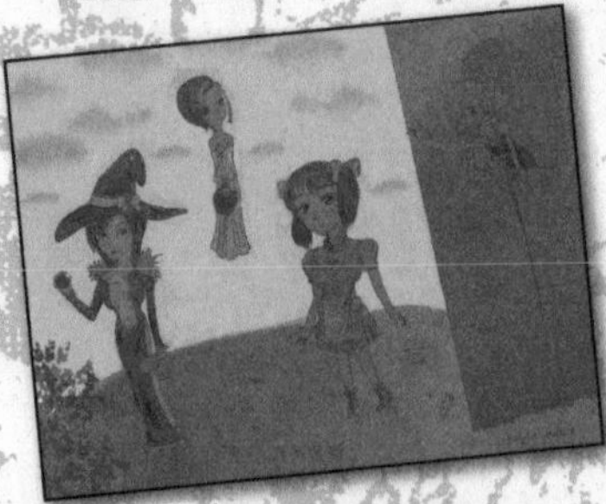

POLAND / JUDYTA MEHLICH-SAN

L "Did you know, Mael? As long as we Four Archangels have our Graces, we cannot die."

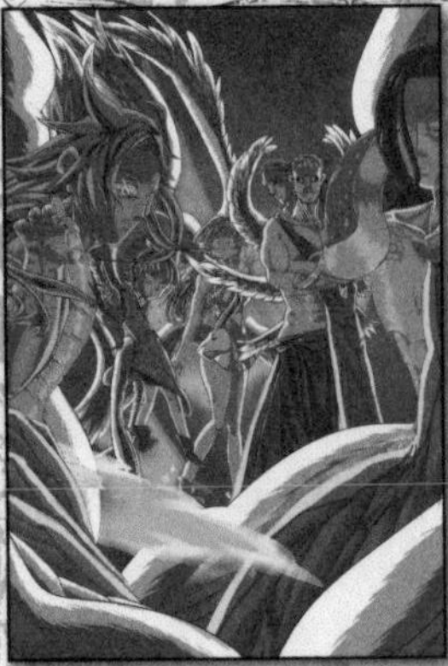

CHINA / LILY ARMY FAILED TO CONQUER THE WEST-SAN

H "I do have a rather regal air about me, don't I? I think I do!"

M "All hail the King of Leftovers!"

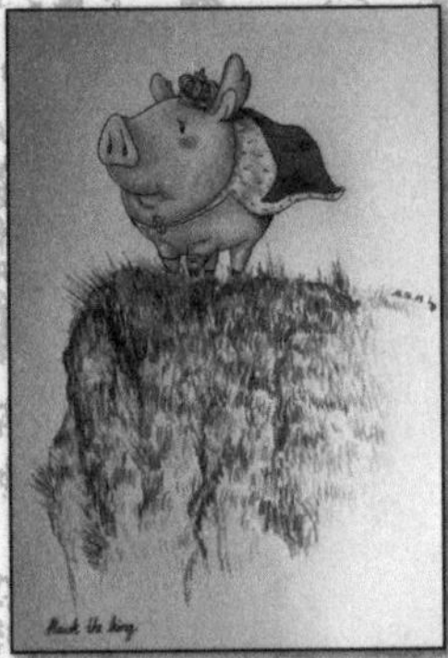

GERMANY / LEAH GERLOW-WEISS-SAN

M "Escanor! I will never forget your friendship...for as long as I live!"

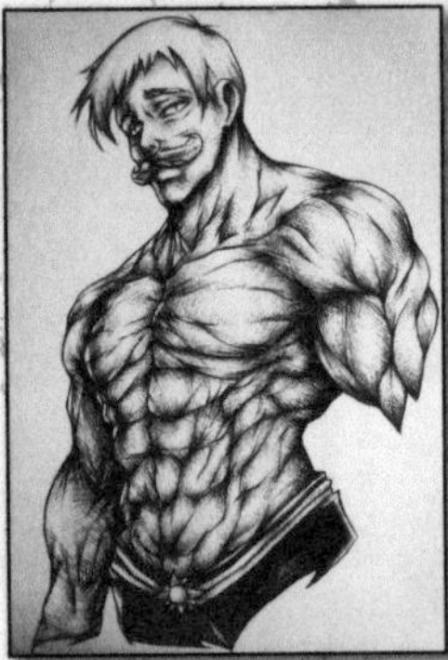

ITALY / RICCARDO CIAFRO-SAN

M "Here, Elizabeth. You can have this."

E "For me? Thank you. I'm so happy..."

H "Give me the sunflower seeds later."

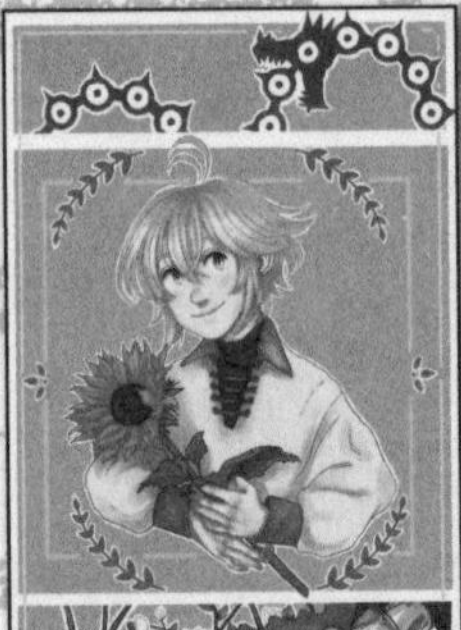

RUSSIA / AMI ALHASOVA-SAN

E "Mael, you were never alone, and you're not alone now."

H "I know that... Thank you."

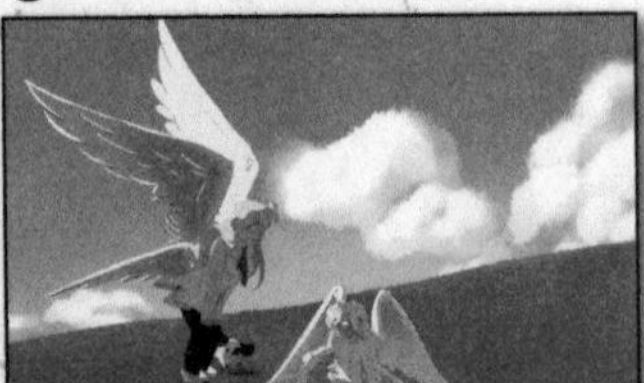

FRANCE / KANEZA HADDAOUI-SAN

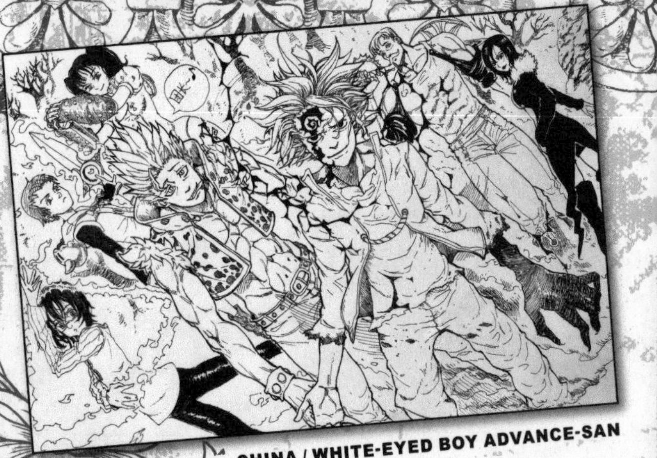

“Let’s knock this guy into next week, Cap’n. ♫”
“Yeah... We’ll give ’em a beating to remember!”
“Shwiiiing!”

CHINA / WHITE-EYED BOY ADVANCE-SAN

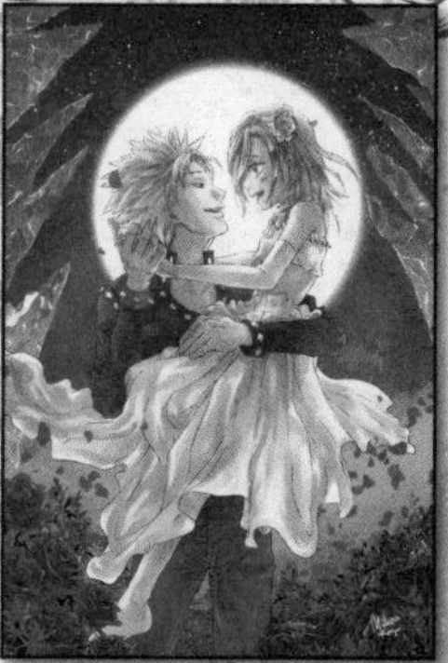

H “O, Fairy Princess. Might I dance with you this fine evening? ♫”
El “Hee hee hee... I’d be delighted!”

POLAND / EMILIA_OLSZEWSKA-SAN

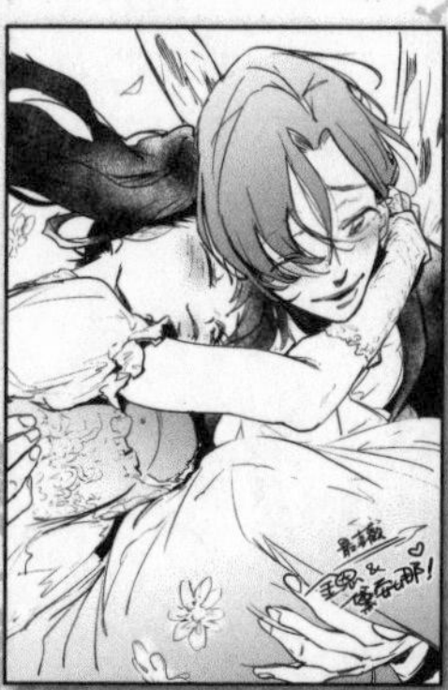

H “King, don’t forget. I’m waiting.”
K “Don’t worry. I promise I’ll propose to you. Just hold on a little longer.”
D “O...Okay!”

TAIWAN / DINNER HSU-SAN

Now Accepting Applicants for the Drawing Knighthood!

- Draw your picture on a postcard, or paper no larger than a postcard, and send it in!
- Don’t forget to write your name and location on the back of your picture!
- You can include comments or not. And colored illustrations will still only be displayed in B&W!
- The Drawing Knights whose pictures are particularly noteworthy and run in the print edition will be gifted with a signed specially made pencil board!
- And the best overall will be granted the special prize of a signed shikishi!!

Send to:
The Seven Deadly Sins Drawing Knighthood
c/o Kodansha Comics
451 Park Ave. South, 7th Floor
New York, NY 10016

- Submitted letters and postcards will be given to the artist. Please be aware that your name, address, and other personal information included will be given as well.

Chobits © CLAMP-ShigatsuTsuitachi CO.,LTD./Kodansha Ltd.

Poor college student Hideki is down on his luck. All he wants is a good job, a girlfriend, and his very own "persocom"—the latest and greatest in humanoid computer technology. Hideki's luck changes one night when he finds Chi—a persocom thrown out in a pile of trash. But Hideki soon discovers that there's much more to his cute new persocom than meets the eye.

KC
KODANSHA
COMICS

The boys are back, in 400-page hardcover that are as pretty and badass as they are!

Saiyuki © Kazuya Minakura / Ichijin

SAIYUKI
THE ORIGINAL SERIES
KAZUYA MINEKURA

"AN EDGY COMIC LOOK AT AN ANCIENT CHINESE TALE." —YALS

Genjo Sanzo is a Buddhist priest in the city of Togenkyo, which is being ravaged by yokai spirits that have fallen out of balance with the natural order. His superiors send him on a journey far to the west to discover why this is happening and how to stop it. His companions are three yokai with human souls. But this is no day trip — the four will encounter many discoveries and horrors on the way.

FEATURES NEW TRANSLATION, COLOR PAGES, AND BEAUTIFUL WRAPAROUND COVER ART!

A Kodansha Comics Trade Paperback Original
The Seven Deadly Sins 38 copyright © 2019 Nakaba Suzuki
English translation copyright © 2020 Nakaba Suzuki

Published in the United States by Kodansha Comics, an imprint of
Kodansha USA Publishing, LLC, New York.

Publication rights for this English edition arranged through
Kodansha Ltd., Tokyo.

First published in Japan in 2019 by Kodansha Ltd., Tokyo
as *Nanatsu no taizai*, volume 38.

ISBN 978-1-63236-922-2

Printed in the United States of America.

www.kodanshacomics.com

9 8 7 6 5 4 3 2
Translation: Christine Dashiell
Lettering: James Dashiell
Editing: Tiff Ferentini
Kodansha Comics edition cover design by Phil Balsman

Publisher: Kiichiro Sugawara
Vice president of marketing & publicity: Naho Yamada

Director of publishing services: Ben Applegate
Associate director of operations: Stephen Pakula
Publishing services managing editor: Noelle Webster
Assistant production manager: Emi Lotto, Angela Zurlo